HEROES
RASCALS
& ROGUES

Published by AA Publishing, a trading name of Automobile Association Developments Limited,
whose registered office is Fanum House, Basing View, Basingstoke, Hampshire RG21 4EA.
Registered number 1878835.

Packaged for Automobile Association Developments Limited by Hunkydory Publishing Ltd.
www.hunkydorypublishing.com

Design by Lise Meyrick
www.lisemeyrick.com

Authors: Rupert Matthews and John Birdsall

Picture research: Sian Lloyd

A CIP catalogue record for this book is available from the British Library.

ISBN: 978-0-7495-5866-6
Special Sales ISBN: 978-0-7495-5888-8

© Automobile Association Developments Limited 2008
Colour separation by Keenes (Andover)
Printed and bound in China by 1010 Printing International Limited
A03650

www.theAA.com/travel

Chapters

Foreword

The world we live in today is the product of the people who live in it, and of those who have lived in the past. Some people affect those around them, some have influence over a wider area—but a few dominate the world and have a profound impact on all those who live in it. It is these people who are the subject of this book.

There have been kings, queens, and rulers who have changed the history of the world on a whim or with a single decision—Caligula, John F Kennedy, Attila the Hun, Genghis Khan, or Catherine the Great to name but a few. Military leaders such as Alexander the Great, Napoleon, or Cortés have altered the world to fit their own untrammelled ambition, and for good or ill they have paid little heed to the consequences of others.

It is not just the rich and the powerful who have shaped our modern world—although there are those in plenty. Others have led by example, inspiring others or filling them with revulsion. Some of these world-shapers have been heroes, others rogues, and not a few absolute rascals. A very few have managed to combine traits of all three.

Beau Brummell was a noted wit who died bankrupt, but his influence is felt today every time a man puts on a suit or ties a tie, or irons his shirt. It was Brummell who revolutionized gentlemen's fashion to such an extent that most men today still wear clothes based on his.

Florence Nightingale had an equally dramatic impact on the nursing profession. She emphasized care, cleanliness, and selflessness. Most hospitals around the world continue to teach her precepts and aim to put her ideas into practice.

Wyatt Earp imposed law and order on the American West at a time when both were in short supply. Although famous for his gunfights, Earp used his dominating personality and an astute mix of threats and charm more than he did his guns.

Pioneers such as Hillary and Tensing, Jacques Cousteau, David Livingstone, and Neil Armstrong have showed by their determination and bravery that humans have the capacity to conquer some of Earth's most daunting challenges, or even transcend the barriers of space to set foot on new worlds.

No less laudable are people such as Andy Green, Roger Bannister, and Amelia Earhart, who broke new records on land and in the air, compelling others follow suit.

Less worthy, but also influential in their way, have been Al Capone, Blackbeard, The Jackal, and Lucrezia Borgia. Through crime, bloodshed, and violence they carved out power and wealth for themselves. Many other people since have sought to emulate them, much to the misfortune of humanity.

In the fields of science, the fame and fortune won by the genius Albert Einstein and by the inventor Thomas Edison not only blazed a trail for the technological 20th century, but also inspired generations of budding scientists to do that little bit of extra work needed for success. And thanks to fellow scientist Alfred Nobel, such innovative thinkers, as well as other people who have left literary or cultural legacies for humankind, are now awarded the ultimate accolade, the Nobel Prize.

This book contains the tales of hundreds of these world-shapers. Be they hero or villain, their skills and abilities are explained and the impact they had on the world explored. Today, as in the past, ours is a world of Heroes, Rogues, and Rascals.

Rupert Matthews

Crime

"Mafia is a process, not a thing. Mafia is a form of
clan cooperation to which its individual members pledge lifelong loyalty."

Joe Bonanno, boss of the Bonanno crime family

MOST FAMOUS CON MAN

By the very nature of their trade, con men work in the shadows and rarely, if ever, court publicity. Even when brought to trial, the confidence tricksters do everything they can to keep a low profile for both themselves and the tricks that they pull.

There are very few who are happy to discuss their successes and failures, their lucrative tricks, and how unsuspecting people fall for them. Those who do are the con men who have decided to go straight and alert the public to the dangers that they face when they come into contact with a con man. Of these, none is so famous as Frank Abagnale. In fact, he wrote a book about his life of crime, which was made into the 2002 Hollywood movie *Catch Me If You Can*. Abagnale was even involved in the film's creation (pictured right, meeting Leonardo DiCaprio who played his adult character).

Abagnale had been involved in petty crime before he ran away from home at the age of 16 in 1964. The news that his parents were divorcing shocked him and, he later claimed, sparked his hasty departure. Arriving in New York, Abagnale soon discovered that people took him to be in his mid-twenties, so he altered his driving licence accordingly and began applying for jobs. However, he had a self-confessed taste for the high life and for impressing the women that he dated.

This led him to his first con,

FRANK ABAGNALE (b.1948)

*"I stole every nickel and blew it on fine threads, luxurious lodgings, fantastic foxes, and other sensual goodies.
I partied in every capital in Europe and basked on all the world's most famous beaches."*

From *Catch Me If You Can* by Frank Abagnale

the elementary business of writing out cheques on his bank account when he knew that he did not have enough money to cover them. The bank, of course, demanded payment, so Abagnale opened other accounts at other banks and wrote fraudulent cheques on those to cover his initial debts. He then developed his first serious con trick: he printed paying-in slips with his own bank account details on them, then left them mixed in with the blank slips found at bank counters. Anyone who paid in

By then, Abagnale had moved on, using one of the several false identities he established for himself.

funds without first examining the slip would find that the money went to Abagnale's account and not their own. He took $40,000 before the bank spotted the con.

By then, Abagnale had moved on, using one of the several false identities he established for himself. One of these was "Frank Williams", a pilot with the Pan Am airline. Abagnale had forged himself a pilot's licence, a university degree in aeronautics, a Pan Am ID card, and a uniform. He spent two years riding passenger jets, staying at staff lodgings, and enjoying himself. When Pan Am realized there was a man with a fake identity using their facilities they clamped down, but Abagnale had moved on again. The press dubbed the false Frank Williams "The Skywayman", and revelled in his exploits.

After numerous ruses posing as a teacher, doctor, and attorney, he was caught in 1969 when an airline stewardess recognized him from a wanted poster. By then he was wanted in 26 countries. He served prison time in France, Sweden, and the USA.

GOING STRAIGHT

Abagnale was released from prison in 1974 on condition that he aid the federal authorities in clamping down on other con men. He later founded Abagnale & Associates, a private security company, through which he has earned more money—helping banks outwit fraudsters—than he did as a con man. He also advises the teachers at the FBI Academy.

Jefferson "Soapy" Smith (1860–1898)

Jefferson Smith was one of the first great con men. He first earned a living as a cheat at card games, then turned to the "soap con". This involved setting up a stall and wrapping up a number of soap bars,

ostentatiously including $10 or $20 bills in with some of the bars. He then sold off the bars at $1 a time, as a form of lottery. In fact, the only people who "won" the money were Smith's associates, while the public gained bars of soap worth 5 cents. This lucrative con gave him his name.

Gregor MacGregor (1786–1845)

When the Scottish soldier Gregor MacGregor returned to Britain a hero in 1820, after fighting in the South American struggle for independence, he announced that he had been appointed governor of Poyais in Honduras, a territory with rich agricultural lands. It is thought he had raised over £700,000 by the time 200 would-be settlers left in January 1823. The settlers found that there was no such place as Poyais.

Robert Hendy-Freegard (b.1971)

Hendy-Freegard (left) is a British con man who posed as an undercover agent for the British secret services. He convinced his victims that they had inadvertently become involved in a terrorist plot and that he could save their lives only if they became an agent. Those he managed to convince were drained of cash and seduced if they were women. He was arrested in 2003.

Matt "The Knife" (b.1981)

Matt "The Knife"—also known as MTK—is a former American pickpocket and con man who has given up his life of crime. He now tours the USA with a stage show and other demonstrations explaining how con men perform dishonest tricks such as memory implantation and removal, three-card monte, pickpocketing, gypsy switches, change raising, speaking with the dead, card cheating, psychic surgery, and so forth.

RENOWNED ESCAPEE

CRIME

Many men held in captivity have sought to break free and head for safety. Some have been criminals, others prisoners of war, and a few kidnap victims.

What they all have in common is a flair for audacity, a skill in subterfuge and the ability to take advantage of circumstances.

British robber Ronald Arthur "Ronnie" Biggs was convicted in 1964 for his part in the Great Train Robbery, a hold-up that gained the gang responsible £2.6 million ($5.2 million).

In 1965, he made a daring escape from Wandsworth Prison using a rope ladder, to be whisked away by a car driven by accomplices outside. Biggs then disappeared, though it was later found that he had gone to Paris to acquire both a forged passport in a new name and a new face through plastic surgery.

In 1970, he was recognized by a visiting reporter working as a set constructor at a TV station in Australia. He vanished again.

In 1974, he was discovered by British police in Rio de Janeiro, but he could not be extradited because the UK did not benefit from reciprocity of extradition to Brazil, and because his new girlfriend was pregnant. He then lived openly under his own name and made a living selling mugs, T-shirts, and other items featuring his name and portrait.

In 1981, Biggs was kidnapped by a gang who took him to

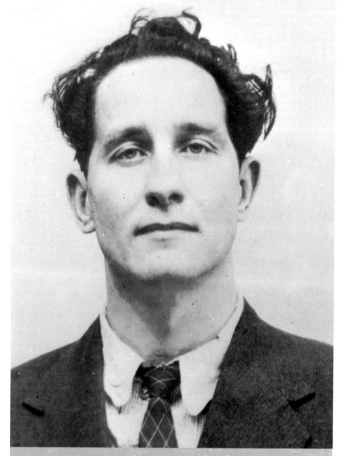

RONNIE BIGGS (b.1929)

"I am a sick man," Biggs told *The Sun* newspaper in 1999. *"My last wish is to walk into a Margate pub as an Englishman and buy a pint of bitter."*

Barbados, hoping to hand him over to British police and so gain the reward. Biggs escaped again, and used Barbados law to ensure his return to Rio. In May 2001, Biggs decided that he wanted to return to the UK at all costs. So he arranged with his son Michael to do a deal with British newspaper *The Sun* which saw him paid for his life story and flown back to England. He was immediately returned to prison, and despite serious ill health in later years, his solicitor has failed to get his sentence reduced or overturned.

In May 2001, Biggs decided that he wanted to return to the UK at all costs.

Roger Bushell (1910–1944)

One of the most famous escapes of all time was The Great Escape, a mass break out of British and other prisoners of war on March 24, 1944. After months of careful planning and lengthy digging, a tunnel was completed without being discovered by the German guards. The mastermind of the effort was Sqn Ldr Roger Bushell (right), a Spitfire pilot who had already broken out twice from other prison camps. About 200 men were equipped with fake ID cards, civilian clothes, and maps. In the event, only 76 got away before a German guard spotted the escapees. Of those 76, three reached Britain and 23 were returned to camp. The other 50, including Bushell, were murdered by the Gestapo.

Squadron Leader Roger Bushell (right) with fellow prisoner of war Wing Commander Bob Tuck.

Richard McNair (b.1958)

One of the USA's most famous fugitives is Richard McNair, a convicted murderer. He first broke out of a North Dakota county jail in 1988, and then again in 1992. He was then moved to a federal prison, but in April 2006 broke out by hiding inside a mail sack inside the mail van. Just hours later he was stopped by a policeman, but managed to convince him that he was a local man out jogging. On October 25, 2007, McNair was recaptured by the Royal Canadian Mounted Police.

Lucien Rivard (d.2002)

Canadian robber and drug smuggler, Lucien Rivard, staged a sensational prison escape in 1965 that had wide political repercussions. Rivard escaped a Montreal jail using a rubber hose to climb the main wall, but other aspects of his escape were decidedly odd and indicated that he had been helped. While on the run, Rivard wrote a series of letters to various politicians and celebrities boasting of his prison break and claiming that he would never be recaptured. He was, in fact, rearrested only four months after the break.

An investigation of the case led to the resignation of Canadian Attorney General Guy Favreau. That, in turn, led to the unexpected promotion of the relatively unknown Pierre Trudeau, who would later become Prime Minister. Rivard was voted 1965 Canadian Newsmaker of the Year.

Kim Philby (1912–1988)

Kim Philby (below) was a British secret agent, who for many years was a spy for the Soviet Union. On January 23, 1963, Philby disappeared. Later it was discovered he had contacted the KGB agent who handled his messages to Moscow and announced that he was about to be unmasked. Philby was given the name of a freighter, the *Dolmatova*, heading for Beirut. While out for a walk, he spotted a man tailing him, gave him the slip, and ran for the port.

BLOODTHIRSTY PIRATE

BLACKBEARD (1680–1718)

Blackbeard tucked lighted matches into his hair so that he was wreathed in smoke and the stench of burning sulphur.

Ask anyone to name a pirate and chances are that they will say "Blackbeard". His reputation for savagery and success is legendary.

Indeed, Blackbeard went out of his way to create a name for invincible ruthlessness because he knew this would encourage his victims to surrender.

Born Edward Teach, the future Blackbeard left his native England around 1706 as a sailor. By 1712 he was serving aboard a British privateer based in Jamaica. Privateers were privately owned warships that were bound by the rules of war and earned their money by capturing enemy merchant ships. Peace came in 1714 but Teach opted to become a pirate—a criminal who attacked and plundered ships of any nation—instead of returning to the dull monotony of legal merchant sailing. It was at this point that Edward Teach created the persona of Blackbeard. Edward Teach had been a violent but undistinguished thief. Blackbeard was to become a legend.

Blackbeard began with his appearance. He grew his hair and his beard long and straggly. When he went into battle Blackbeard was said to have tucked lighted matches into his hair so that he was wreathed in smoke and the stench of burning sulphur. He wore fine quality clothes, including a gold-brocaded coat that hung to his knees. He habitually carried a razor sharp cutlass at his hip and had a shoulder belt from which hung six pistols.

Cruising north along the east coast of North America, Blackbeard captured numerous merchant ships. These he emptied of their cargoes before setting free the ships and their crews. By May 1718 he was back in the Gulf of Mexico, snapping up more prizes. Then he headed north and by the summer entered Charleston, South Carolina, blockading the port and capturing eight ships. He left only when the governor paid him a huge bribe.

Flush with treasure, Blackbeard then betrayed his own crew.

He ran his ship aground, then fled in a small sloop with his trusted lieutenants and the loot.

He ran his ship aground, then fled in a small sloop with his trusted lieutenants and the loot. Most of the crew were left behind, penniless. Blackbeard now reverted to being Edward Teach. He bribed the governor of South Carolina into giving him a pardon, bought a house and got married. But he could not give up his lawless ways. When pirate Charles Vane paid a visit, Teach decided to return to sea once again as Blackbeard.

> *Edward Teach had been a violent but undistinguished thief. Blackbeard was to become a legend.*

This time his luck ran out. Governor Alexander Spotswood of Virginia was determined to stamp out piracy in his waters. He bought a number of fast, well-armed sloops and put them under the command of Lieutenant Maynard of the Royal Navy. On November 22, 1718 Maynard spotted Blackbeard's new ship off Ocracoke and attacked. Maynard's crew was larger and the pirates were gradually overwhelmed. Blackbeard fell to a pike thrust, but not before he had been shot five times and wounded twenty times by sword. Maynard had Blackbeard's head cut off and tied it to his bowsprit as he sailed back to Virginia.

Captain William Kidd (c.1645–1701)
William Kidd turned pirate in 1697 after a successful career as a privateer. When no French ships were found on a privateering voyage to the Indian Ocean in 1697, Kidd began attacking Portuguese and British ships. In 1798 he sailed to Massachusetts where he tried to bribe the governor into giving him and his crew a pardon. The governor refused and sent Kidd to London for trial and execution. He is said to have buried his vast treasure somewhere on the American coast. So far as is known, it has never been found.

Henry Avery (c.1653–1696)
Avery was probably the most successful pirate of all time—and he got away with his treasure. In 1695 he captured a ship carrying the daughter of the Moghul Emperor of India. The treasure on board was vast; the gold bullion alone would today be worth about $160 million. Avery divided the spoils and disbanded his crew. He then went to his native Cornwall and gave some of his treasure to relatives. Where he went next was never discovered. It is presumed he began a new life with his vast wealth.

Anne Bonney (fl.1720)
Anne Bonney was born the illegitimate daughter of a rich lawyer in South Carolina. As a teenager she ran away to marry a sailor, James Bonney, and went to sea with him. In May 1719, the Bonneys fell in with noted pirate "Calico" Jack Rackham. In 1720 Rackham and his crew were captured as they were sleeping off a drunken night. The male pirates were hanged, another female pirate, Mary Reade, died in prison, but Anne escaped the noose as she was pregnant. Where she went after her release is unknown.

DARING FRAUDSTER

CRIME

Horatio Bottomley was one of the most audacious and successful fraudsters in British history.

Not content with swindling people out of money, he set about making himself a highly respectable member of British society.

Bottomley was born in London in 1860 and grew up in an orphanage. He trained as a lawyer, but chose to go into the stock exchange. In 1888 he founded the *Financial Times* newspaper. He established it as a reputable commentary on the banking and stock market activity of the City of London. But he also slipped in fictitious stories that boosted the market price of stocks he was trying to sell, or undermined the value of those he was buying. He then joined the Liberal Party and in 1905 was elected a Member of Parliament for Hackney.

> *But he also slipped in fictitious stories that boosted the market price of stocks he was trying to sell.*

In 1908, Bottomley was arrested and charged with fraud relating to Australian gold-mining shares that he had been selling, but which were worthless. The case dragged on for four years before he was acquitted. The failure of the prosecution was largely due to the fact that Bottomley had kept almost no written records. He had, instead, remembered the details of thousands of deals in

HORATIO BOTTOMLEY (1860–1933)

A prison visitor came across Horatio Bottomley at work stitching mailbags and said: "Ah, Bottomley, sewing?" Bottomley replied: "No, reaping."

his head. Although acquitted, the details that came out ruined his reputation in the City. The Liberals ousted him from his seat.

When World War I broke out, Bottomley turned a magazine he was running, *John Bull*, into an unofficial journal for the rank-and-file soldiers. Bottomley went on a series of recruitment drives, using his magnificent oratorical skills and flair for publicity to recruit tens of thousands of volunteers into the army. Throughout the war he maintained a patriotic stance, while earning a fortune from the

So powerful an advocate was Bottomley that after one trial the judge offered him his wig.

magazine and the products it promoted. On several occasions he was accused of profiteering from this but each time he sued for libel and in most actions he won. So powerful an advocate was he that after one trial the judge, Mr Justice Henry Hawkins, offered Bottomley his wig.

In 1918 he stood as an independent candidate for his old seat of Hackney and won a landslide victory. He then began the John Bull Victory Bond Club, a form of savings club in which investors were not paid interest, but instead given the chance to win large cash prizes.

In 1921 he was charged with fraudulently siphoning funds out of the Bond Club into his own bank account. This time, however, he was convicted and sent to prison for seven years. After his release, Bottomley went on the stage with a one-man show in which he recounted the story of his life. By this means he was amassing a third fortune when he died suddenly in 1933.

BOTTOMLEY & NOEL COWARD

There have been persistent rumours that the great British musical writer Noel Coward, was considering writing a comic musical based on Bottomley's career. Evidence of this comes from the fact that in May 1931 Coward lost his wallet at the Theatre Royal, London. It was found in 1981 lodged inside a broken tuba. Inside was Coward's money, plus a photo of Bottomley.

OTHER NOTABLE FRAUDSTERS

Tino De Angelis (b.1915)

Tino De Angelis (right) created the great salad oil scandal of the 1960s. He established a company, Allied Crude Vegetable Oil, which for some years traded legitimately in salad oils. In 1962 De Angelis built a new warehouse in which the vast tanks of oil were linked by a complex system of pipes and pumps that allowed him to move oil quickly from one tank to another. This made it appear as if they were all full, while other tanks were filled with water with a layer of oil on top. He then borrowed vast amounts of money, using the non-existent oil as collateral. By the time the scam was uncovered around $175 million had gone missing. He was given a seven-year jail sentence.

Nick Leeson (b.1967)

Nick Leeson (left) was a British banker whose fraudulent dealings caused the collapse of Barings, one of Britain's oldest independent banks. At Barings, Leeson became the 'star' of the Singapore futures market. At first he made large profits for his employer, and he was awarded a bonus of £130,000 ($260,000) on his salary of £50,000 ($100,000). His trading then began to turn a loss. On February 23, 1995, Leeson left a note reading "I'm sorry" on his desk. An investigation found that his losses totalled £827 million ($164 million). Barings was declared insolvent on February 26 and sold for £1 ($2). Leeson was sentenced to 6 years in prison.

VIOLENT GANGSTER

No gangster in the world is better known than Al Capone. His criminal career ended more than 70 years ago but his image as a ruthless yet stunningly successful crime boss has never diminished.

Al Capone's grip over the Chicago underworld was enforced by clever diplomacy, bribery, and lethal violence. Helped by movies and books, Al Capone's career has acted as an inspiration to generations of criminals.

Capone was born in New York to parents who had emigrated from Italy a few years before. He entered organized crime when he got a job as a bartender at a bar owned by gangster Frankie Yale. Capone's talents quickly led to his rise in Yale's gang and by the age of 20 he is thought to have carried out at least two murders.

In 1919, Yale sent Capone to Chicago to help his friend Giovanni "Johnny" Torrio, who ran much of the Windy City's vice business. When Prohibition arrived, Torrio promoted Capone to run his illegal alcohol business. By 1923, Capone was heading his own mini criminal empire in the town of Cicero.

Meanwhile, Torrio was engaged in a war with the North Side Gang. In 1925, when he was badly injured in a gun battle, he named Capone as his successor. Capone quickly established control over Torrio's gang and established a firm grip on the city's government through bribery and blackmail.

AL CAPONE (1899–1947)

Politicians and senior police officers were in his pocket; his empire of vice operated virtually unhindered by the law.

Politicians and senior police officers were in his pocket, and Capone's empire of vice, gambling, and alcohol operated virtually unhindered by the law. He quickly became the richest man in the city. But if Capone and his gang were beyond the law, they were not beyond the reach of other gangsters. The North Side Gang, led by Bugs Moran, was continually trying to encroach on Capone's territory. There were frequent outbreaks of violence. In 1928 Bugs Moran tried unsuccessfully to have Capone murdered.

Capone plotted revenge, and gave the job of carrying it out

Indirectly, the St Valentine's Day Massacre as it became known, also destroyed Capone.

to his chief executioner, Jack "Machine Gun" McGurn. McGurn discovered that on February 14, 1929 all the gang leaders were to be at a garage to receive a consignment. McGurn had his hired gunmen dress as policemen and burst into the garage.

The gangsters lined up as instructed. The fake policemen then opened up with machine guns and shotguns with such savagery that several of the victims were almost cut in two. The St Valentine's Day Massacre, as the mass killing became known, destroyed the North Side Gang.

> But if Capone and his gang were beyond the law, they were not beyond the reach of other gangsters.

Indirectly, the massacre also destroyed Capone. The killings were so brutal and so open that they prompted a backlash by the citizens of Chicago, and caused the federal government to take an interest. The famous Elliot Ness of the US Treasury discovered a book that detailed payments made to Capone. In 1931, Capone was convicted on five charges of tax evasion. The judge imposed the harshest sentence possible: 11 years in federal prison and one year in the county jail, plus fines.

In prison, Capone's grip on his criminal empire slackened. By 1938, the onset of tertiary syphilis led to a steady decline in Capone's health. He was released in 1939 and died January 25, 1947.

Charles "Lucky" Luciano
(1897–1962)
Charles "Lucky" Luciano (right) was an American gangster from a Sicilian family. He established the Genovese crime family, still one of the most powerful in America, and is credited with having developed the international heroin trade. In 1947 Luciano was declared to be Capo Di Tutti Capi ("Captain of all Captains" or "Boss of Bosses") by the Italian crime families of America. He held the position until his death from a heart attack in 1962 at the age of 64.

Giuseppe Masseria (c.1887–1931)
Giuseppe "Joe The Boss" Masseria moved to America in 1903 to avoid a murder charge in his native Sicily. He joined the Morello Gang, and in 1924 became its boss. By 1929 he had established himself as the head gangster in New York. In 1931 he moved to take control of the Castellamarese mafia family, sparking a war that cost him his life. He was shot by two gunmen while eating lunch.

The Kray Twins
The Kray Twins (left), Ronnie (1933–1995) and Reggie (1933– 2000), ran The Firm, which dominated London's crime world in the 1950s and 1960s. Officially the Krays ran a number of fashionable nightclubs, in which they mixed with celebrity and showbiz customers, but most of their wealth came from armed robberies, protection rackets and arson. In 1969 they were convicted of the murders of two other gangsters, Jack "The Hat" McVitie and George Cornell. Ronnie died in prison. Reggie died three months after being released.

RUTH ELLIS (1926–1955)

"When you fired that revolver, what did you intend to do?" She replied: "It's obvious that when I shot him, I intended to kill him."

of a nightclub where she met David Blakely, three years her junior. He was a well-mannered former public-school boy, but also a hard-drinking racing driver with expensive tastes. Within weeks he had moved into her flat.

Blakely became progressively jealous of Ellis's attentions to male customers, and stayed in the club to keep an eye on her. She, in turn, was jealous of his female friends. Rows fuelled by alcohol became increasingly violent.

On Good Friday, April 7, 1955, Blakely left the house and promised to return in the evening to take Ellis out for a drink. When he had not returned by Sunday evening, she set out to look for him, finally tracking Blakely to The Magdala pub in north London.

As he emerged from the pub, she took a .38 calibre revolver from her handbag and fired six shots. Blakely died almost instantly. Ellis made no attempt to leave the scene. She was arrested and charged with Blakely's murder. Her fate was sealed at her trial when the prosecution asked her:

Ruth Ellis was the last woman to be executed in the UK, and the last woman to be hanged in the English-speaking world.

Born Ruth Neilson in the Welsh seaside town of Rhyl, Ellis left home at the age of 17 to become

a nightclub hostess. She had an illegitimate child, then a short-lived marriage to George Ellis and a second child, but worked steadily at her nightclub career.

In 1953, Ruth became manager

The front page of the Daily Mirror newspaper on July 13, 1955—the day of Ellis's execution.

Ellis made no attempt to leave the scene. She was arrested and charged with Blakely's murder.

"When you fired that revolver at close range … what did you intend to do?" Ellis replied: "It is obvious that when I shot him, I intended to kill him." The jury took just 14 minutes to convict her; she received the death sentence calmly. The case caused widespread controversy. A petition to the Home Office asking for clemency was signed by 50,000 people, but the Home Secretary, Major Gwilym Lloyd George, rejected it. She went to the gallows at Holloway Prison on July 13, 1955, aged 28.

In July 2007, a new petition was published on the 10 Downing Street website. The British Prime Minister is being asked to reconsider the case and grant a pardon in light of new evidence that the jury in 1955 was not asked to consider.

OTHER VICTIMS OF THE HANGMAN'S NOOSE

THE LAST MEN TO BE HANGED IN THE UK

Peter Anthony Allen and Gwynne Owen Evans were the last men to be hanged in Britain.

The murder victim was John Alan West, a 53-year-old laundry van driver who lived alone in Workington, Cumbria. At about 3am on April, 7 1964 his neighbour heard a commotion coming from West's home and saw a car being driven off at speed. The police found West dead on the floor with a stab wound to his chest and head injuries. They soon found a medallion engraved with Evans's name on it in the pocket of a raincoat. He was already known to them as a petty criminal. Within 48 hours of the killing, Evans was under arrest, along with his known partner in crime Peter Allen. Under questioning both men blamed each other for the killing. It seems the pair were short of money and had gone to rob West. At some stage Allen had turned violent and beat him mercilessly.

Whether or not Evans had joined in the assault was never clear but both men were convicted and hanged on August 13, 1964—Evans at Manchester's Strangeways Prison and Allen at Walton Prison in Liverpool.

THE LAST MAN TO BE HANGED IN THE USA

In 1979, Billy Bailey broke out of prison and went on an armed spree that culminated in the deaths of an elderly couple, Gilbert Lambertson and his wife Clara. At that time, Delaware offered prisoners the choice of death by lethal injection or hanging. Bailey opted for hanging and was executed in January, 1996. Delaware has since removed the choice of hanging.

THE SILKEN ROPE

Traditionally, noblemen were able to opt for hanging by a silk rope if sentenced to death in England. There has never been a law on the subject but the right has been invoked several times. The use of silk has little to do with its higher status, however. Hanging with a hemp rope doesn't guarantee a broken neck, which means slow strangulation. A silk rope is thinner and bites into the neck, so cutting off the blood supply to the brain and leading to swift unconsciousness.

Lawrence Shirley, 4th Earl Ferrers, the last peer to be hanged in England, in 1760, was reportedly hanged with a silken rope.

CRIMINAL MASTERMIND

The American mafia boss Carlo Gambino was born in Sicily but moved to the USA at an early age. Unlike many other mafia bosses, he remained largely ahead of the law and, although widely credited with numerous murders and other crimes, he spent little time in prison.

Gambino is thought to have been the main inspiration behind the figure of "The Don" in the *Godfather* novels and movies.

As a cousin of the mobster Paul Castellano, Gambino was given a head start in the American mafia. As a teenager he became a violent enforcer for the mafia chief Charlie "Lucky" Luciano, a period of time when he is thought to have committed several murders on the orders of Luciano.

In 1931, Luciano, and therefore Gambino, inadvertently became involved in a gang war between Luciano's colleague Joe Masseria and another powerful Italian mafia family, the Castellammarese Clan. The resulting Castellammarese War lasted four years and by the end cost hundreds of lives among Italian gangsters.

In 1931, Luciano and Gambino made contact with junior mobsters in the rival camp and persuaded them that the war had to end if the mafia was to survive as an organization. It was eventually brought to a close when the juniors in each clan murdered their seniors in a bloodbath of terrible proportions.

CARLO GAMBINO (1902–1976)

"Mafia is a process, not a thing.
Mafia is a form of clan cooperation to which its individual members pledge lifelong loyalty."
Joe Bonanno, boss of the Bonanno crime family.

After the end of the war, Gambino was placed by Luciano into the Mangano crime family, which specialized in gambling but also hired itself out to other criminal organizations as a murder squad. By 1957, Gambino had worked his way up to head this powerful and lucrative organization, which soon became known as the Gambino Family. Over the next few years, a number of arrests and killings gave Gambino the opportunity to use his wealth and violence

By 1964, it is estimated that he controlled 30 gangs, with a turnover of about $500 million.

to take over a number of smaller Italian gangs in cities outside of his homebase in New York. By 1964, it is estimated that he controlled, either directly or indirectly, 30 gangs with a full-time membership of 1,000 men and a turnover of about $500 million.

During this time, Gambino was manoeuvring against rival mafia bosses Joe Bonanno, Joseph Magliocco, and Stefano Magaddino. Details of these moves are hazy as Gambino always preferred to work behind the scenes.

> *The juniors in each clan murdered their seniors in a bloodbath.*

In 1965, the power play became a shooting war. Bonanno began picking off men loyal to Gambino. Gambino retaliated, but was not getting the best of the violence when Bonanno suffered a heart attack, sold up his interests, and retired from crime. The end of the "Bonanno War" left Gambino as the richest and most powerful mafia boss in America.

TOTAL CONTROL

Gambino exercised control and influence from behind the scenes right to the end, and there was no doubt that by the 1970s his power extended to a greater or lesser extent over every Italian criminal organization in the USA. It was a position that he never relinquished, only nominating his successor, Paul Castellano, months before his death of a heart attack in 1976.

Thomas Blood (1618–1680)
Irish Colonel, Thomas Blood, fought alongside Oliver Cromwell in the English Civil War. When he lost his estates, he organized a gang, and in 1671 tried to steal the Crown Jewels of England. King Charles was so amused by the episode that he returned the confiscated estates. Blood was, in part, the inspiration for the Sabatini novel *Captain Blood* and has featured in the *Flashman* books.

Adam Worth (1844–1902)
The writer Conan Doyle made German-born Worth the model for the fictional criminal genius Professor Moriarty in the *Sherlock Holmes* stories. By 1869, Worth was organizing bank robberies in New York. He moved to London in 1873 where he organized a gang of burglars. His greatest theft was Thomas Gainsborough's portrait of the Duchess of Devonshire.

Jonathan Wild (c.1683–1725)
Jonathan Wild was a famous English criminal, who ran one of the most successful gangs of thieves in 18th-century London while posing as the enemy of crime. Wild was the inspiration for John Gay's *The Beggar's Opera*. He is also a character in the David Liss novel *A Conspiracy of Paper*.

Charlie Peace (1832–1879)
It was his ability to adopt different identities and personas that made the Victorian English crook Charlie Peace so difficult to catch. A notorious burglar and murderer, his somewhat remarkable life later spawned dozens of romanticized novels and films. Peace is mentioned by name in the Sherlock Holmes short story, *The Adventure of the Illustrious Client*.

MEDIEVAL OUTLAW

Dashing through the forests clad in a green outfit with Little John, Friar Tuck, Will Scarlett, and the glamorous Maid Marian, Robin Hood is the most well-known medieval outlaw of all time.

He famously stole from the rich, only to give to the poor and never harmed a woman or child. He was a crack shot with a longbow, the finest archer in England, and fought tenaciously against the corrupt Sheriff of Nottingham. He was the Saxon Lord of Loxley who had been deprived of his rightful inheritance by the wicked Prince John and his gang of Norman nobles.

Such is the legend, but the truth about Robin Hood is rather more difficult to discover. In the search for the real Robin Hood it is necessary to look first at the earliest references to him. These are all fictitious stories dating to the late 15th and early 16th centuries. They do not claim to be true stories, but do state that they are stories about the famous outlaw Robin Hood.

In these stories, Robin Hood is a rather different character than he is in the developed legends with which we are familiar. There is no reference to him being a Saxon lord. Instead he is a quite ordinary country man. His weapons of choice, the longbow and quarterstaff, were those most used by farmers and foresters during the period 1300 to 1450. There is no trace

ROBIN HOOD (fl.13th or 14th century)

The stories told about Robin Hood articulated a general hatred of corruption and dishonesty in government, portraying as hero an honest peasant who takes the law into his own hands to right those wrongs.

of Maid Marian nor Friar Tuck in these tales, though Little John and Much the Miller's Son are there.

In these stories, Robin Hood does not rob from the rich to give to the poor. His motives are more subtle. His enemies are the corrupt and greedy who occupy positions of power. The Sheriff of Nottingham in these early tales is not so much evil as corrupt. He takes bribes to decide court cases and denies justice to poor farmers who cannot afford to pay

The Sheriff of Nottingham in these early tales is not so much evil as corrupt.

him. It is this that earns Robin's enmity, not his wealth. Likewise, Robin attacks and robs rich bishops and abbots who flaunt their jewels and mistresses when they should be poor, humble, chaste servants of Christ.

Robin himself is represented as pious in a conventionally Christian way. Such concerns were those of the medieval peasants from which the stories about Robin sprang.

> Robin himself is represented as pious in a conventionally Christian way.

The stories told about Robin Hood articulated a general hatred of corruption and dishonesty in government, portraying as hero an honest peasant who takes the law into his own hands to right those wrongs. The early tales are quite definite that Robin Hood really did exist, and that he did so during the reign of King Edward. Moreover, there is a persistent belief that he was forgiven by the King, who dismissed the corrupt Sheriff and took Robin into his own service.

THE REAL ROBIN?

Records from the medieval period are patchy at best. However, we do know that in 1323 King Edward II visited Nottingham to sort out some unspecified legal business that concerned the Sheriff of Nottingham. The payroll for the Royal Household records that immediately after this visit a man named Robert Hood was employed as a senior official in the stables.

Sir Eustace Folville (fl.1330–1340)

In 1332, the eminently respectable knight Sir Eustace Folville became involved in a dispute with neighbours over the ownership of a piece of land. The argument turned violent and Sir Eustace found himself declared an outlaw as a result, he always claimed, of a bribed judge. He spent the next four years terrorizing his neighbours, but was eventually given a hearing in front of King Edward II who pardoned him and his men on the condition that they join the English army fighting the Scots.

Thomas Dun (fl.1150s)

Thomas Dun was an outlaw active in Bedfordshire, England during the anarchy of the reign of King Stephen in the 12th century. He and his gang robbed only travellers on the Great North Road, never bothering the locals from whom they bought provisions with their loot. It was this that ensured he escaped justice for 20 years. Dun was famously hostile to lawyers, who he blamed for his having been outlawed in the first place, and he targeted them whenever possible.

Juro Janosik

(c.1690–1713)

Described as the "Slovak Robin Hood", Juro Janosik (right) served in the Hapsburg army for a while, but in 1710 deserted and joined a bandit gang. He quickly killed the chief, took over leadership of the gang, and led them on a career of robbery and murder through the Carpathians. He specialized in attacking Hapsburg officials and distributing some of the spoils to local peasants. The Hapsburg army caught and hanged him in 1713.

A statue of Juro Janosik in Terchova, Slovakia

"THE JACKAL" (b.1949)

"I'm not a sadist or a masochist—I don't enjoy the suffering of others. When we had to eliminate them it was in a cold, simple way with the least pain possible." Carlos the Jackal

Most assassins are famous more for the people they kill than in their own right. One notable exception was the man who became an internationally wanted fugitive under the name of Carlos the Jackal.

"Carlos" was, in fact, a Venezuelan named Ilich Rámirez Sánchez who in 1959 joined the Communist Party at the age of ten and later attended a guerrilla warfare training camp run by Castro's regime on Cuba. After attending university in Moscow,

he moved to Jordan to join the Popular Front for the Liberation of Palestine (PFLP), where he took the name of Carlos. He subsequently took part in a number of military and terrorist campaigns in Israel, Britain, and France. When the French police tried to arrest him in 1975, he shot two of them dead and fled.

Carlos became established as a leading assassin when he planned and carried out a raid on the headquarters of OPEC in Vienna in December 1975. With five others he took more than 60 hostages and had them flown to Algiers. From there, he flew the gang and some of the hostages to Baghdad and Tripoli before returning to Algiers where the gang collected a ransom and was allowed to go free. Carlos then went to Aden to meet the high command of the PFLP where he explained the loss of some of the ransom money, which others had accused him of stealing.

In September 1976 Carlos established a link to the East

TALKING BIG

During his career, Carlos the Jackal claimed responsibility for numerous terrorist acts. The most famous of these were the attack on the Israeli athletes at the 1972 Munich Olympics and the hijacking of an Air France jet to Entebbe in 1976. At the time, Western news agencies and the secret services believed that Carlos had been involved, but it is now known that he had nothing to do with them.

His fame was becoming something of an embarrassment for those who supported him.

German secret police and set up his own terrorist group, which he called the Organisation of Arab Armed Struggle. The group was, in fact, open for hire by anyone prepared to pay cash. One job was to kill dissidents abroad for the Romanian government; another was to work for the Baghdad government killing political opponents living in exile. He also attacked a nuclear power station and several trains in France, though who hired his group for these attacks is not clear. It was widely alleged that he was operating on behalf of the KGB, but this was never proved. In 1985 he moved to Syria.

By this time his fame was becoming something of an embarrassment for those who supported him. When he was caught discussing an operation with Iraqi secret services in 1990, Syria expelled him. He moved to Jordan then on to the Sudan. Unknown to him, however, the Sudanese government was in talks with the French and on August 14, 1994, he was handed over to the French authorities.

In December 1997 he was tried for the murder of the two policemen he had killed in 1975, found guilty, and sentenced to life imprisonment. He remains in jail.

OTHER DEADLY HITMEN

Jimmy Moody (d.1993)

Moody was a London killer, an "enforcer" for the notorious Richardson gang in the 1950s and 1960s. He was credited with many beatings and a few killings before he was convicted of manslaughter in 1967. He was released in 1972 and became an armed robber, founding the notorious "chainsaw gang". Before he came to trial he escaped from prison to Ireland where he became one of the IRA's most feared assassins. In 1983 he was shot dead in London.

Pausanias of Orestis (d.336BC)

Pausanias (above) was an obscure Macedonian nobleman who gained fame for killing King Philip II, father of Alexander the Great. Philip was at a wedding when Pausanias struck, using his position as a royal bodyguard to get close. As soon as Philip fell, Pausanias fled and was well ahead of his pursuers when he tripped and was killed by another bodyguard Attalus.

Yigal Amir (b.1970)

The killer of Yitzhak Rabin, Prime Minister of Israel, in 1995, Amir (below) was a law student involved in protests against Rabin's attempts to build peace with the Palestinians. He became convinced that only by killing Rabin could such a betrayal of Israel be prevented. On November 4, Amir managed to get close to Rabin's official car during an event and shot him twice and a bodyguard once. He was sentenced to life imprisonment. There have been numerous accusations of a wider conspiracy, but none of these has yet been proved.

INFAMOUS BANK ROBBER

Of all the gunmen of the Wild West, it is Jesse James that has proved to be the most enduringly famous.

His career of bank robbery, murder, and train hold-ups was a spectacular one that outranked the exploits of any other bad man. Yet Jesse James might have spent his life as a quiet farmer had it not been for his less well-known brother, Frank.

When the American Civil War broke out, the state of Missouri sided with the Confederate states. Many men were recruited to join the army, but Frank James opted instead to join a guerrilla force led by a man named Quantrill. Quantrill's Marauders raided deep into Federal territory to the north, their activities more akin to those of bandits than of soldiers.

> *Yet Jesse James might have spent his life as a quiet farmer*

When the war ended, the victorious Federal government declared that Quantrill's men would be treated not as enemy soldiers but as criminals and set a date for their trial. Four of them decided to go on the run. They were the brothers Jim, John, and Cole Younger, plus Frank James; Frank's young brother Jesse decided to join them.

The gang's first raid was a bank robbery in Liberty Missouri, when they got away with $15,000 in gold coins. The Younger-James Gang went on to rob 24 other banks over the next 16 years. Throughout this time they kept the sympathy of the rural farming folk of Missouri, which enabled them to gain supplies and hide from the law. It was well known that the Youngers' father and sister had been killed by Federal soldiers in the war. Moreover, the Federal authorities often behaved with brutal oppression against Missouri folk who had actively supported the Confederate cause. The gang was seen as a small team of brave men fighting back.

That sympathy began to wane in the 1870s when the gang robbed Missouri banks of Missouri money, and shot dead a number of loyal southerners in the course of their robberies. It seems that Jesse James was the one responsible

JESSE JAMES (1847–1882)

Some call the outlaw Jesse James America's Robin Hood, while others see him as a cold-blooded killer.

His hold-ups were spectacular ones that outranked the exploits of any other bad man.

for most of the killings. The gang decided that if they were to keep the support of locals they had to start robbing outside the state. The first raids were a success, then the gang moved against the bank in Northfield, Minnesota in 1876. The raid was a disaster. Three of the eight-man gang were killed and all the Youngers captured. Only the James boys got away.

Jesse and Frank fled to Mexico, but returned in 1879. Their first crime was a train hold-up near Kansas City, but they soon returned to bank robbery. They often brought in other outlaws to aid them in their more spectacular raids but never formed a real gang. This habit of using short-term allies proved to be the James's undoing. After ten years of successful raids and bank robberies, Frank and Jesse recruited the two Ford brothers to help them in a raid. But the Fords were more interested in the $10,000 reward offered by the governor of Missouri for Jesse James, dead or alive.

Robert Ford called on Jesse James at his home. As they talked about the planned raid, Jesse noticed a picture on the wall was crooked. When he turned to put it straight, Ford shot him in the back of the head. James died instantly. Frank James fled, but gave himself up six months later. He was spared execution as there was no evidence that he had ever shot anybody. He spent a few years in prison then went back to his family farm and raised crops until his death in 1915.

BONNIE & CLYDE

Bonnie and Clyde were a pair of lovers who acquired a quite undeserved reputation for glamour and romance during their murderous career in the midst of the Great Depression. Clyde Barrow (1909-1934) was a small time thief when he met Bonnie Parker (1910-1934) in 1930. He was arrested and put in prison, but Bonnie smuggled a gun to him, allowing him to escape. The pair went on the run together with Barrow's brother and his wife. The four shot and robbed their way across the Midwest until May 23, 1934 when Bonnie and Clyde died in a shoot-out with officers of the law.

OTHER WILD-WESTERN OUTLAWS

John Dillinger (1903–1934)
Dillinger (right) was the greatest bank robber of the 1930s, and coined the term of G-Men for the FBI. He specialized in armed bank robberies, always carefully planning the attack in advance to scoop the greatest reward for the least risk. In 1934 his girlfriend betrayed him to the police and Dillinger was shot dead. There is some evidence that he had set up a fellow criminal to take his place, and that Dillinger actually escaped with his loot.

Joaquin Murieta (1832–1853)
A 19-year-old farmer when the USA annexed California from Mexico in 1848, Murieta (left) was thrown off his farm by American immigrants, and his brother shot dead for objecting. He set out to kill the men responsible, funding his campaign with a series of robberies. By 1852, he was leading a gang of 90, and took at least $50,000 from bank robberies and other crimes. He was shot dead on July 25, 1853 by an army patrol.

LEGENDARY HIGHWAYMAN

Dick Turpin was the last of the great highwaymen. He swaggered and fought his way across England creating a legend of cunning, daring and glamorous exploits that has endured for centuries.

Richard Turpin was born in 1705 as the son of an Essex farmer. As a boy he was apprenticed to a London butcher and at the age of 21 set up his own shop in Waltham Abbey. He married the daughter of a local innkeeper and seemed set to lead a fairly routine life. But he was already involved in crime. When he was caught stealing a cow to be killed and taken to his butcher's shop, Turpin went on the run.

He managed to steal a uniform belonging to a Revenue Officer and spent the next six months extorting money from smugglers in Norfolk. When they discovered Turpin was a crook himself, the smugglers swore revenge and Turpin fled south to join the Gregory Gang, a band of housebreakers operating in Suffolk and Essex. During one attack on a

DICK TURPIN (1705–1739)

Highwaymen were distinctive figures in the English underworld. They thrived in England in the 17th and 18th centuries, becoming legendary, romantic figures. It was a bold and daring lifestyle that Dick Turpin embraced enthusiastically.

NOBLE VILLAINS

Highwaymen were expected to dress beautifully, ride fine horses, and to spend their loot with abandon. Courage and audacity were their hallmark. In return they expected the homage of their fellow criminals and to have their pick of food and women. Generally, they got it all. Death was the usual punishment and few highwaymen survived for long on the road.

country inn, Turpin persuaded the landlady to reveal where her cash was hidden by the brutal method of holding her over a fire. In April 1735, three members of the gang were caught and hanged, and the brutal gang was broken up.

Accompanied by a fellow survivor of the Gregory Gang named Thomas Rowden, Turpin changed his tactics and decided to become a highwayman. The duo struck first on July 10, 1735, when they held up a gentleman

He walked bravely to his execution, chatting with the crowd and executioner.

riding between Wandsworth and Barnes, just south of London.

Turpin embraced the bold, daring, and dangerous lifestyle of the highwayman, but Rowden did not, and soon left to take a safe and legal job. Turpin then teamed up with an equally notorious highwayman named Tom King. The pair were astonishingly successful at both robbery and evading capture. Their luck ran out in April 1738 when they were drinking at the Green Man Inn at Epping. The landlord recognized King and grabbed him from behind. Turpin drew his gun and in the scuffle that followed accidentally shot King.

> *The pair were astonishingly successful at both robbery and evading capture.*

Turpin then gave up being a highwayman. He travelled to Yorkshire where he took the name John Palmer and became a horse trader. In February 1739, he was arrested on suspicion of handling stolen horses. While in York prison, he wrote to his brother asking for help. The letter was intercepted and Palmer's true identity was revealed. Having been sentenced to death, Turpin reverted to bold highwayman style. He sold all his property and spent the money on a new suit in which to be hanged, as well as a series of parties in prison. He walked bravely to his execution, chatting with the crowd and executioner. He did not wait for the executioner, but jumped off the scaffold himself.

Captain James Hind (1616–1652)

Captain James Hind established the lifestyle of crime that became known as that of the highwayman. He was born in 1616 and took to the road in 1644 amid the anarchy of England's civil war. Until then, highway robbers had been called "footpads", and looked down upon as savage ruffians. Hind made a point of riding a horse, avoiding violence whenever possible, and exhibiting good manners. He claimed to be a royalist gentleman fallen on hard times, and dressed the part.

William Nevison (c.1639–1685)

William (also known as John) "Swift Nick" Nevison was one of the few highwaymen who actually was a gentleman by birth. He left for London as a teenager and became a highwayman in the 1670s, earning fame for his great Ride to York. He held up a coach outside Rochester in Kent at dawn but was recognized, so decided to establish an alibi by riding as far away as possible. Nevison rode to York by sunset and made a point of asking the mayor, no less, what the time was. When accused of the Rochester robbery, Nevison produced the Mayor of York as a witness. Nobody believed the 230-mile (370km) ride was possible in such a short space of time, and Nevison was acquitted.

Claude Duval (1643–1670)

The Frenchman Duval came to England in 1660 as a servant of King Charles II. In 1661 he was sacked for theft and became a highwayman. Duval distinguished himself by his excellent manners and the fact that he led a gang, unlike most highwaymen who operated alone. His most famous exploit was in 1666 when he stopped a coach on Hounslow Heath. He was so struck by the beauty of the lady he was robbing, that he got one of his men to play a tune while he danced with her, and then returned her money.

Human Endeavour

*"Don't be afraid if things seem difficult in the beginning.
That's only the initial impression. The important thing is not to retreat;
you have to master yourself."*

Olga Korbut

FIRST MAN TO THE SOUTH POLE

ROALD AMUNDSEN (1872–1928)

More than any other man, Norwegian Roald Amundsen pushed back the frontiers of the unknown at both Poles.

Long after most of the Earth's surface had been explored, the two Poles and the areas surrounding them remained shrouded in mystery and full of unknown dangers.

The lure of the frozen wastes proved to be irresistible to a new breed of hardy explorers who were prepared to risk their lives to expand human knowledge. More than any other man, Norwegian explorer Roald Amundsen pushed back the frontiers of the unknown at both Poles.

After abandoning his training as a doctor, Amundsen joined an 1897 expedition to the Antarctic led by Adrien de Gerlache. The team was the first to endure the perpetual darkness of a bitterly cold southern winter.

He returned to Norway and fitted out a small sailing ship, the *Gjoa*, for Arctic exploration. Between 1903 and 1906, he used her to become the first man to navigate the Northwest Passage around the top of North America in both directions. Along the way he became the first man to locate the magnetic North Pole.

> *Roald Amundsen pushed back the frontiers of the unknown at both Poles.*

Amundsen's next expedition proved to be his most controversial. He announced a plan to sail towards the North Pole, using ocean currents to move his ship through the pack ice, and then completing the journey on dog sleds. He persuaded his fellow Norwegian explorer Fridtjof Nansen to lend him the icebreaker *Fram*, but gathering funds for the expedition proved difficult.

In 1909 came news that Americans Robert Peary and Matthew Henson had reached the North Pole first. Undeterred, Roald Amundsen continued to raise funds for his trip. Finally, in August 1910, everything was ready and Amundsen set off.

His plan called for him to enter the Arctic Ocean by way of the Bering Straits, so nobody on board thought it odd that they first headed south down the Atlantic. What Amundsen had not told them was that before setting off he had sent a telegram to Captain Robert Scott who was setting off with a British team to

On his return to Europe, Amundsen found himself a controversial figure.

explore Antarctica. In his message Amundsen announced that he was heading for the South Pole.

When the news broke, Scott was disappointed but Nansen was furious. He demanded that Amundsen bring back the *Fram*, but the ship had already left. Amundsen reached the Pole on 14 December, 1911, took a few photos, and planted the Norwegian flag then set off for home. He arrived back having been away for just 99 days.

On his return to Europe, Amundsen found himself a controversial figure. Some hailed him as a hero for his achievement, others as a villain for his deceit. Shrugging off the disputes, he turned north again. In 1925 he flew an airship over the North Pole with the airship's designer Umberto Nobile. The pair were beaten to first place over the Pole by American Lincoln Ellsworth.

It was another trip over the Pole with Nobile in 1928 that proved fateful for Amundsen. Nobile's airship went missing, so Amundsen set off to search for it. Ironically, Nobile returned but Amundsen was never heard from again.

OTHER FAMOUS POLAR EXPLORERS

Matthew Henson (1866–1955) **& Robert Peary** (1856–1920)
The Americans Matthew Henson (far right) and Robert Peary (right) are usually credited with being the first people to reach the North Pole, though the expedition also included three Innuit. Peary was an officer in the US Navy who became obsessed with Polar exploration when on a trip to Greenland. He spent the years 1888 to 1902 on Arctic survey work. In 1909 he set off for the Pole with 133 dogs, 19 sledges and 24 men. He returned on September 7 to announce that he had succeeded, reaching the Pole on April 6. His claim has since been challenged due to navigational discrepancies in his log book, but not definitively disproved.

Captain Robert Scott
(1868–1912)
Robert Falcon Scott was the leader of the second team to reach the South Pole. In 1910 he led a research expedition to Antarctica that had as a secondary aim to reach the South Pole. Scott and four companions set off for the Pole on November 1 and reached it on January 17, 1912 only to find Amundsen's flag already there. Disappointed, they set off on their return but were overtaken by bad weather. Lawrence Oates was suffering from frostbite and, fearing he was slowing down the party, heroically walked out to his death, but to no avail. The entire party died of exhaustion and frostbite.

Ernest Shackleton
(1874–1922)
Alone among Arctic explorers, Shackleton never lost a single man on any of his expeditions. His greatest trip was the Imperial Trans-Antarctic Expedition of 1914. In January 1915 his ship got stuck in ice and was crushed. Using boats, he got his team to Elephant Island. Then he set off with six men in a single boat to sail and row the 900 miles (1,448km) to the nearest manned station, on South Georgia Island. The journey took three weeks, but they made it and a rescue team was dispatched to Elephant Island.

FIRST MAN ON THE MOON

NEIL ARMSTRONG (b.1930)

"It suddenly struck me that that tiny pea, pretty and blue, was the Earth. I put up my thumb and shut one eye, and my thumb blotted out the planet Earth. I didn't feel like a giant. I felt very, very small."

At 2.56 GMT on July 21, 1969, a cumbersomely clad figure climbed down the ladder of his spacecraft, watched by an audience estimated to be over 500 million. History was being made, and it was on TV.

As Neil Armstrong set his booted foot down into the silver-grey dust of the lunar surface, he uttered the now famous words, "That's one small step for man, one giant leap for mankind." More than 236,000 miles (380,000km) away, millions

cheered. President Kennedy's 1961 promise had finally been fulfilled. The United States had put a man on the moon.

The slight slip in Armstrong's speech (it should have been "…one small step for a man…") was uncharacteristic of a man unaccustomed to making errors. The cool, confident commander of the Apollo 11 space mission had prepared the speech while sitting inside the Lunar Module *Eagle* only minutes after demonstrating why he had been given the job. For, as the lunar lander had begun its descent, it was obvious to Armstrong that all was not well with the onboard guidance system. As they headed over a huge crater filled with rocks, Armstrong seized the controls and guided them to a safer landing site. The Earth held its breath in tense anticipation, until finally Armstrong's calm voice came over the radio: "Houston, Tranquility Base here. The Eagle has landed."

Neil Armstrong's historic journey began in his home state of Ohio when, aged 16, and still unable to drive a car, he passed his pilot's licence. Five years later he was a fighter pilot flying combat missions in the Korean War. During the next 17 years Armstrong flew more than 200 kinds of aircraft. In 1966, now an astronaut, Armstrong flew aboard *Gemini 6* on his first space mission. It was very nearly his last.

Armstrong's mission was to dock with the Agena Target Vehicle—the first ever space

The slight slip in Armstrong's speech was uncharacteristic of a man unaccustomed to making errors.

docking. Armstrong achieved the link-up perfectly, but soon after, the coupled craft began to spin. Fearing he and his crew member might lose consciousness, he undocked and aborted the mission. Two years later, Armstrong found himself commander of Apollo 11, and aged 38 began preparing for the four-day flight to the Moon.

> "Houston, Tranquility Base here. The Eagle has landed."

NASA had employed 400,000 people and spent $24 billion to achieve what many had thought impossible. Armstrong and his co-pilot Aldrin were the first to leave their footprints in the lunar dust, but in the next three years ten others would follow.

In his 70s, the man who once rode a 160-million horsepower (120-million kilowatt) rocket into the history books, now flies gliders. "It's the closest you can come to being a bird," he says.

MEN ON THE MOON

Since Neil Armstrong's famous first "small step", 11 other astronauts have set foot on the moon. And while Armstrong and Aldrin spent just 2 hours 53 minutes outside their Lunar Module, on each subsequent Apollo mission this time increased. On the final mission, Apollo 17 astronauts Eugene Cernan and Harrison Schmitt spent more than 22 hours exploring the moon. In that time they covered around 18 miles (29km) in their moon buggy.

Yuri Gagarin (1934–1968)

In 1961 the Soviet Union was winning the Space Race. Four years earlier it had successfully launched the first satellite, *Sputnik 1*. Now, on the morning of April 12, as *Vostok 1* stood on the launchpad of the Baikonur cosmodrome, it was about to trump this success by sending the first man into space. One hundred and eight minutes later, having travelled at a speed of 17,000mph (27,000km/h) and completed a single orbit, Major Yuri Gagarin returned to Earth and a hero's welcome.

John Glenn (b.1921)

Just 10 months after Gagarin's historic space flight, on February 20, 1962, NASA won back some US pride when John Glenn became the first American to orbit the Earth. Launched from Cape Canaveral, Florida, in the space capsule *Friendship 7*, Glenn attained an altitude of 162 miles (260km), circling the Earth three times and completing his flight in 4 hours 55 minutes, 23 seconds. In 1998, aged 77, Glenn became the oldest person in space when he left Earth again for nine days aboard the space shuttle *Discovery*.

Valeriy Polyakov (b.1942)

Russian cosmonaut Valeriy Polyakov holds the record for the longest time ever spent in space. From January 8, 1994 to March 22, 1995 he stayed aboard the *Mir* space station for 437 days, 17 hours and 58 minutes. Add this to his previous time in space, and he has spent more than 678 days in space. A trained doctor, while aboard *Mir* Polyakov actively pursued a programme of research into the effects of micro-gravity on the human body and ways in which astronauts could stay fit and healthy in space.

FIRST MAN TO BREAK THE FOUR-MINUTE MILE

For nearly nine years Gunder Hägg's record for the mile had stood at 4 minutes, 1.4 seconds. Perhaps it would not have lasted so long had World War II not provided a more serious preoccupation for the world's young men.

But stand it did, so tantalizingly close to the numerically neat four minutes, that the challenge of breaking it grew in the minds of athletes and journalists alike.

Roger Gilbert Bannister was born in Harrow, Middlesex in the UK on March 23, 1929. As a child he claimed he found running easy—easier than walking—and he soon discovered that he was good at it, winning several 800m races at school. But his running career really took off when he went to Oxford aged just 17. Before long he was selected as an Olympic possible for the 1948 London Games. But he declined, believing he was not yet ready. Instead, he set about training for the 1952 Helsinki Games.

That Bannister had enormous natural talent is undisputed. His initial successes were achieved with remarkably little training. But as his aspirations rose, so too did his willingness to train harder. At Helsinki, however, Bannister was only placed fourth in the 1500m.

Some believe that it was Bannister's "failure" at the 1952 Olympics that prompted him to focus on running the first sub four minute mile. Working with Austrian coach Franz Stampfl,

ROGER BANNISTER (b.1929)

"As a child, instead of walking, I would run. And so running, which is a pain to a lot of people, was always a pleasure to me because it was so easy." Roger Bannister

Bannister began interval training with increasing intensity.

On May 2, 1953 Bannister ran a storming race, shattering the British mile record with an impressive 4.03.6. "This race made me realize that the 4-minute mile was not out of reach," he said afterwards.

The next year, Australian John Landy notched up similar times and, when slated to run in Finland later in the year, Bannister decided it was now or never.

The meet he chose was held on May 6, 1954, in Oxford, between Oxford University and the British

His initial successes were achieved with remarkably little training.

Amateur Athletic Association. The day dawned wet and windy with cross winds blowing up to 25mph (40km/h).

> *As his aspirations rose, so too did his willingness to train harder.*

Bannister was twice on the point of postponing but just before 6pm, when the race was scheduled to begin, the winds abated and Bannister said, "Let's do it!" With Chris Brasher and Chris Chataway setting the pace, he took his marks. Bannister was going well and still looked comfortable as Chataway took over on the third lap. With 275 yards (250m) to go, Bannister kicked for home. By the time he crashed through the tape, his face was white and drawn. The crowd only heard the announcer say, "three minutes…" before their cheers drowned out the rest.

Bannister had run the mile in 3.59.4 minutes. But 46 days later in Finland John Landy also broke through the four-minute barrier, pushing the record to 3.57.9.

THE MIRACLE MILE

Few races have generated the sense of anticipation as the mile held at the 1954 British Empire & Commonwealth Games in Vancouver. In the line-up were the only two men to have broken 4 minutes: Bannister and Landy. Landy led for most of the race but made the disastrous error of glancing over his shoulder to check on his rival. Bannister streaked to the line in another sub 4-minute time.

Michael Johnson (b.1967)

Widely regarded as the greatest sprinter of all time, Michael Johnson is the only sprinter in history to be ranked number one for the 200m and 400m in the same year—a distinction he achieved an incredible four times, in 1990, 1991, 1994 and 1995. At the 1996 Atlanta Olympics, he won gold in the 400m in a new Olympic record time of 43.49 seconds; in the 200m he also claimed gold, dropping the world record time to an unbelievable 19.32 seconds.

Yiannis Kouros (b.1956)

Kouros inhabits the rarefied world of the ultra-runner, runners who compete at distances beyond the marathon—distances that push human endurance to its very limit. Kouros, however, doesn't simply compete, he dominates. In a career spanning three decades, he has held every world record at distances from 100–1,000 miles (160–1,609km) and in events spanning 24 hours to 6 days. But this Greek-born Australian athlete's most apposite achievement is winning the Spartathlon four times. This 153.85 mile (246km) race traces the footsteps of Pheidippides, an Athenian messenger sent to Sparta in 490BC to seek help in the Battle of Marathon. Kouros ran and won the first-ever Spartathlon in 1983 and then won it again in 1984, 1986, and 1990. In every race he won in a time that has yet to be beaten.

Jim Hines (b.1946)

Born in Dumas, Arkansas, as a youth James Hines preferred baseball to running. As he matured, however, his speed became obvious and he took up sprinting. At the 1968 US National Championships in Sacramento he entered the record

books when he became the first person to run the 100m in under 10 seconds. He confirmed his ability at the Mexico Olympics just a few months later. With race riots in the US, and controversy over South Africa's admission to the Games, tensions were running high. The 100m final was the first in Olympic history in which all the athletes were black. Hines not only won the race but he also set a new world record of 9.95 seconds.

UNDERWATER EXPLORER

For over half a century, the kingdom of Neptune communicated with us in a soft French accent.

Its spokesperson, the charismatic Commander Jacques Yves Cousteau, drew us through the portholes of our television screens into his undersea world and made us love its beauty.

He was born on June 11, 1910 in Saint-André-de-Dubzac, France. At school he was at first unruly and unfocused, so his parents sent him to a boarding school with a reputation for discipline. There he excelled, and after a spell at the French Naval Academy, he joined the Navy as a gunnery officer. In 1935 his hopes of becoming a navy pilot were dashed when he suffered a car accident. To strengthen his injured arms Cousteau returned to swimming, and the sea.

Eager to capture this mysterious underworld on film, in 1936 he invented a waterproof enclosure for his movie camera. When

JACQUES YVES COUSTEAU (1910–1997)

"From birth, man carries the weight of gravity on his shoulders. He is bolted to earth. But man has only to sink beneath the surface and he is free." Jacques Cousteau

DIVING SAUCER

Although Cousteau will always be remembered for inventing the aqua-lung with Emile Gagnon, he didn't stop there. His desire to dive ever deeper and explore parts of the ocean never seen before led him to develop with Jean Mollard the *SP-350 Soucoupe plongeante* or "diving saucer", christened Denise. One of the most successful submersibles ever built, the SP-350 allowed two people to explore depths down to 1,150 feet (350m).

World War II began, Cousteau soon had plenty of work filming shipwrecks for the Navy. At that time, divers were attached to a cumbersome air tube that ran back to the surface. Cousteau wanted to be able to swim freely, so together with engineer Emile Gagnan, he developed a valve that allowed a diver to breathe from a tank of air he could carry on his back. They called it the Self Contained Underwater Breathing Apparatus—SCUBA. It was an incredible breakthrough and it helped to make them very rich.

He introduced his viewers to the denizens of the deep as if they were his friends.

The war over, Cousteau threw himself into his new-found passion of oceanography. His enthusiasm soon won him the support of a wealthy sponsor who bought him an old British minesweeper—the *Calypso*—and had it refitted as a floating laboratory. With a team made up of scientists and film-makers Cousteau began perfecting the art of underwater film-making. For millions of people around the globe the image they have of the underwater world is that captured through the lens of Jacques Cousteau.

> *The war over, Cousteau threw himself into his new-found passion of oceanography.*

Modestly, Cousteau referred to himself as an "ocean technician" but he was much more than that; he was an interpreter, a guide, an enthusiast. His subjects were famously anthropomorphized and he introduced his viewers to the denizens of the deep as if they were his friends.

Over the many years he spent on and under the sea, Cousteau became acutely aware of human impact on his "blue continent". In 1974, he set up the Cousteau Society and in 1992 he attended the UN conference on the environment in Rio de Janeiro. By the time he died on June 25, 1997, he had become known not only as Captain Cousteau but also as "Captain Planet".

OTHER MEMORABLE AQUANAUTS

Lloyd Bridges (1913–1998)
Father of actors Beau and Jeff, Lloyd Bridges Jr (below) became a big star of the small screen thanks to his starring role in 155 episodes of *Sea Hunt*. In 1958 scuba-diving was new and exciting and the undersea adventures of Mike Nelson, became one of the most popular syndicated TV series ever. Once the show ended, Bridges became a certified diver and fervent environmentalist.

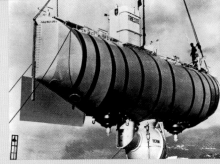

Sylvia Earle (b.1935)
Warmly referred to as "Her Deepness", Sylvia Earle (above) is one of the most accomplished oceanographers ever. She made her first dive aged 17 and over 50 years has logged about 7,000 hours underwater. She led the first team of women divers to participate in the Tektite Project, which explored the possibility of establishing underwater communities. In 1979 she made a dive wearing an armoured JIM suit, setting a women's depth record of 1,250 feet (381m).

Jacques Picard (b.1922) & **Lt Donald Walsh** (b.1931)
The Everest of the oceans is the Challenger Deep in the Mariana Trench. First discovered in 1951, the first divers to explore this area southwest of Guam were Swiss scientist Jacques Picard and US Navy Lieutenant Donald Walsh. On January 23, 1960 they made their descent in the bathyscaphe *Trieste* (above). After descending for five hours, when they reached the seabed 35,797 feet (10,911m) below, *Trieste* withstood pressure of 16,000psi.

FIRST EUROPEAN TO REACH INDIA BY SEA

HUMAN ENDEAVOUR

Vasco da Gama was a Portuguese nobleman who commanded the first European fleet to sail around the southern tip of Africa to reach India. The voyage opened the route for European merchants.

Da Gama studied mathematics at university and took up naval navigation as a hobby. In 1497 King Manuel appointed him to command a fleet of four ships and gave him the mission of discovering a sea route to India. Other Portuguese captains had explored much of the west coast of Africa, and in 1490 Bartolomeo Diaz had discovered a cape beyond which the coast seemed to head north. We now know that this was the Cape of Good Hope, but when da Gama set out he didn't know if this really marked the southern tip of Africa.

Two of da Gama's ships had been specially designed for the trip by Diaz, a third was a rigged merchant ship, and the fourth was a smaller store ship that it was intended to abandon when it had been emptied of food. Da Gama left home on July 8. Following advice from Diaz, he did not sail down the African coast, where a north-flowing current would have slowed him, but sailed south down the centre of the Atlantic until he thought he had reached the latitude of the Cape of Good Hope. He then turned east to find himself only a few dozen miles north of his objective.

VASCO DA GAMA (c.1460–1524)

"The road was crowded with a countless multitude anxious to see us. Even the women came out of their houses with children in their arms and followed us."
Da Gama's diary entry for the day they arrived in Calicut.

On November 25, he rounded the cape and headed north. Finally they reached Mozambique, then a thriving trading colony of the Arabs. The Arabs were not pleased to see Christian ships and attacked, but were driven off. Da Gama seized a local sailor by force and persuaded him to show the Portuguese the route to India as the price of his freedom. On May 20, 1498 the small fleet reached Calicut on India's southwest coast.

The ruler of Calicut was willing to trade, but the port was

The Arabs were not pleased to see Christian ships and attacked, but were driven off.

dominated by Muslim traders who spread all sorts of rumours about da Gama and the Christians. After a few weeks in port, da Gama set off for home with a few sacks of spices and a couple of locals whom he persuaded to accompany him to Europe. He eventually reached Portugal on September 9, 1499. Da Gama was given a hero's welcome, made a count, and given a massive cash reward.

> *Finally they reached Mozambique, then a thriving trading colony of the Arabs.*

In 1502, he led a second fleet to India. This was 20 ships strong and included warships designed to overawe the Arabs that had caused trouble on the first voyage. Da Gama used his power ruthlessly to massacre Arabs and force Indian ports into granting favourable trading terms. The trading stations he established formed the base for subsequent Portuguese power in the area.

BIRTH OF AN EMPIRE

The true importance of da Gama's voyage did not become apparent for some years. By finding a direct sea route from Europe to India, da Gama cut out the previous lengthy overland route, and the Muslim states that controlled it. In the longer term it starved the Ottomans and other Muslim states of trading wealth, allowing the Europeans to overtake them in terms of wealth and sophistication. Da Gama's voyage began the European domination of the world.

Sir Francis Drake (c.1540–1596)

Sir Francis Drake is usually remembered as a privateer attacking Spanish treasure ships, but he was the first European to sail over many areas of sea. He sailed from the Pacific coasts of South and Central America northwards at least as far as northern California, then headed west across the Pacific to become the first man to captain his ship around the world.

Leif Erikson (fl.990–1010)

Leif Erikson was the first European to set foot on American soil. In 1000, he set sail south from the Viking settlements on Greenland in search of a forested land that had been sighted 14 years earlier by another Viking sailor. Greenland had no trees, and the settlers needed wood for building houses and ships. An account of Erikson's voyage has survived, so we know that he called at Baffin Island and Labrador. He then pushed on to a land that might have been Newfoundland or even Cape Cod. After spending the winter there, he returned home.

Christopher Columbus (1451–1506)

Christopher Columbus is remembered as the first European to sail to the Americas in 1492. In fact, Columbus had been trying to reach China, but the lands he found were different from descriptions travellers had brought back about the country. It was on his fourth voyage to the Americas in 1502 that he guessed he had found a new landmass that lay between Europe and China.

Captain James Cook (1728–1779)

Captain James Cook made three great voyages of exploration to the Pacific Ocean. On the first voyage of 1768 to 1771 he visited New Zealand and mapped the east coast of Australia. On the second voyage of 1772 to 1775 he explored the Antarctic, then headed north to Polynesia. On the third voyage, which began in 1776, he mapped the west coast of North America, then discovered the Hawaiian islands.

HUMAN ENDEAVOUR

AMELIA EARHART (1897–1937)

Earhart became a household name in 1932 when she became the first woman to fly solo across the Atlantic.

In 1928 she got a call from Captain Hilton H Railey who was organizing a publicity flight over the Atlantic and wanted to take a woman along to gain extra press coverage. She accepted the offer and flew as a passenger. The flight changed her life. Book publisher and publicist George P Putnam took her on and carefully crafted her image as Queen of the Air. She flew solo across the USA and back, and undertook a variety of other high profile pioneering flights, as well as entering a number of air races. Over the next eight years she was to set seven world records for women flyers.

> *The flight changed her life.*

She then began planning something never before attempted—a round-the-world flight. She bought a Lockheed 10E Electra twin-engined aircraft and hired pilot Fred Noonan to be her co-pilot and navigator. The pair set off from Miami on 1 June, 1937. They flew down to South America, across the Atlantic to Africa and then on to the Indian subcontinent and Southeast Asia. On 2 July, 1937, the pair took off from Lae in New Guinea heading for Howland Island, their first refuelling stop on their route over the Pacific. They never arrived. During the flight, Earhart was heard over the radio several times. The final message came at 8.45am when Earhart broadcast: "We are running north and south."

Flying in experimental aircraft was dangerous as well as exciting, and many pilots lost their lives. Among these was the pioneering airwoman, Amelia Earhart.

Amelia was born into a wealthy Kansas family, though her father's career as a lawyer was not especially successful. On December 28, 1920 she had her first flight in an aircraft at a show and immediately decided on a career involving aircraft. She scraped together the money for flying lessons and by the end of 1921 had her own machine.

Another signal was later picked up near Gardner Island, but it wasn't definitely from Earhart. As soon as the staff listening for her at Howland Island realized that Earhart and Noonan were lost, the coast guard ship *Itasca* was sent out to search for them. Ships from the US Navy were summoned to search remote islands around the area in case the aviators had crash-landed. No physical evidence of the pair or their aircraft was ever found.

Most people believe that Earhart and Noonan missed Howland Island for navigational reasons, then ditched into the sea and died. Others think that she may have reached Gardner Island about 350 miles (560km) from Howland.

In 1941, a woman's skeleton was found on Gardner Island. Unfortunately, it was lost during the war and so was never DNA-tested. We will never know if it was Amelia's.

Chuck Yeager
(b.1923)

Chuck Yeager was the first pilot to fly at supersonic speed. He joined the US Air Force before the outbreak of World War II and served with distinction as a fighter pilot based in Britain from 1943 to 1945. After the war he became a test pilot for the air force and it was in this role that he was chosen to fly the rocket-powered Bell X-1. He broke the sound barrier on October 14, 1947. Yeager later returned to fighter squadron service and held a series of commands. He continued to work in civilian aviation well into his 80s.

Charles Lindbergh (1902–1974)

American pilot Charles Lindbergh became famous for his solo flight across the Atlantic on May 20, 1927. He set off from Roosevelt Airfield, New York, in a specially constructed aircraft named the *Spirit of St Louis* that was packed with massive fuel tanks and sophisticated navigational equipment. On his return to the USA, Lindbergh was given a ticker-tape welcome and the Distinguished Flying Cross. He went on to chart civilian air routes and to develop high-altitude flying techniques. In 1932 his son was kidnapped and murdered, leading to a controversial trial and conviction. Lindbergh worked to keep the USA out of World War II and was subsequently the subject of accusations of pro-Nazi leanings. He later devoted himself to environmental causes and died in 1974.

Steve Fossett (1944–2007)

Steve Fossett was a pioneering balloon pilot famous for being the first person to fly solo non-stop around the world in a balloon. After setting numerous other records in gliders and balloons, Fossett set off on his round-the-world trip from Northam, Western Australia on June 19, 2002. The flight took 13 days 8 hours, covering more than 20,0000 miles (32,000km). On September 3, 2007, Fossett took off in a private aircraft to fly from Nevada to California. His aircraft vanished and has never been found.

FIRST TO BREAK THE SOUND BARRIER ON LAND

In the cool dawn of the Nevada desert a plume of dust streaked across the horizon, at its head a sleek black car. But it was a car like no other. With its arrow-shaped nose cone and twin turbo-prop engines, it looked more like a jet fighter shorn of its wings.

Fittingly, at its controls was RAF squadron leader Andy Green. Suddenly, the desert air was rent by the sound of a whip cracking —twice. It was the sound of a record being broken for ever.

Piloting the ThrustSSC at an average two-way speed of 763.035mph (1,227.953kph), Andy Green wrote his name indelibly into the record books. Indelibly, because although his record may one day be beaten, he will always be remembered as the first man to break the sound barrier on land.

The final run was the culmination of six years' hard work by Richard Noble. Not simply the man behind the ThrustSSC record attempt, Noble was the previously unbeaten holder of the land speed record, which he set in 1983 when he drove Thrust 2 across the same desert at 633mph (1,018.715kph).

It was the morning of October 15, 1997 and the team had decided to make an early start. The cool, crisp air would not only give the twin-turbo fan engines more thrust, but curiously, the speed of sound also drops with air

ANDY GREEN (b.1962)

"It's been a magic morning. We've just achieved what we set out to do all those years ago. Undoubtedly this is the greatest day of my life. It's been a hell of a campaign. It's a hell of an achievement."
Andy Green immediately after his record-breaking sprint.

temperature, so an early start was essential. To eliminate the effects of wind or gradient, the landspeed record rules require two runs to be made, in opposite directions, within an hour. The team had

already failed this challenge once, and were eager not to make the same mistake again.

The first run went brilliantly, with the jet car punching through the sound barrier and reaching

"It's been a hell of a holiday job, but fighter flying is the best job in the world."

759.333mph (1,221.995kph). But as the technicians raced to refuel the car and re-arm the parachutes, the minutes and seconds were ticking away. With 54 minutes and 48 seconds on the clock, it was beginning to look like another failed attempt. But then the big black car began its return run—and in a minute it was all over.

Seconds later the radio crackled to life as timing officials called in: "Pit station, this is USAC timing. I can confirm you completed both runs with a little over five minutes left." The relief was palpable. Then came the figures everyone was waiting for: Andy Green had hit a top speed of over 770mph (1,240kph) and set an average two-way record speed of 763.035mph (1,227.952kph)—not bad for a man who confessed later, "I sharpened my reactions with a Game Boy computer game and a set of juggling balls."

DIGGING FOR GOLD

Almost nine years after his supersonic success in ThrustSSC, Andy Green, now Wing Commander Green, was back in the cockpit of a car designed entirely by computer. The yellow and black, dart-shaped projectile (main picture) was designed to break the landspeed record for a diesel-powered car. And it did—the run made the previous record of 235mph (378.186kph) look positively pedestrian. On August 23, 2006, Green streaked across Bonneville Salt Flats at 350.092mph (563.403kph).

Count Gaston de Chasseloup-Laubat (1867–1903)

The first-ever holder of the land speed record was Count Gaston de Chasseloup-Laubat who set his record on December 18, 1898, driving a Jeantaud electric car at Achères, near Paris. He completed a single kilometre in just 57 seconds, giving an average speed of 39.23mph (63.13kph). Three months later, on March 4, 1899, the Count raised the record to 57.60mph (92.69kph).

Donald Campbell (1921–1967)

Between 1956 and 1959, Donald Campbell raised the water speed record no fewer than four times, to 260.35mph (418.98kph). He then turned his attention to the land speed record and in appalling conditions at Lake Eyre in South Australia, on July 17, 1964, drove at a record-breaking 403.10mph (648.71kph). Incredibly, later the same year, he set a new water speed record of 276.30mph (444.65kph).

Ken Warby (b.1939)

Ken Warby first broke the world water speed record on November 20, 1977 at the helm of *Spirit of Australia*, a wood and fibreglass boat he had built in his backyard and powered by a jet engine bought at a military surplus sale for just $69. Then, on October 8, 1978, at Blowering Dam, New South Wales, Australia, he smashed his own record and became the first person to exceed 300mph (482.79kph) on water and live to tell the tale.

OLYMPIC MEDAL-WINNING GYMNAST

HUMAN ENDEAVOUR

Olga Korbut was the first of a number of teenage gymnastics stars to come out of the Communist bloc during the 1970s. Together they were credited with boosting the popularity of the sport, especially among younger audiences.

Korbut was born in Belorussia (now Belarus) in the USSR. She took up gymnastics at school and by the age of 11 was moved to the state sports academy at Minsk for intensive training. In 1969 she came fifth in the Soviet championships and the following year won the vault event. However, injury and illness meant that her performances in competitions were inconsistent. It was not at all certain that she would join the Soviet team at the 1972 Munich Olympic Games, but in the end she did win a place.

Once in Munich she displayed a technical mastery that dazzled the judges, while the audiences loved her displays of emotion and acrobatic skills. She was dubbed "The Minsk Sparrow" due to her diminutive size. She was the first person ever to perform a backward somersault on the beam, the first to do a backward somersault on bars, and the first to perfect a backward somersault off the beam to finish her routine. She finished the Games with three gold medals and one silver and returned to the Soviet Union a national hero. She was awarded the Honoured

OLGA KORBUT (b.1955)

"Don't be afraid if things seem difficult in the beginning. That's only the initial impression. The important thing is not to retreat; you have to master yourself." Olga Korbut

Master of Sport in Athletics—the youngest person ever to have received this accolade.

The stunning success of Korbut changed gymnastics radically. Until 1972 the emphasis had been on grace and elegance, but the high scores given to Korbut ensured

that henceforth acrobatics and athletic ability would become the dominant features in all high-level gymnastic routines. Women's gymnastics also began to be dominated by younger entrants.

The following year she won a silver medal in the all-round event

At the Munich Olympic Games she displayed a technical mastery that dazzled the judges.

> *"Sometimes I say, 'Enough...
> all my life I've done gymnastics.
> Let's do something else.'
> But I was born in gymnastics,
> and it is in my heart."*
> Olga Korbut

Olga's poise and balance earned her the nickname "The Minsk Sparrow".

at the European Championships. As the 1976 Olympic Games approached, Korbut seemed to be at the top of her powers. But a last-minute minor injury meant that she was not really fit and her performances were below what was expected of her. She won one gold and one silver but went home disappointed.

In 1977 she retired from competitive gymnastics, finished college, and became head coach of the Belarusian team.

OTHER GYMNASTIC PRODIGIES

Oksana Chusovitina (b.1975)

Chusovitina was only 13 when she swept the boards in the junior division at the 1982 USSR National Championships. She rose to become a key member of the Soviet team and won a gold medal at the 1992 Barcelona Olympics. She also scooped every gold except one at the 1990 World Sports Fair. In 1993 she joined the Uzbekistan team and won a string of medals.

Nadia Comaneci (b.1961)

The Romanian gymnast Nadia Comaneci (right) was the first gymnast to be awarded a perfect score of 10 at an Olympic gymnastics event. She entered the European Championships at the age of 13 and won four gold medals. At the 1976 Montreal Olympics she was given no less than seven scores of 10, going on to win three gold medals and one silver. She retired in 1981 to take up coaching.

Lilia Podkopayeva (b.1978)

One of the most successful Ukrainian gymnasts to emerge since the break up of the USSR, Lilia Podkopayeva (left) competed at the World Championships in 1993, aged only 14. At the 1995 World Championships she won the all-round gold medal, then a gold at the vault, plus two silver medals. At the 1996 Olympics, Podkopayeva gained the highest score of the Ukrainian team in every event and won the gold medal for the all-round event. In 1997, injuries forced her to retire.

AFRICA'S GREATEST EXPLORER

Early expeditions made by explorers overland could be extremely hazardous as they involved arduous journeys, often through areas inhabited by hostile peoples. More than one explorer was to disappear without trace, or would escape only by good luck.

Dr David Livingstone was born an impoverished Scot, but he later proved himself to be a tower of strength and religious determination. Born in 1813, Livingstone began work at the age of ten at a local cotton mill.

He went to school for two hours each evening after a 12-hour shift at work. In this way, he learned Latin, Greek, and mathematics and so won a place at Glasgow University. His aim was to become a doctor and missionary, to take what he firmly believed to be the benefits of European science and religion to uncivilized parts of the world.

He went to school for two hours each evening after a 12-hour shift at work.

In 1841, Livingstone arrived in Africa as part of a mission to the Batswana tribe, later heading north to the Kalahari desert, where he preached to the Bakaa people. In 1843, he was attacked by a lion and lost the use of his left arm. In 1849, he headed north again 600 miles (966km) to Lake Ngami and the lands of the Makololo, which had never before

DAVID LIVINGSTONE (1813–1873)

He devoted his life to missionary journeys through the heart of Africa, returning periodically to areas settled by Europeans.

been visited by Europeans. His first attempt to reach there failed but he succeeded in 1851. Thereafter, he devoted his life to missionary journeys through the heart of Africa, returning periodically to areas settled by Europeans.

He explored the Zambezi and Luanda rivers, then went up the Ruvuma to reach Lake Nyasa. There he first came across Arab slave traders and was disgusted by the cruelty of their trade.

In 1865 he set off for lake

There he first came across Arab slave traders and was disgusted by the cruelty of the trade.

Tanganyika, to try to find the source of the Nile. He spent the following years wandering around the headwaters of the Congo and Nile rivers. As far as the civilized world was concerned, Livingstone had vanished, so in 1871 the *New York Herald* newspaper hired explorer Henry Stanley to try to find him. Stanley set off into the interior and after eight months found the Scotsman at a town called Ujiji and greeted him with the immortal words, "Dr Livingstone, I presume".

Stanley headed back to Zanzibar but Livingstone refused to leave, despite the fact his health was failing. He begged supplies and porters, then set off southwest to explore Lake Bangweulu. He died on May 1, 1873. His dedicated porters embalmed his corpse and carried it to Zanzibar with all his books and notes. His body was buried in Westminster Abbey, but his heart was cut out and left in Africa.

In his last years, Livingstone's private porters had to carry him everywhere on a litter.

Meriwether Lewis (1774–1809) & William Clark (1770–1838)

Meriwether Lewis (left) and William Clark (below left) were hired in 1803 by US President Thomas Jefferson to explore a vast tract of land that the USA had just bought from France. This Louisiana Territory, as it was known, stretched from the Mississippi to the Pacific and was totally unexplored by Europeans. Lewis and Clark set off with their expedition in May 1804. Their first objective was to reach the Mandan tribe on the Missouri River, a people regularly visited by fur trappers. They spent the winter of 1804–05 among the Mandan, collecting details of the lands further west. Beyond the Mandan, the team entered unexplored lands. They discovered the Yellowstone River, then pushed on to the Marias, where they turned south to follow the upper Missouri. By July, they were marching up the Jefferson River and in August entered the Bitterroot Mountains. In October they reached the Snake River, arriving at the Pacific Ocean on November 7, 1805. By the time they reached St Louis in September they had been away for two years. Before long, the USA would begin to send traders, settlers, and soldiers westward in the wake of Lewis and Clark.

Robert Burke (c.1820–1861) & William Wills (1834–1861)

Robert Burke (right) and William Wills (far right) set out to do for Australia what Lewis and Clark had done for North America. They failed, but in doing so explored a vast region of the continent. They left Melbourne in August 1860 with camels, pack horses, and masses of equipment. Their aim was to reach the Gulf of Carpentaria on Australia's north coast, and explore all the land in between. Things soon began to go wrong and the expedition split at Cooper's Creek. Burke, Wills, Charles Gray, and John King headed north on camels for the Gulf while the rest stayed behind to explore the area. Burke and Wills eventually reached the coast, but disaster struck on the way back. Gray died of dysentery on April 17. The three survivors struggled on to Cooper's Creek only to find that the base team had left that morning. Burke and Wills died soon afterwards, and King only survived by joining a band of Aborigines who gave him food and shelter until he was rescued.

INTREPID MOUNTAIN CLIMBER

When Sir Edmund Hillary and Tenzing Norgay stood on the roof of the world in 1953, they had not only climbed the Earth's highest mountain, they had also redefined the possible for all those who came after them.

But one man later set his sights even higher. Not content with the possible, Reinhold Messner would redefine the impossible.

Everest stands 29,035 feet (8,850m) above sea level. Here the air is thin, containing only a third of the oxygen found at sea level. According to the world's medical experts, the only way climbers could survive above 26,247 feet (8,000m) was to take their own oxygen supply.

Reinhold Messner didn't agree. And in 1978, together with Peter Habeler, he set out to prove the world wrong. When their plans became public they elicited widespread criticism. Undeterred, the pair pressed on with their audacious plan, climbing with the Austrian Everest Expedition.

When their plans became public they elicited widespread criticism.

After suffering a series of setbacks, they made rapid progress. Arising at 3am on May 8, the altitude was beginning to take its toll. It took them four hours to reach Camp V but with the weather worsening, they decide they had to press on.

REINHOLD MESSNER (b.1944)

"That solo ascent is the most remarkable attempt on Everest ever. Add to it what he achieved later and he is undoubtedly one of the greatest mountaineers of all time."
Sir Chris Bonington

Despite having to lean on their ice axes and rest after every step, the climbers somehow reached the Hillary Step. Messner said afterwards that it was like his mind had died, and only his soul compelled him to move forward.

So it was that Habeler and Messner, finally reached the summit in the early afternoon. Their success was a defining moment in the history of mountaineering. They had achieved a physical feat deemed medically impossible. Two

Messner said it was like his mind had died and only his soul compelled him to move forward.

years later, to prove it was no fluke, Messner climbed Everest without oxygen again—this time alone.

Born in Brixen-Bressanone, South Tyrol in 1944, Messner reached his first alpine summit aged only five. By the time he was 22, he and his younger brother Günther were among the best climbers in Europe. But in 1970 Günther was killed in an avalanche as the pair were returning from an ascent of Nanga Parbat. Reinhold survived, only to find that many believed that he had abandoned his younger brother.

He was forced to give up pure rock climbing due to his injuries. Messner channelled his energies into conquering the "eight thousanders"—the 14 highest mountains on Earth. One by one they fell to his skill and single-mindedness, until on October 16, 1986, when he stood atop Lhotse on the Tibet-Nepal border, he became the first man to climb them all. It was an incredible feat.

IN SEARCH OF THE YETI

To many, Messner's obsession with the Yeti is proof that he has climbed one mountain too many without oxygen. But in 1986 Messner saw one of these elusive beasts himself, in Tibet. His first glimpse was of a shadow, but the 14in (35cm) wide footprints were real enough. For a week he searched for 12 hours a day. His next sighting was of a female yeti with young. After talking to locals and analyzing the evidence, Messner not only believes the Yeti is real, but that it is a rare species of nocturnal Tibetan bear.

Edmund Hillary (1919–2008) **& Tenzing Norgay** (1914–1986)
At 11.30 on the morning of 29 May, 1953 two men stood where no one had stood before. At 29,035 feet (8,850m) above sea level, Edmund P Hillary, a New Zealand beekeeper, and Tenzing Norgay, a Nepalese Sherpa, had reached the summit of Mount Everest.

Led by Colonel John Hunt of the King's Royal Rifle Corps, this was the 11th assault on the summit and the 9th by a British team. It had begun on March 10, when the expeditionary force of 12 climbers, 20 sherpas, and 362 porters, carrying over 10,000lbs (4500kg) of equipment had set out from Kathmandu and trekked 170 miles to Nanche Bazar.

After a period of acclimatization, Hunt pressed on up the Khumbu Glacier, establishing camp after camp ever higher. The last—Camp VIII—at 27,500 feet (8,382m) on the South Col, was from where a hand-picked pair of climbers would make their final assault on the summit.

On May 26, Charles Evans and Tom Bourdillon launched the first summit attempt. But at just above 28,750 feet (8763m) one of their oxygen sets malfunctioned and they were forced to turn back. Next it was Hillary and Tenzing's turn. After a fitful night at 27,900 feet (8503m), the pair arose at 6.30am and by 9am they had reached the South Summit. Surmounting a 40-feet (12m) high rocky step, later called the Hillary Step, they zig-zagged across the summit ridge until the vast plateau of Tibet opened up before them. As Hillary would say afterwards, "A few more whacks of the ice axe in the firm snow, and we stood on top." There, the pair unfurled three flags: the British Union Jack, the flag of the United Nations and the flag of Nepal.

ICONIC SOCCER HERO

In the football firmament, one star shines more brightly than any other. Born Edson Arantes do Nascimento, he is known to millions as Pelé.

In 2000, Pelé was voted Athlete of the Century by the IOC and Player of the Century by FIFA.

In a career spanning 22 years, he played more than 1,360 matches, scored over 1280 goals and is the only player to win three World Cup gold medals. A virtuoso, he personified the Brazilian style of football that so mesmerized the world.

Born in Três Corações, Brazil, Pelé's footballing father, Dondinho, encouraged his boy to kick a ball as soon as he could walk. Spotted by Brazilian International Waldemar de Brito, by the time he was 15 he had joined Santos FC—the club he would stay with for most of his playing career.

> *A virtuoso, he personified the Brazilian style of football that so mesmerized the world.*

PELÉ (b.1940)

In 1967, Pelé stopped a war when Nigeria's warring factions agreed on a 48-hour ceasefire so that they could watch him play an exhibition match in Lagos.

Making his debut in 1956, he scored in his first match. At the age of just 16 he was the top scorer in the league. Less than a year after turning professional he was called up to the Brazilian national team and, still only 16, he scored his first goal when Brazil lost to Argentina 2-1 in 1957.

A year later he was playing in the World Cup: the youngest player ever to do so, the youngest ever to score, the youngest to score a hat trick—and then the youngest to play in a final, in which he scored twice against Sweden.

Pelé's incredible ability so captivated Europe that many of the big clubs tried to tempt the youngster. Fearful of losing their star, the Brazilian government declared him a national treasure, effectively blocking a move.

In Pelé's next World Cup he scored in the first match, but picked up an injury that kept him out of the rest of the tournament. The 1966 finals were even more of a disappointment when Brazil

A year later he was playing in the World Cup: the youngest player ever to do so.

went out in the first round after a series of brutal challenges against Pelé. Having vowed never to play in a World Cup again, Pelé was finally persuaded to join Alberto, Jairzinho, Rivelino, and Tostão in what is widely believed to be one of the greatest teams ever seen. His performance in Mexico was electrifying, the young player scoring six times including a header in the final against Italy.

Pelé played on at Santos until 1972 when he retired. In 1975, however, he was persuaded to join the New York Cosmos. As the Cosmos general manager, Clive Toye put it, "I told him don't go to Italy, don't go to Spain, all you can do is win a championship. Come to the US and you can win a country." Pelé did both, leading the Cosmos to the 1977 NASL championship and raising the profile of soccer immeasurably.

Pelé ended his glittering career appropriately at the Giants Stadium, in an exhibition match between Santos and Cosmos. Playing one half with each team, he scored once for Cosmos who finally won the game 2-1.

WHAT'S IN A NAME?

Edson Arantes do Nascimento was named after Thomas Edison, the inventor. As a boy, Edson was an admirer of the goalkeeper, Bilé. Whenever Edson played in goal he would call out his hero's name each time he made a save. To one of his classmates the name sounded like "Pelé", so he taunted him with the nickname. Edson punched the boy—but the name stuck.

Diego Maradona (b.1960)

Only one player repeatedly challenges Pelé for the title of best player of all time: Diego Maradona. When FIFA were choosing their Player of the Century in 2000, they ended up honouring both players. While the Argentine number 10 is most often remembered for his "hand of God" goal, it was his Goal of the Century against England that characterized his talent and brought him such adulation from the fans.

Franz Beckenbauer (b.1945)

Known as "der Kaiser", Beckenbauer was capped 103 times for Germany. He is one of only two players to hold bronze, silver, and gold World Cup medals and the only person to have won a World Cup as both a player, in 1974, and as manager, in 1990. His authority on the pitch was matched only by the panache with which he could pass the ball. His long attacking runs from defence even led to Beckenbauer being credited with the creation of the modern sweeper role, a style of play that had never been seen before.

Johan Cruyff (b.1947)

Voted European Footballer of the Year three times, Johan Cruyff was not only blessed with tremendous speed and control, he was also a master tactician. A central attacker, he was an early proponent of "Total Football". He is also credited with the eponymous Cruyff Turn, a classic trick, where the attacker feigns a shot, drags the ball back with his foot and turns, leaving the defender left for dead.

TOP BASEBALL STRIKER

"A figure unprecedented in American life. A born showman off the field and a marvellous performer on it, he had an amazing flair for doing the spectacular at the most dramatic moment."

So wrote *The New York Times* of George Herman Ruth Jr—known to millions of sports fans simply as Babe Ruth, and arguably the first celebrity athlete whose fame transcended his sport.

Born on February 6, 1895, George Herman Ruth Jr didn't have an easy start in life. His parents ran a bar and had so little time for their young son that at the age of seven they sent him to the Catholic missionaries who ran a local school. George hated the restrictive environment and used sport as an outlet. He grew to become a powerful pitcher and skilful catcher, and when he was 19 was spotted by Jack Dunn, owner of the Boston Orioles.

George hated the restrictive environment and used sport as an outlet.

By this time George Ruth Jr was over 6 feet (1.8m) tall and powerfully built, so when he was referred to as "Jack's newest babe" the ironic nickname stuck. Within five months the Boston Red Sox had bought his contract and Babe Ruth began playing Major League baseball. On the field he was an almost immediate success. In his first World Series game in 1916

BABE RUTH (1895–1948)

"No one hit home runs the way Babe did. They were something special. They were like homing pigeons. The ball would leave the bat, pause briefly, suddenly gain its bearings, then take off for the stands."
Yankees team mate, Lefty Gomez

he pitched 13 scoreless innings for the 2-1 win—a record that still stands today. In 1918 he notched up another World Series win. But after a poor 1919 season, Boston's new owner, Harry Frazee, sold Ruth to the New York Yankees for $100,000. It was a huge sum at the time—but history was to prove that the Yankees got a bargain.

Ruth's success came at a turbulent time in baseball's history.

When Yankee Stadium opened in 1923 it was nicknamed "The House that Ruth Built".

In 1919, eight Chicago White Sox players were accused of throwing the World Series, and the public's faith in the game was at an all-time low. Ruth's hard-hitting, gritty style of play was just what was needed to get the game back on its feet. In 1920, during his first season with the Yankees, Ruth smashed 54 home runs. When Yankee Stadium opened in 1923 it was nicknamed "The House that Ruth Built", and Ruth fittingly slammed a home run in the stadium's inaugural game.

In his 22-year career Babe Ruth's statistics were awesome.

In 1927 he hit 60 home runs in a 154 game stretch, a record that stood for 34 years. His career total of 714 home runs stood unmatched for 39 years, and his .690 lifetime slugging percentage may never be equalled.

In 1948, Babe Ruth donned his famous pinstripe uniform for the last time to celebrate the 25th anniversary of the opening of Yankee Stadium. And on that day, to honour the player who had made the Yankees and baseball known around the world, the club retired his number 3 shirt.

THE CURSE OF THE BAMBINO

When Ruth played for the Red Sox they were one of the most successful teams in Major League baseball. But that all changed when Ruth was sold to the New York Yankees in 1919. In what became known as "The Curse of the Bambino" the Yankees went on to win 26 World Series titles, while the Boston Red Sox did not win a World Series title for the next 86 years.

When Babe Ruth died of cancer later the same year, more than 100,000 people came to Yankee Stadium to pay their respects to the baseball hero.

OTHER BASEBALL LEGENDS

Ted Williams (1918–2002) Boston Red Sox star Ted Williams was the best left-handed hitter of the live ball era, scoring a .406 in 1941. Nicknamed the "Splendid Splinter", Williams was a consummate technician and at the end of his career he wrote *The Science of Hitting*, a manual that is still studied today. He was, however, unpopular with the press for his often abrasive nature.

Lou Gehrig (1903–1941) Batting in the shadow of the great Babe Ruth, Gehrig once said, "It's a pretty big shadow, it gives me lots of room to spread myself." And spread himself he did. In 14 years he played 2,130 consecutive games for the Yankees, earning himself the nickname "The Iron Horse". In that time he hit 493 homers, batted in 1,990 runs and achieved a lifetime slugging percentage of .632.

Joe DiMaggio (1914–1999) Nicknamed the "Yankee Clipper", DiMaggio helped the Yankees to win nine World Series titles and ten American League championships. He sealed his reputation just before the USA joined World War I in 1941, when he managed a hit in 56 straight games. Already popular on the field, DiMaggio's fame exploded following his nine-month marriage to Marylin Monroe.

Ty Cobb (1886–1961) Ty Cobb, the "Georgia Peach", set around 90 Major League records. His career batting average of .367 remains the highest in the history of the game today. He was also the first to be inducted into the baseball Hall of Fame, receiving 222 out of a possible 226 votes. Careful with his cash, he invested wisely and is believed to have become one of the first baseball millionaires.

GREATEST OLYMPIC SWIMMER

MARK SPITZ (b.1950)

"There's nothing better in the world, when you're trying to be the best in the world, than to actually say, 'I am the world record holder. I am the best in the world.'" Mark Spitz

By the time Mark Spitz stood poolside at the 1972 Munich Olympic Games, he knew he was the best in the world.

And in a matter of days he would prove it, winning seven gold medals and setting seven world records—an incredible feat that may never be beaten.

Spitz was just two years old when his parents left California for Hawaii, and it was in the warm waves of Waikiki Beach that he learned to swim. By the time he was six, now back in California,

he was swimming competitively at the Sacramento YMCA. Three years later he joined the Arden Hills Swim Club where he was coached by Sherm Chavoor. By the following year he held 17 national titles and one world record. When his training schedule clashed with his Hebrew classes, his father reportedly told the rabbi, "Even God likes a winner".

In 1965 Spitz got his first taste of gold. Aged 15 he entered the Maccabiah Games in Tel Aviv, Israel, and won four gold medals. Two years later he broke his first world record—the 400m freestyle. It was a great boost to his preparations for the 1968 Mexico Olympics. Brash and full of confidence, he boasted he would win six medals. In the end he won only two golds, a silver, and a bronze. For many that would have been a career high. Spitz described it as "the worst meet of my life".

Out of the pool Spitz had set his sights on becoming a dentist, and in 1969 he enrolled at Indiana University. The school had a great reputation for aquatic sports, and while there he trained with former national swimming champion James 'Doc' Counsilman. His preparations for the 1972 Munich Olympics were focused and meticulous.

As the Games approached the only surprise was that Spitz had grown a moustache. It had taken him four months and he decided to keep it as a talisman. When asked by a Russian coach if the

Between 1965 and 1972, he won nine Olympic gold medals, one silver, and one bronze.

moustache didn't slow him down, Spitz improvised, claiming that it deflected water from his mouth, allowed him to keep his head lower and so swim faster. Within weeks several Russian swimmers were sporting similar facial hair.

His father reportedly told the rabbi, "Even God likes a winner".

Spitz's Olympic performance appears textbook perfect. From his first event, the 200m butterfly, to the last, the 4 × 100m medley relay, he not only won gold in every race, but in each one he also set a new world record. In later accounts he would claim that he lost confidence after winning his fifth event and even considered sitting out the 100m freestyle. But his old coach Sherm Chavoor urged him not to quit—the rest is history.

After the games Spitz, still only 22, and having set an incredible 33 world records, retired from swimming and made his living from product endorsements and television appearances.

TERRORIST ATTACK

Mark Spitz's incredible seven-gold-medal achievement should have been reason enough for the 1972 Munich Olympics to be remembered. But, tragically, there was second reason. Palestinian Black September terrorists attacked the Israeli team headquarters. By the end of the ordeal, the terrorist group had killed 11 Israeli athletes and coaches.

Johnny Weissmuller (1904–1984)

Throughout the 1920s Johnny Weissmuller was the fastest freestyle swimmer in the world. He set 67 world records and won 3 gold medals at the 1924 Paris Olympics in the 100, 400, and 800m freestyle, and two more at the 1928 Olympics for the 100 and 800m freestyle. His acting career took off in 1932 when he exchanged his swimming trunks for a loincloth, and took the starring role in *Tarzan the Ape Man*.

Captain Matthew Webb (1848–1883)

On August 25, 1875, aged 27, Captain Matthew Webb became the first person to swim the English Channel—a feat that at the time was thought impossible. Smothered in porpoise grease, and given beef tea and strong ale from his support boat, he swam for 21¾ hours. For a few years, Webb was an A-list celebrity, but as his fame dimmed he was driven to perform outrageous stunts. His attempt to swim the rapids below Niagara Falls led to his death.

Alison Streeter (b.1964)

Since Captain Webb first proved the Channel could be swum, more than 600 other attempts have been successful. Alison Streeter, nicknamed "Queen of the English Channel", can lay claim to 43, plus the record of having swum it more times than anyone else. She first swam the 21 miles (34km) in 1983 aged just 18. In 1989, she set the women's record for a crossing from France to England in 8 hours 48 minutes. In 1990, she also became the first woman to swim the Channel three ways, non-stop.

Benoît Lecomte (b.1967)

After his father died, French-born long-distance swimmer Lecomte decided to swim the Atlantic in tribute and to raise money for cancer research. In 1998 he completed the 3,736 nautical miles (5,600km) in 72 days. Lecomte trained up to six days a week for two years to develop his endurance. Accompanied by a 40-foot (12m) yacht crewed by just two French sailors, he swam for 6 to 8 hours a day, in 2-hour sessions.

Military

"Rules are for the the obedience of fools
and the guidance of wise men."

Douglas Bader

GREAT EMPIRE-BUILDER

King Alexander III of Macedon set out at the age of 20 on a military expedition that would see him conquer the largest empire ever known until that date.

Although the political unity of his empire would collapse soon after his death, the Hellenistic culture that he established, and which spread rapidly, proved more enduring. Indeed, it has been argued that our current Western culture is largely a descendant of Alexander's Hellenistic vision.

The basis of Alexander's success was the professional and superbly trained Macedonian army that had been created by his father, King Philip II. But it was Alexander's innate talent for military operations combined with an astute tact in diplomacy that enabled the young man to lead his men on a career of conquest that has no equal.

Alexander's first campaign was to crush the rebellious city of Thebes that had risen up against the Macedonian hegemony over Greece. That was achieved with brutal thoroughness. In 334BC he set out to invade the vast Persian Empire at the head of a force of around 40,000 men. The heart of his army was the professional Macedonian force, but he also had highly effective Thessalian cavalry units and Thracian skirmishers as well as contingents of men from most Greek states.

His first campaign led to the Battle of the Granicus and

ALEXANDER THE GREAT (356BC–323BC)

It has been argued that our current Western culture is largely a descendant of Alexander's Hellenistic vision.

Alexander's capture of the key cities of Halicarnassus, Miletos, Sardis and Ephesos. This Granicus Campaign is often overlooked, but it showed Alexander at his most inventive. The campaign was won largely by Alexander's command of logistics, which allowed his army to move quickly.

The next year he defeated Emperor Darius III with the Persian Royal Army at the Battle of Issus. Alexander spent the following years attacking Phoenician cities and securing his hold on the grain fields of Egypt. He then turned east to defeat Darius once more at the Battle of Gaugamela.

The campaign was won largely by Alexander's command of logistics, which allowed his army to move quickly.

At this battle, Alexander may have been outnumbered by as many as four to one, but his tactical genius and the training of his soldiers won out.

Darius was murdered soon afterwards by Bessus, one of his own commanders, who went on to try to establish himself in power in the eastern part of the Persian Empire. Alexander took three years to defeat Bessus, then launched himself into the invasion of India that led to the Battle of the Hydaspes in 326BC. Alexander then turned back towards Babylon.

> *At this battle, Alexander may have been outnumbered by as many as four to one, but his tactical genius and the training of his soldiers won out.*

Back at the heart of his newly won empire, Alexander dismissed his veterans with lavish gifts and set about recruiting a new army that he planned to lead into Arabia or, perhaps, to Sicily and Italy.

A LASTING LEGACY

On returning to Greece after his travels, Alexander began reorganizing the administration of his vast empire and set about trying to fuse the learned Greek culture that he admired so much with his native Macedonian warrior ethos and the sophisticated Persian luxury of his new subjects. This task was still incomplete when he died, apparently of typhoid fever exacerbated by alcoholism, at the age of 32.

Tamerlane (1336-1405)

Tamerlane, or Timur, was the founder of Muslim Timurid Empire of Asia. Timur was born into the Barlas tribe of Turks, which he took over in 1369, but claimed to be a descendant of Genghis Khan. He then began his career of conquest, crushing the Mongol Golden Horde to seize control of the Silk Road and its wealth, and even invaded the Ottoman Empire.

Zahir ud-Din Mohammad (1483–1530)

Babur meaning "Tiger" was the nickname of the Islamic conqueror Zahir ud-Din Mohammad, a descendant of Tamerlane. In 1494 he inherited from his father the small territory of Fergana. He spent the next few years conquering Herat, Kabul, and Samarkand for the powerful Shah of Persia. Then, in 1526, he struck out on his own to invade India with 12,000 men. By 1529 he was master of all of northern India.

Augustus (63BC–AD14)

Augustus, the title by which Gaius Octavius Caesar is usually known, founded his empire by reforming the system of government rather than by outright conquests. After disposing of his uncle, Julius Caesar's, enemies, Augustus renounced all formal offices, keeping only the right to veto any government decisions, which became the basis of power for the next three centuries.

Shih Huang-Ti (259BC–210BC)

Sometimes known as Qin Shi Huang-Ti, Shih Huang-Ti inherited the Chinese state of Zhao in 247BC. He then set out to conquer the other Chinese states to unify all the Chinese peoples under his own rule by 221BC. Determined to avoid civil wars, Shih Huang Ti destroyed the old system of noble landowners, replacing them with governors and other officials appointed by himself.

INSPIRATIONAL WAR HERO

Douglas Bader became one of the greatest fighter pilots and leaders of the British Royal Air Force during World War II. He achieved this remarkable feat despite having lost both his legs in a pre-war flying accident.

Bader was born into a military family, but chose to ignore the army and join the RAF instead. He passed through training as an above-average pilot and seemed set for a career in the RAF. But on December 14, 1931, he crashed his aircraft while performing aerobatics at Reading Airfield. Both his legs were amputated, one above and one below the knee. He was fitted with a pair of experimental metal legs and by the spring of 1932 could walk and drive a modified car.

When war was declared, Bader volunteered and demanded that he be given a medical test.

He was passed as fit to fly and spent the winter retraining on modern combat aircraft. In February 1940, he joined No. 19 Squadron at RAF Duxford, then in June took command of No. 242 Squadron, a Canadian unit that had suffered heavy losses in the German invasion of France. He rapidly rebuilt the squadron with new pilots, new aircraft—and a massive boost to morale.

During the Battle of Britain, Bader operated his squadron out of Duxford with great success. He then became involved in a bitter controversy—known as the Big

DOUGLAS BADER (1910–1982)

*"Rules are for the obedience of fools
and the guidance of wise men."*
One of the key lessons that Bader instilled in his pilots.

Wing Argument—within Fighter Command. Bader favoured waiting until a wing of three fighter squadrons was assembled before launching a massed attack, and opposed sending squadrons in piecemeal. Critics pointed out that it took so long to form up a wing that the Germans sometimes escaped from a raid without being attacked.

In 1941, Bader was promoted to Wing Commander and given command of the all-Spitfire wing, based at Tangmere in Sussex, south east England. This new

Bader proved to be a troublesome prisoner. He tried to escape several times.

formation was equipped with Spitfire VBs, which had two 20mm cannons and four .303 machine guns. However, Bader insisted on flying a Spitfire with just eight machine guns and no cannons, as he considered machine guns to be better against fighters.

By August 1941 he had shot down 22 enemy aircraft, making him the 5th-highest-scoring RAF fighter pilot. On August 9, he baled out over France after his Spitfire collided with another aircraft. In doing so, Bader lost one of his artificial legs. As a result, the Germans gave a British aircraft a "free pass" to fly a replacement leg across the Channel.

Bader proved to be a troublesome prisoner, making so many attempts at escape that the Germans threatened to take away his legs. He also became an enthusiastic "goon-baiter", meaning that he teased and annoyed the German guards, or "goons". Eventually, he was sent to the "escape-proof" Colditz Castle until spring 1945.

POST-WAR CAMPAIGN

After being released from Colditz, Bader could have quit the forces, but instead chose to remain in the RAF until the summer of 1946, when he left to return to work in the oil business. He subsequently devoted much of his time to campaigning for those with disabilities and, in particular, for those who had lost limbs for whatever reason. It was for this charitable work, not his war record, that he was knighted in 1976. He died of a heart attack in 1982.

OTHERS WHO TRIUMPHED OVER ADVERSITY

Ludwig van Beethoven
(1770–1827)
The great German composer Beethoven began to lose his sense of hearing at the age of 26. He was profoundly deaf by 1814 when he was 44 years old. He overcame his deafness when composing by gripping in his teeth a rod that was attached to the soundboard of his piano.

Francisco Goya
(1746–1828)
The Spanish artist Francisco Goya was struck deaf by a fever in 1792 at the height of his fame. He refused to be deterred by the sudden handicap and went on to become a court painter to the royal family as well as producing a series of idiosyncratic works that in many ways anticipated modern art.

Franklin Delano Roosevelt (1882–1945)
Roosevelt (above) was paralysed from the waist down by polio in 1921. He didn't allow the extent of his handicap to become public and took great care to avoid being photographed in his wheelchair. In 1932 he ran for President of the USA and won by a landslide that saw him take all but six states.

RETREATING MILITARY LEADER

Military retreats are rarely popular with the soldiers or successful, though some can mean that an even worse defeat is avoided.

None was more disastrous than Napoleon's retreat from Moscow in 1812. The disaster was all the more severe as it was a catastrophe entirely of Napoleon's own making. It was a defeat that precipitated the great military leader's downfall.

Bonaparte had worked his way up from being an army officer to become first the dictator and then, from 1804, Emperor of France. He achieved this meteoric rise through hard work and a genius for military operations. By 1810 all of Europe other than Portugal and Britain had been either defeated or cowed into an alliance favourable to France.

He achieved this meteoric rise through hard work and a genius for military operations.

NAPOLEON BONAPARTE (1769–1821)

"However skilful the manoeuvre, a retreat will always weaken the morale of an army." Napoleon.

In 1811, Russia broke a treaty with France that banned trade with Britain. Napoleon decided to punish Russia by invading the country at the head of the largest army Europe had ever seen. He mustered an invasion army of 400,000 men, supported by flank guards, rear guards and supply line guards totalling another 400,000 men. More than half these men came from allies of France.

Napoleon did not take enough food for the campaign, believing his men could pillage what they needed. They crossed into Russia on June 24, heading for Moscow. Commanded by the veteran Mikhail Kutuzov, the Russian armies retreated before this vast host. As Napoleon advanced he was forced to detach troops to guard towns and bridges, as well as to search for food. Kutuzov turned on September 7, at a strong defensive position at

Borodino, but Napoleon smashed his way through the defences and marched into Moscow. The Russians had evacuated the city, and now set it on fire. About 80 per cent of the wooden city was reduced to ashes, depriving the French of shelter.

Aware that the Russians were bringing up reinforcements, and disappointed that he had not forced them to surrender,

Of his 800,000 men, around 400,000 were killed, and 100,000 taken prisoner.

Napoleon ordered a retreat out of Russia. Kutuzov moved quickly to close in on the flanks of the retreating army, forcing them to go back the way they had come. That area had been stripped of food on the march to Russia. Thousands of horses died from starvation, which crippled the French supply system and led to mass starvation among the men and a shortage of ammunition.

The Russians launched numerous raids and attacks, inflicting heavy casualties. Finally, all French discipline collapsed and the bitter Russian winter weather struck. Napoleon's casualties were huge. Of his 800,000 men, around 400,000 were killed, and 100,000 taken prisoner. Many thousands of the survivors were so badly injured that they were no longer fit for front line service. Napoleon never recovered from the disaster and was ousted from power three years later.

WOLVES

The aftermath of the retreat from Moscow caused great problems for the farmers of eastern Germany. Vast numbers of wolves followed the column of starving men and horses out of Russia. It has been estimated that the wolf population of Prussia and Poland tripled in 1812. The wolves then turned to hunting livestock and, allegedly, people. It took more than five years to reduce their numbers again.

George Washington (1732–1799)
During the American War of Independence, George Washington retreated to Valley Forge in the autumn of 1777, after losing the Battle of Brandywine on September 11 and launching an unsuccessful raid on the British garrison at Germantown in early October. He stayed there for the winter, during which time he lost 25 per cent of his men to disease and the cold. The next spring, however, Washington began a thorough retraining, aided by the Prussian soldier Baron von Steuben. That summer he manoeuvred the British out of Philadelphia and laid siege to New York City. He went on to win the war and become the first President of the USA.

Xenophon (c.435–354BC)

In 402BC, 10,000 Greek mercenaries, among which was the noted veteran Xenophon, were hired by the Persian prince, Cyrus the Younger, to help him take the throne of Persia from his elder brother, Artaxerxes. At the Battle of Cunaxa, just outside Babylon, Cyrus was killed and most of his army promptly fled. Xenophon was faced with leading the mercenaries on a 1000-mile retreat north to the Black Sea. The Greeks not only had to fight off the Persian army, but force their way through the territory of hostile tribes, find a route over the mountains, and endure cold and hunger before meeting Greek merchant ships that carried them home.

General Sir John Moore (1761–1809)

In 1808, the British sent an army led by General Sir John Moore to assist the Spanish to fight off a French invasion. General Moore had reached Salamanca before he learned that his Spanish allies had been defeated and that Napoleon was marching against him. Moore decided to retreat to the port of Corunna where the British fleet would evacuate him and his army. On January 15, 1809 Moore turned to face the French just outside the walls of Corunna and inflicted a sharp enough defeat to allow his troops to embark on the waiting ships. Moore himself was killed when struck in the chest by a cannonball and was buried on the ramparts of Corunna.

HISTORY'S MOST VICIOUS QUEEN

BRUNHILDA OF THE FRANKS (d.613)

In Germanic legend Brunhilda became an almost supernatural figure of towering emotions, deadly violence, and hideous revenge.

Brunhilda was a princess of the Visigothic tribe, then holding power in Spain, who came north to marry Sigebert, a prince of the Franks around 570.

Her sister, Galswintha, married Sigebert's half brother Chilperic. In 576, the king of the Franks died and his lands were divided between both sons. Sigebert took the east and Chilperic the west.

Galswintha was murdered in 580 by her husband's younger lover, Fredegond. Brunhilda swore vengeance for her sister's death. She began by launching an army to invade Chilperic's lands, but after much savage fighting the invasion failed. In the aftermath, Chilperic had Sigebert murdered and took Brunhilda captive.

Brunhilda managed to seduce Chilperic's son and enticed him into letting her escape. Back home,

Brunhilda raised a fresh army and launched a new invasion. The war dragged on until 597 when Fredegond died. Thousands had been killed and vast areas of land laid waste. In 613, Brunhilda, now an elderly lady, was tricked into captivity by Fredegond's son Clotaire. After torturing her, he had Brunhilda's arms and legs tied to horses. The horses were whipped to a gallop, causing the ropes to snap tight. Brunhilda died instantly but her fame lived on.

KILLER QUEEN

Queen Fredegund of Neustria (d.597) was young, beautiful, and utterly ruthless when in 579 she became the lover of elderly King Chilperic I of Neustria. She murdered Queen Galswintha so that Chilperic was free to marry her, which he did. As soon as she had produced a son and heir, she had Chilperic's existing five children murdered. After Chilperic was murdered in 584, she proclaimed herself regent for her son. She ruled until her death in 597.

Thousands had been killed and vast areas of land laid waste.

Queen Mary I of England (1516–1558)

Queen Mary I of England came to power in 1553 determined to undo the religious reforms of her brother, Edward VI, who had introduced a more radical form of Protestantism than their father Henry VIII. Mary was a devout Catholic and she soon began to introduce Catholic bishops. In 1554, she married King Philip II of Spain and invited the hardline Catholic, Cardinal Reginald Pole, to come to England to serve as Archbishop of Canterbury. With Pole at her side, she began the persecution of Protestant clergy. More than 300 Protestants, including three bishops, were executed for religious crimes during Mary's reign.

Empress Irene of Byzantium (752–803)

Empress Irene of Byzantium took power when her husband, Emperor Leo IV died and she became regent for their son Constantine VI. She introduced economic reforms, but caused controversy for her support of iconography. In 790, Constantine took power, but he proved incompetent and in 797 Irene overthrew him, blinding him so that he could not return to rule.

Cleopatra III (161 BC–101 BC)

Cleopatra III seduced her uncle, Ptolemy VII, and bore him two sons. She then murdered Ptolemy VII's only legitimate son by his sister-wife Cleopatra II to ensure her sons' succession. When Ptolemy VII died, Cleopatra killed her aunt Cleopatra II. She then took power as regent for her sons. When the elder boy turned 18, she tried to have him killed, and then ruled in her second son's name.

Queen Aelfthryth of England (c.945–1000)

Queen Aelfthryth of England was the second wife of King Edgar. When Edgar died, his son, Edward, by his first wife became king instead of Aelfthryth's son. So, on March 18, 978, when Edward paid a visit to his stepmother, at her home in Corfe, Dorset, she gave him a cup of wine. But, as he leaned forwards to take it, one of her servants stabbed him in the back.

Queen Catherine de Medici (1519–1589)

Catherine de Medici came to France in 1533 as the 14-year-old bride of the Dauphin Henri. In 1547, Henri became king. When he died in 1559 Catherine took over as regent for her son, Francis II. In 1572, she helped organize the notorious St Bartholomew Day's massacre when 50,000 French Protestants were murdered.

Queen Jezebel (d. c.843 BC)

Queen Jezebel (right)—a princess from Sidon—married King Ahab and so became Queen of Israel. She used her influence over Ahab to introduce the pagan gods Baal and Asherah to Israel. When the Israelite religious leaders protested, she had several of them executed. In 841 BC Ahab was killed by his senior general, Jehu, who then ordered her immediate execution.

BLUNDERING GENERAL

LT GENERAL CHELMSFORD (1827–1905)

The Zulus would be defeated by a later British invasion but Chelmsford's disastrous campaign remains the worst defeat the British suffered during the entire 19th century.

Chelmsford ranks as a blunderer for two reasons: he led his army into an ambush that resulted in the worst defeat suffered by a European army at the hands of colonial enemies, and he was partly responsible for starting the war in the first place.

When Sir Frederic Thesiger, 2nd Baron Chelmsford, arrived in Cape Town in March 1878 to command the British armies in South Africa, he found the colonies in a state of upheaval. There was a serious drought, food shortages, and refugee problems. To the east lay the vast Zulu Empire with a standing army of around 50,000 and at least as many again available as reserves. Chelmsford thought that the Zulu king Cetshwayo might invade British territory. He decided to attack first to gain the elements of surprise and initiative.

Chelmsford left one force in British territory to guard against a Zulu counter-invasion, while he marched at the head of a powerful invasion force, crossing the Buffalo River that formed the border at Rorke's Drift. To the north a smaller column formed a flank guard and a second similar force was to the south.

By January 22, the British had sighted only a few Zulu scouts. Chelmsford had no idea where the main Zulu army was. That afternoon one of his cavalry units came across 1,500 Zulus in the Nquthu Hills. Chelmsford leapt to the conclusion that this was the main Zulu army.

He then made the fatal mistake of dividing his army. He took any fast-moving troops to the Nquthu Hills, leaving the rest to guard his main camp on the slopes of a rocky massif named Isandhlwana. Around noon, Chelmsford arrived on the Nquthu Hills to find the 1,500 Zulus retreating. Meanwhile, the main Zulu army had hooked around behind him and launched an attack on his base camp. The British had rifles and artillery, the Zulus only spears and clubs. It should have been a British victory, but Chelmsford had failed to set up defensive lines around the

The Zulu army attacked and annihilated the central British column at Isandhlwana.

camp. The Zulu onslaught was so sudden and so massive that the defenders were overwhelmed.

Within less than an hour almost the entire British force had been wiped out. In total, 600 British soldiers plus more than 100 local troops and 600 allied tribesmen were killed. The Zulus lost around 2,000 men. They then swept on to Rorke's Drift where they spent the next 24 hours attacking the 100-strong British garrison.

> *Within less than an hour almost the entire British force had been wiped out.*

The Zulu main army (impi) then moved north. Unlike Chelmsford, Colonel Charles Pearson—leader of the British coastal flank—had stopped each night in a position that he could defend. When the Zulus attacked, his men drove them off and then dug in for a siege lasting two months.

Chelmsford was relieved of his command but went on to defeat the Zulus at the Battle of Ulundi before the arrival of his replacement, Viscount Wolseley.

Chelmsford also had Natal auxiliaries, volunteers, and irregulars under his command.

Maxime Weygand (1867–1965)

Weygand had served most of his career as a staff officer, earning a reputation for superb logistical ability, but he had little experience commanding in action. Nevertheless, it was Weygand the French government chose to take over the defence of France as the Germans broke through the French defences in May 1940. Arriving at a moment of crisis, Weygand decided that his first priority should be sorting out the paperwork and supply system. By the time he turned his attention to fighting it was too late—his armies had already been defeated.

Publius Quintilius Varus (46BC–AD9)

Publius Quintilius Varus was the commander responsible for the worst military defeat of the Roman Empire, until Rome itself fell to the barbarians. In AD7 he was made governor of the newly conquered province of Germania, which covered much of what is now western Germany. In AD9 there was a small revolt, which Varus decided to put down with overwhelming force. He marched three legions—the XVII, XVIII, and XIX—plus assorted auxiliary units into the Teutoburg Forest, near modern-day Osnabrück. He was guided by a German prince named Arminius. In fact, the revolt was merely a lure to get Varus and his men into the forest. A major uprising had been planned, and the man behind it was Arminius. Varus marched straight into an ambush. Of the 50,000 men he had with him, barely 800 survived the three-day battle.

Douglas MacArthur (1880–1964)

For many, Douglas MacArthur (second from left) was a great general, but to others he was a coward who earned the nickname "Dugout Doug". In 1941, he was commander of the forces in the Philippines. On December 7, when Japan attacked Pearl Harbor, air reconnaissance gave him eight hours' notice of a Japanese attack on the Philippines the next day. MacArthur did nothing, allowing his entire air force to be destroyed on the ground. He also herded his remaining troops into pre-war bunkers and because he had forgotten to stock the defences with enough food, the men had to surrender in April 1942. By then, he had evacuated to Australia.

MILITARY ADVENTURER

HERNÁN CORTÉS (1485–1547)

In his quest to discover the New World, Cortés discovered and ultimately destroyed a formerly unknown civilization.

Hernán Cortés was born in 1485 as the younger son of an impoverished Spanish knight.

He was given a good education then packed off to the American colonies, namely the island of Hispaniola (now Santo Domingo), to earn a living. Then, in 1518, he was put in charge of 500 men and sent to establish a new fort on the mainland coast to serve as a base for trading with the inland tribes. He had been in present-day Mexico only a few weeks when a column of men arrived carrying lavish gifts of gold and silver. The ambassadors said they had come from the Aztec emperor Montezuma and promised Cortés more gifts on the condition that he stayed where he was and did not set off to visit Montezuma. Cortés, however, set out at once to visit Montezuma, taking with him his small army of 500 men.

On the way to the Aztec capital of Tenochtitlán, Cortés met several tribes subject to the Aztec ruler. Cortés promised to free them from Aztec rule if they joined him. He therefore arrived to meet Montezuma at the head of a sizeable force. Montezuma, meanwhile, thought that Cortés was a god and welcomed him. Cortés quickly put himself in charge of the Aztec state.

> *Cortés promised to free them from Aztec rule if they joined him.*

In 1520, Spanish soldiers interrupted an Aztec religious festival that involved human sacrifice. This led to an Aztec uprising, in which Montezuma was killed by his own people when he appealed for peace. Cortés and his men were driven out of Tenochtitlán with heavy losses—about 70 per cent of the Spaniards were killed. Cortés then recruited more local allies and Spanish adventurers before returning to Tenochtitlán. The war that followed lasted 20 years but ended with the Spanish in firm control of the entire Aztec state. Cortés then retired to Spain to live on his hard-won wealth.

Cortés set out at once to visit Montezuma, taking with him his small army of 500 men.

Jørgen Jørgensen (1780–1841)

The Danish sea captain Jørgen Jørgensen was nothing if not ambitious. In 1809 he was commanding a privateer—a privately owned naval ship and paid for in loot. On June 21 he sailed into Reykjavik, capital of Iceland. Finding the place unguarded, Jørgensen announced that he was taking control of Iceland in the name of the King of Denmark. He then looted the State Treasury of everything it had and took up residence in the Governor's mansion. He was in the process of imposing new taxes on the Icelanders when a British Royal Navy ship arrived. He was taken to Britain, later to be transported to Australia.

Giuseppe Garibaldi (1807–1882)

Garibaldi (left) believed passionately in Italian nationalism and hated the way that, in 1860, large parts of Italy were ruled by Austria or by foreign-born noblemen. He raised a private army of 1,000 men and equipped them with red shirts, arms, and equipment. He then hired a ship and took his men to Sicily where they joined a local revolt against King Francis II of Naples. Declaring himself to be Dictator of Sicily, Garibaldi raised an even larger army and invaded southern Italy. He crushed the Neapolitan army and ousted King Francis. He then marched north and met King Victor Emmanuel of Piedmont heading south. Italy was then united under Victor Emmanuel, though Rome was not added until 1870.

John of Gaunt (1340–1399)

In 1366 a French army put the pro-French Prince Enrico on the throne of Castille. The ousted King Pedro asked the English for help and gave his daughter in marriage to John of Gaunt (right), son of Edward III, to seal the pact. Pedro died soon after, so John of Gaunt claimed the Castillian throne in the name of his wife. In 1385 he took an English army to attack Castille. After four years of fighting, a treaty was arranged that saw John's daughter marry Pedro's son while another daughter married the King of Portugal. Gaunt thus ended up as the grandfather of two kings.

An Lushan (c.707–757)

An Lushan joined the Chinese army in about 735 as a mercenary recruited from the nomadic tribes north of the Great Wall. He proved to be a loyal and competent commander so rose to command the 130,000 strong Chinese army on the northern frontier. When Yang Kuo Chung became Chief Minister he was jealous of An Lushan. In 755 orders for An Lushan's arrest were issued. An Lushan moved first, marching his army south to crush the central Chinese army and declare himself Emperor. He was murdered by his own son after ruling for only one year.

Porfirio Díaz (1830–1915)

Díaz (above) became a soldier in 1855 and joined Benito Juárez in the Mexican civil war. In 1867 Juárez gained complete power. When he died in 1872 his two lieutenants, Díaz and Lerdo, both claimed the presidency. After winning the Battle of Tecoac in 1876, Díaz became President of Mexico. He began an enlightened rule of liberal trade policy and reform, but one that was enforced by harsh military control. In 1910 one of his chief supporters, Francisco Madero, raised a rebellion and Díaz fled to France.

RENOWNED USURPER

In 521 BC the great ruler of the Persian Empire, Cambyses, died during a campaign to conquer Egypt. His place was quickly taken by his younger brother, Smerdis.

According to later official records, this succession was puzzling, as Smerdis (also known as Bardiya) had been absent for many years following a quarrel with Cambyses. The story goes that Smerdis refused to see anyone who knew him, and Darius—a former friend—became suspicious.

One day, Darius and six other noblemen marched to the doors of the royal audience chamber and, when they were refused entry, killed the guards. They burst into the room to confront Smerdis. Darius said he knew instantly that the man on the throne was not Smerdis. He claimed the pretender was a priest named Gaumâta who was impersonating Smerdis. And so, the priest was killed instantly.

> *Darius said he knew instantly that the man on the throne was not Smerdis.*

However, Cambyses had left no legitimate children and there was no obvious heir. The Persians decided to leave the choice to the gods. The leading noblemen gathered together. Each man brought with him a horse, which was tethered in a line facing the noblemen; the man whose horse whinnied first would be the next

DARIVS.

3

DARIUS THE GREAT (c.549 BC–485 BC)

The leading noblemen gathered together. Each man brought with him a horse, which was tethered in a line along with the others, facing the noblemen; the man whose horse whinnied first would be the next ruler.

ruler. By a trick of horsemanship, Darius ensured that his horse was the first—and so he became ruler of the vast Persian Empire.

Darius was not widely accepted at first, and had to impose his rule with force—suppressing rebellions throughout the empire. Once established, however, he began a series of reforms. He gave the empire a coinage for the first time, built roads, reorganized the civil service, and overawed his neighbours with a vast army.

Darius was not widely accepted at first, and had to impose his rule with force.

Selim the Grim
(c.1465–1521)

Selim I, also known as "the Grim", usurped power in the Ottoman Empire in 1512. Selim was one of many sons of the ruler Bayazid. He poisoned his father, then accused his brothers of the murder and had them all killed on the spot. All his male relatives were killed, plus any officials that he did not like. About 300 died in those two days and Selim took power.

Francesco Sforza
(1401–1466)

The Italian mercenary captain Francesco Sforza (above) married the daughter of Duke Filippo of Milan in 1441. When Filippo died, the Milanese council declared a republic, which Sforza outwardly supported while plotting its overthrow. In 1450, he used his troops to put him on the throne to rule in the name of his wife.

Juan Vincente Gómez
(1857–1935)

Gómez (above) was head of the Venezuelan army under President Cipriano Castro. He grabbed power when Castro died in 1908 and ruled as a military hardman until his death. He reformed the economy to great effect, but creamed off vast sums for himself and pandered to foreign big business.

Zimri (d. c.876BC)

Zimri usurped power in Israel in about 876BC. Zimri was commander of the bodyguard to the unpopular King Elah. One night Elah became hopelessly drunk, so Zimri took the opportunity to stab him to death then have himself proclaimed king by a carefully organised palace coup. The army, however, preferred their own commander Omri. Zimri was dead within weeks.

Mahapadma (fl.360BC)

Mahapadma usurped power in Magadha in 363BC. Born the illegitimate son of a barber and a prostitute, Mahapadma worked his way up through the bureaucracy of the Indian state of Magadha through talent and hard work. In 363BC he staged a coup, murdered all his rivals and rewrote all the contemporary chronicles to hide exactly how he had become king.

King Henry I (c.1068–1135)

Henry I (below) of England was the younger brother of King William II and Duke Robert of Normandy. On August 2, 1100 William was shot dead with an arrow when out hunting. Henry, who was in the hunting party, raced off to be crowned king before Robert, who was away, could intervene. In 1105, Henry threw Robert into prison and seized Normandy as well.

DEVASTATING BOMB COMMANDER

Air Chief Marshal Sir Arthur Travers Harris led the bomber wing of the British Royal Air Force for most of World War II.

His uncompromising belief in the ability of bombers to seriously damage enemy war industries and his insistence on the primacy of strategic bombing over battlefield air support earned him the nickname of "Bomber" from his men and the public.

Harris served in fighter squadrons for most of World War I and stayed in the RAF when peace returned. He became a convert to the power of bombing when serving in India and fighting against tribal enemies on the Afghanistan border. When World War II broke out he returned to Britain to take command of No 5 Group of Bomber Command, based in Lincolnshire. His expertize in night bombing led to his promotion to leader of all of Bomber Command in 1942.

He became a convert to the power of bombing when serving in India.

SIR ARTHUR HARRIS (1892–1984)

He developed the tactic of area bombing. This involved choosing an area where several factories or other targets were close together and bombing the general area.

Harris knew that navigating at night for hundreds of miles over blacked-out enemy territory made finding individual factories or rail junctions virtually impossible except on nights of a clear full moon. He therefore developed the tactic of area bombing. This involved choosing an area where several factories or other targets were close together and ordering his men to bomb the general area, usually the centre of an industrial city. This inevitably involved civilian casualties, but at first these were low due to good German bomb shelters and the limited bomb loads carried by British bombers.

In August 1943, Harris concentrated his entire bomber force on the city of Hamburg for successive raids. The city centre was destroyed and thousands of civilians killed. Due to poor weather and the need to support

His expertize in night bombing led to his promotion to leader of all of Bomber Command in 1942.

the D-Day landings in Normandy, Harris did not send his main bomber force back to Germany on major raids until the autumn of 1944. By that time new, larger bombers could carry more bombs, while navigational aids and improved tactics meant that huge bomb loads could be dropped on to city areas with precision.

The damage to Germany's war industries and civilian casualties rose quickly. On February 16, 1945 the city of Dresden was heavily bombed and tens of thousands of Germans killed.

After the war the awesome damage inflicted by Bomber Command became clear, as did the large numbers of civilians killed. Harris was furious that Bomber Command alone did not get a special medal, and refused the honours offered to him in protest. He resigned to write his memoirs and died in 1984.

OTHER INFAMOUS "BOMBER BOYS"

Hermann Göring (1893–1946)

While other airmen formulated the principles of a bomber offensive, it was Hermann Göring (right) who first put it into practice. He fought as a fighter pilot in World War I and ended it as a hero. As head of the Luftwaffe from 1934, Göring set about creating an effective armed air force. It was his bombers that launched the first air assaults on a massive scale, tearing the heart out of Warsaw then Rotterdam, and contributing to the decision of the French government to abandon Paris. He was proved correct in his prediction that the Luftwaffe would fail in the vast spaces of Russia. Göring was sentenced to death at the Nuremberg Trials but committed suicide.

Curtiss LeMay (1906–1990)

The American commander who formulated the strategy of the bomber war against Japan, Curtiss LeMay (left) transferred to the Pacific in 1944. On March 9 he launched a raid on Tokyo, using incendiary bombs dropped from low altitude; up to 100,000 people were killed. Over the next 5 months his aircraft bombed 64 cities killing 330,000 people, injuring 476,000 and leaving 8.5 million homeless. He retired in 1965.

Guy Gibson (1918–1944)

In 1939, the career RAF bomber pilot Guy Gibson flew one of the first bombing missions to Germany. He had flown an amazing 176 missions before he was chosen to lead the 617 Squadron on the famous Dambuster Raid in 1943. Both the Moehne and the Eder Dams were destroyed, and two others damaged. Two other dams were attacked but not breached. Only 11 of the bombers survived the mission; 53 crew members died in the raid.

TOP FIGHTER ACE

The most successful fighter pilot of all time, and a hero in his country, was Major Erich Hartmann of the German Luftwaffe in World War II.

In a combat career of almost three years he shot down an astonishing 352 confirmed enemy aircraft. His exemplary image was enhanced in post-war years by his committed stance against Nazism.

Born in 1922, Hartmann joined the Luftwaffe at the age of 18 but didn't graduate as a trained fighter pilot until 1942. He was then sent to join Fighter Squadron (JG) 52, which was then flying Messerschmitt Bf109 fighters in southern Russia.

He flew his first mission on October 14, and within 30 minutes was diving on Russian aircraft that were strafing a column of German troops. After expending all his ammunition without scoring a single hit, Hartmann then found himself surrounded by Soviet fighters.

He flew his first mission on October 14, and within 30 minutes was diving on Russian aircraft.

ERICH HARTMANN (1922–1995)

By the end of 1943, Hartmann had become known to the Russians as the "Black Devil". Whenever his unit was sighted in an area, the Russians would move in their most experienced fighter units with orders to shoot him down.

Eventually escaping into cloud cover, he realized he'd run out of fuel and had to crash land. He hitched a ride back to base, where he was taken off flying duties.

Hartmann returned to combat on November 5, and was flying a patrol with three comrades when they spotted a formation of 18 Russian Sturmovik bombers escorted by 10 fighters, and dived to attack. He poured shots into a Sturmovik, but to no effect. He then remembered his instructor telling him that the crew of Soviet bombers were protected by armour plate, so he switched his attack to the starboard engine. This caught fire at once and exploded, sending the bomber crashing to the ground. Hartmann went on to shoot down a

Hartmann developed a theory of aerial combat.: "Detect–Decide–Attack–Disengage".

further 61 Sturmoviks, each time by targeting the engines.

In the course of his long combat career, Hartmann developed a theory of aerial combat that he tried to teach to all new recruits. His doctrine was simple: "Detect–Decide–Attack–Disengage". The key thing he taught was knowing when NOT to attack. He believed it was better to avoid a combat that you were not certain of winning than to attack regardless. Hartmann himself was not a particularly good shot so he always closed the range until the enemy aircraft filled his windscreen before firing.

By 1943, the Germans were on the defensive on the Eastern Front, and Hartmann's unit was moved repeatedly to fight off attacking Soviet bomber formations. By the end of that year he had become known to the Russians as the "Black Devil". Hartmann was decorated several times in the war, culminating in the Knight's Cross with Oak Leaves, Swords, and Diamonds—Germany's highest award for bravery in combat.

SHOT DOWN

Hartmann's log book shows that he flew 1,400 war missions and was involved in 800 air combats. He was himself shot down several times and failed to return to base 14 times. How many of these were occasions on which he was shot down is a matter of dispute. He accepted that he'd been shot down three times, but some of his other crashes were certainly caused primarily by enemy action.

Manfred von Richthofen (1882–1918)
Richthofen (right), better known as "The Red Baron", was the top-scoring ace of World War I. He began the war as a professional cavalry officer but transferred to the air force in 1915. It was Richthofen who developed the idea of a "hunting squadron", a large force of single-seat fighters.

James McCudden (1895–1918)
Major James McCudden was the highest scoring British ace of World War I, with a confirmed 57 kills plus another 16 probables. He joined the Royal Flying Corps (RFC) in 1915 as a mechanic and taught himself to fly on leave.

William Bishop (1894 - 1956)
William Avery "Billy" Bishop was the top-scoring Allied ace of World War I, with 72 confirmed kills. After the war, he joined the Royal Canadian Air Force (RCAF) and became its first commander and Air Marshal, in charge throughout World War II.

Marmaduke Pattle (1914–1941)
Pattle was the most successful Allied ace of World War II, with 40 confirmed kills and 18 probables. He was born in South Africa of British parents and returned to Britain in 1936 to join the RAF.

Johnny Johnson (1918–2001)
Johnson was the highest-scoring British fighter pilot in World War II, with 38 kills. He joined the RAF in 1939 and was posted to 616 Spitfire Squadron during the Battle of Britain. What's truly amazing about his "score" is that all 38 victories were against single-engined fighters.

CONQUERING WARLORD

GENGHIS KHAN (c.1162–1227)

He brought the nomadic tribes of Mongolia under one rule and then extended his empire across Asia to the Adriatic Sea.

Perhaps the greatest warlord in history, Genghis Khan rose from poverty to rule the greatest contiguous empire the world has ever seen.

Genghis Khan was born in 1162 with the name Temüjin as the son of a minor Mongol chieftain. His father was murdered when he was ten and he was abandoned by his tribe as they did not wish to be ruled by a boy.

For several years, Temüjin survived by hunting marmots as a bandit and picking wild fruits. He then turned bandit and began recruiting a small band of followers. By the age of 16 he was the leader of a sizeable force and was able to marry Börte of the Konkirat tribe. By 1190, Temüjin had become the accepted warlord of the various Mongol tribes. He then led them on a series of campaigns to subdue the other nomadic peoples of central Asia: the Naimans to the west, the Merkits to the north, Tanguts to the south, the Jin and Tatars to the east. One campaign involved killing his childhood friend Jamuka, who led a rebel faction of Mongols.

> *By 1190, Temüjin had become the accepted warlord of the various Mongol tribes.*

By 1206 all the nomads had been defeated or cajoled into alliance. A grand council of all the nomadic tribal leaders appointed Temüjin to be Genghis Khan, or "supreme ruler" of all the nomads. He then invaded China, at that time divided into several warring states. By 1209, the Mongols had defeated the smallest of these, the Xia. Next to fall was the much larger Jin, their capital of Beijing falling in 1215. Genghis Khan then turned west to destroy the khanate of Kara-Khitan and the Khwarezmid Empire with an army of 200,000 men. The vast army then divided to raid successfully into Persia, Armenia, Afghanistan, northern India, and Russia.

In 1227 Genghis Khan turned again to China, but in August he died—apparently of pneumonia brought on by a riding accident.

A grand council of nomadic tribal leaders appointed him to be Genghis Khan, or "supreme ruler".

Attila the Hun (d.453)

Attila (above) became King of the Huns and one of their most powerful rulers in 445, at a time when the tribe ruled the plains from the Danube to the Aral Sea. He at once invaded the eastern Roman Empire. In 450 he proposed marriage to the sister of Valentinian, Western Roman Emperor. When the woman refused his offer, he invaded to claim half the empire as her dowry. The Roman commander Aetius managed to patch up an alliance with various other barbarian tribes and met Attila at the Battle of the Catalaunian Plains. The Huns were defeated and retreated, but Attila was not finished. In 452 he invaded Italy and devastated the Po Valley.

Hengist (d. c.488)

Hengist (right, first left) came to Britain in about 449 to lead a band of Germanic mercenaries hired by the post-Roman British government to fight off invasions from the Picts. Based in Kent in southeast England, he became a legendary leader, but in 455, after not being paid for his services, he launched a rebellion, which was at first successful, but his brother Horsa was then killed and his forces confined to Kent. Hengist stayed independent King of Kent.

Matilda of Tuscany (1046–1115)

Countess Matilda inherited her lands as a child and became instantly wealthy. In 1061, at the age of just 17, she raised an army and led it to defend Rome and the pope against an invading German army. She personally led a cavalry charge beneath the walls of Rome that broke the invading army. Then in 1077, Matilda again raised a fresh army and used it to support Pope Gregory VII against the Emperor Henry.

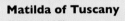

Gaiseric the Vandal (c.390–477)

Gaiseric became King of the Vandals in 427. Originally a Germanic tribe, by the time they reached southern Spain in the 420s the Vandals were a vast band of pillaging barbarians from many tribes. Gaiseric led them into North Africa, capturing Hippo and Carthage. He then became interested in setting up a kingdom. He built a fleet of warships with which he terrorized the Mediterranean, capturing Rome in 455. He died undefeated in 477.

Jan Zizka (c.1370–1424)

Jan Zizka (left) was a famous military commander of many years when, in 1419, he was chosen to lead a rising of the Czechs against Poland. The Poles were staunchly Catholic, while the Czechs backed calls for reform of the church initiated by Jan Huss. With 4,000 men, Zizka ran rings around King Sigismund's army of 40,000 to capture Prague and the fortress of Tabor. In 1421 he was blinded at the siege of Raby, but he had by this date perfected his tactic of a mobile wagon fortress and went on to win 12 battles. He died of the plague in 1424.

ANCIENT MILITARY MARTYR

In 480BC, Xerxes the ruler of Persia invaded Greece to punish the Greek states for having supported a rebellion in what is now Turkey. The invasion was blocked at the pass of Thermopylae by a small Greek force led by King Leonidas of Sparta.

The size of the vast Persian army is said to have numbered 100,000 men. To supply this vast horde, Xerxes had a large fleet of merchant ships loaded with food creeping along the coast. The key to the position of Thermopylae was that there were no convenient ports for several days' march to the north. If the Persians could be held there, they would run out of food and be forced to retreat. The pass between the cliffs and the sea was only 40 yards (37m) wide at its narrowest point and Leonidas was confident he could hold it with his 300 Spartans and 700 Thespians.

Leonidas arrived several days before the Persians. He repaired a defensive wall, dug pits to trip horses, and blocked a stream to create a marsh over which Persian siege engines could not advance. A scout came back and told Leonidas that there were so many Persians that their arrows would block out the sun. One of the Spartans joked, "Oh good. Then we can fight in the shade."

When the Persians arrived, Xerxes launched an immediate attack with his elite Immortal Guards. This was thrown back

LEONIDAS (d.480BC)

His heroic defence of the narrow pass at Thermopylae is often invoked as the epitome of bravery against overwhelming odds.

with humiliating losses. On the second day Xerxes sent forward wave after wave of troops, but none of them were able to drive the Greeks off their wall.

> *On the second day Xerxes sent forward wave after wave of troops.*

That night, a shepherd came to Xerxes and offered to show him a narrow path over the mountains that came down behind the wall.

Xerxes sent his Immortals to follow the shepherd.

The next morning, the Immortals appeared behind Leonidas' position. Leonidas sent his allies south to alert the Greeks that the position was falling but chose to stay with his 300 Spartans. The final hours saw the heavily armoured Spartans inflict massive casualties on the lightly armed Persians but the end was never in doubt. Leonidas and all his men were killed.

Leonidas was confident he could hold it with his 300 Spartans and 700 Thespians.

Colonel Anthony Durnford (1830–1879)

Colonel Anthony Durnford was commanding a force of over 100 locally raised cavalry, including both white and black men, during the British invasion of Zululand in 1879. On January 22, the main British invasion column was suddenly attacked by an overwhelming force of Zulus. Durnford and his men were a few miles out of the camp when the blow fell. He rushed back and took up a defensive position near to a rocky promontory that the Zulus called Isandhlwana. When he saw the left wing infantry collapse, Durnford ordered his men to mount and galloped them to where the road back to British territory crossed over a ridge.

There, Durnford halted his men and formed a defensive ring to hold the road as long as possible. Dozens of fleeing men got away, but Durnford refused to leave until it was too late. A fresh force of Zulu came up behind the ridge to surround Durnford and his men (below). Durnford held out for another half hour. One Zulu said later: "They stood back to back and were surrounded. Their ammunition was gone when I arrived, but they still fought with swords and pistols. We were unable to break their formation until nearly all of them were dead. We killed the last ones with spears."

Colonel George Armstrong Custer (1839–1876)

Colonel George Armstrong Custer, who distinguished himself in the American Civil War, was killed with all of his men at the Battle of the Little Big Horn—also known as Custer's Last Stand—on June 25, 1876. Custer had been sent forward with his 7th Cavalry by General Alfred Terry to find and scout the camp of the hostile Sioux. Custer, however, decided to attack the Sioux camp as soon as he found it, without realizing that he faced around 2,000 warriors, many armed with modern rifles. Of the more than 200 men who followed Custer into battle, not one lived to tell the tale. It is thought that Custer died in the early stages of the retreat, but this is unclear.

Harold Godwinson of England (c.1022–1066)

King Harold II, the last Anglo-Saxon king of England, made his last stand at the Battle of Hastings on October 14, 1066. The English infantry held off the armoured knights of the Duke of William of Normandy for most of the day, but as dusk came on, a final assault of archers and knights broke the English formation. Harold was wounded but chose to fight on as his army disintegrated. Aided by his housecarls, a highly trained band of professional warriors, Harold held out until sunset, giving his retreating army time to get away under cover of darkness. He was eventually killed when a group of Normans cut their way past his guards.

MAD COMMANDER

"MAD MITCH" (1925–1996)

"A great many Arabs are alive today because we used these methods and a great many Argylls are alive today because we used them." Mitchell, a few years before his death.

British Army officer Colin Campbell Mitchell (above right) earned himself the nickname of "Mad Mitch" for his successful, high profile, but extremely controversial exploits in the British colony of Aden in the 1960s.

Born in London as the son of a Scottish lawyer, Mitchell always regarded himself as Scottish and loved the more flamboyant accessories of highland culture. In 1943, he was called up into an English regiment, and quickly worked his way up through the ranks. When he gained an officer's commission, he asked for, and was given, a transfer to the Argyll and Sutherland Highlanders. He served with that regiment in Italy in 1944 and 1945, then opted to stay with them after the war.

> *He quickly worked his way up through the ranks.*

In 1966 he was promoted to Lieutenant Colonel of the regiment and led it to Aden, a British colony in the Yemen. The British government had decided to grant independence to Aden under certain conditions, but Arab nationalists wanted unconditional independence and in 1964 began an armed uprising.

In June 1967, the local police force in the town of Crater rebelled against the British to join the nationalist insurgency. They killed 22 British soldiers, mutilated their bodies, and put them on public display. Major-General Philip Tower sent for Mitchell and ordered him to lead a small probing force into Crater to see if it would be feasible to re-establish control, emphasizing that he was to take no risks.

Mitchell called a meeting of his officers. He told them that they were going to reassert control of Crater and impose what he called "Argyll Law". He then marched his men into the town with the regimental band playing a medley of Scottish marches. One Arab appeared with a gun and was shot dead but there

Mitchell himself took to driving around the city in an open-topped truck equipped with loudspeakers.

were no other casualties. Once in Crater, Mitchell divided the town up into districts, separated by barriers and patrolled by his men. Townspeople were allowed to pass between districts only with special permission. Mitchell himself took to driving around the city in an open-topped truck equipped with loudspeakers. His delighted men dubbed him "Mad Mitch".

Mitch shrugged off allegations of strong-arm tactics. Tower sent Mitchell an order telling him to scale down his operation but Mitchell stepped it up. By this time, the world's press had descended on Crater, to be welcomed by Mitchell in his Scottish uniform and bagpipers.

In November 1967, Aden was granted independence. Mitchell arrived home in typically flamboyant style, marching his men to the sound of bagpipes. He was, however, given a severe rebuke by the Labour government instead of the honorary OBE he had expected. Mitchell left the army to become a politician.

RISE OF A DICTATOR

When serving in East Africa, Mitchell insisted that the local black soldiers should be promoted and rewarded on the basis of merit. One of the enthusiastic and competent young soldiers that he favoured was Idi Amin, who would later rise to be the Defence Minister of Uganda. Amin used his position and military backing to launch a coup and so become dictator and President of Uganda.

General Joseph Hooker
(1814–1879)

General Joseph Hooker served in the Unionsit army during the US Civil War. He famously wrote a dispatch reading: "I have the finest army the sun ever shone on. If the enemy does not run, God help them." Just days later he lost the Battle of Chancellorsville by leaving his right flank exposed. He ran a loose headquarters that was described as a blend of a "bar-room and a brothel". The American slang term of "hookers" for prostitutes is thought to derive from his headquarters.

General James Wolfe (1727–1759)

General James Wolfe was a British army officer who captured Quebec in 1759 and destroyed French power on the continent, but it cost him his life. Throughout his career he had a reputation for nervousness and unconventional hobbies such as writing poetry and flower arranging. When a courtier once remarked that Wolfe was mad, King George II retorted, "Mad, is he? Then I hope he will bite some of my other generals."

James Brudenell
(1797–1868)

James Brudenell, 7th Earl of Cardigan, earned great fame as the man who led the heroic, but futile, Charge of the Light Brigade in 1854. He insisted on aristocratic manners and once court-martialled an officer for ordering beer instead of wine at dinner. He challenged another to a duel for turning up for dinner with unpolished buttons. Though brave, his prickly temperament and unpopularity led to his retirement in 1866.

MOST DECORATED WAR HERO

Audie Murphy remains the most highly decorated soldier in American military history, having been awarded the Medal of Honor, along with 32 other US medals, plus five from France, and one from Belgium.

Murphy was born into a poverty-stricken farming family in Texas in 1924. When his father abandoned the family, Murphy dropped out of school to work for a dollar a day on farms to bring in extra income for his family. In 1942, he falsified his age and volunteered for the steady pay of the military. The US Marines turned him down as he was under 5 feet 6 inches (1.67m) tall but the infantry accepted him.

He first saw combat in Sicily in July of that year. Murphy soon attracted notice when he shot dead two Italian officers with two shots at a distance of half a mile as they galloped by on horses.

Murphy then moved on to the Italian mainland, earning medals and promotions as he went. He won the Distinguished Service Cross for single-handedly wiping out three German machine gun nests and four other positions. He was commissioned to be an officer on the battlefield at the end of 1944 and then transferred to the French front. It was there that he won the Medal of Honor.

He returned to Texas to a hero's welcome, featuring on the cover of *Time* magazine, and left the army in September 1945.

AUDIE MURPHY (1924–1971)

Murphy first saw combat in Sicily in July of 1942. He soon attracted notice when he shot dead two Italian officers with two shots at a distance of half a mile as they galloped by on horses.

Murphy agreed to appear in a movie promoting the work of the Variety Club charity, and this caught the eye of Hollywood producers. For several years he struggled to make it as an actor, eventually starring in *Beyond Glory* in 1948. He went on to make a total of 44 war adventure films, including a fictionalized version of his war record called *To Hell and Back* that was a huge hit.

On May 28, 1971, he was killed in an air crash.

He returned to Texas to a hero's welcome, featuring on the cover of Time *magazine…*

MURPHY'S MEDAL OF HONOR CITATION

RANK & ORGANISATION:
Second Lieutenant, US Army, Company B 15th Infantry, 3rd Infantry Division.

PLACE & DATE:
Near Holtzwihr France, 26 January, 1945.

EXTRACT FROM CITATION:
Second Lt. Murphy commanded Company B, which was attacked by six tanks and waves of infantry. 2d Lt. Murphy ordered his men to withdraw to a prepared position in a woods, while he remained forward at his command post and continued to give fire directions to the artillery by telephone. With the enemy tanks abreast of his position, 2d Lt. Murphy climbed on the burning tank destroyer, which was in danger of blowing up at any moment, and employed its .50 caliber machine gun against the enemy. He was alone and exposed to German fire from three sides, but his deadly fire killed dozens of Germans and caused their infantry attack to waver. He received a leg wound, but ignored it and continued his single-handed fight until his ammunition was exhausted. He then made his way back to his company, refused medical attention, and organized the company in a counterattack, which forced the Germans to withdraw.

John Travers Cornwell
(1900–1916)

John Cornwell, Boy Seaman First Class, won his Victoria Cross (VC) at the age of just 16 and remains the youngest recipient of Britain's highest award for courage in battle. In the spring of 1916 he joined the crew of the cruiser HMS Chester. On May 31, 1916 the ship entered the Battle of Jutland, the largest naval action of World War I. Cornwell took up his position as gun-layer. As the ship emerged from fog, it found itself faced by four German cruisers. In the ensuing battle, Chester was hit 17 times and a German shell wiped out his entire crew. Despite his wounds, Cornwell stayed at his gun. He later died of his wounds.

Noel Chavasse (1884–1917)

Only three men have ever been awarded the Victoria Cross twice. Noel Chavasse was awarded the VC for rescuing wounded men under fire at Guillemont, France, on August 9, 1916. He was awarded a second VC for carrying a wounded colleague to a hospital, despite being wounded himself at Wieltje, Belgium. He died of his wounds a few days later.

Arthur Martin-Leake (1874–1953)

Surgeon Captain Arthur Martin-Leake was awarded his first VC after he dressed the wounds of two men under fire at Vlakfontein, South Africa, on February 8, 1902, during the Boer War. He was awarded his second VC for rescuing three wounded men from no-man's-land under heavy German fire near Zonnebeke, Belgium, in November 1914.

Charles Upham (1908–1994)

Charles Upham won his first VC in March 1941 for an action on Crete when he held a defensive position single-handed for five hours, killing 22 Germans. His second VC came in July 1942 for an offensive action near El Alamein in North Africa. Armed only with a rifle and grenades he destroyed one German tank, several anti-tank guns, and five lorries. He was wounded twice during this action and was captured.

ADMIRAL TRYON (1832–1893)

Captain Bourke asked Tryon twice if he should alter course. He was ignored. When he asked a third time, Tryon told him irritably to put his engines astern. By then it was too late.

Few commanders have ended their careers with quite so much ignominy as did Admiral Sir George Tryon. It was most unfortunate that in ending his career, and his life, Tryon ended the lives of more than 350 of his men.

Entering the British Royal Navy as a boy cadet in 1848, Tryon saw a few days of desultory action in the Crimean War, but otherwise served out his entire career in peacetime. His administrative

abilities were highly regarded. He held a number of prestigious postings before in 1891 he was given command of the Mediterranean Fleet, the most powerful force in the Royal Navy.

On June 22, 1893, Tryon led his fleet's 11 main battleships into a series of manoeuvres. He led one column of six ships in his flagship *Victoria*, while a second column was led by his deputy, Admiral Hastings Markham, in the *Camperdown*.

The manoeuvre to be carried out was for the lead ships to turn inwards towards each other so that by the time they had completed a semi-circle they would be steaming in the opposite direction, about 400 yards (366m) apart. Given the turning circle of the big battleships, it was usual to begin this move with the columns a minimum of 1,600 yards (1,463m) apart. However, Tryon gave the order to close the gap to 1,000 yards (914m).

Tryon ordered the turning manoeuvre to begin. Markham, seeing how close the ships

The disaster was reported around the world.

He assumed that Tryon was intending to give an order to change direction at some point.

were, asked that a signal be sent querying the order. Before the signal could be sent Tryon sent a second order that read simply: "What are you waiting for?"

Markham then gave the order for his column to start turning. He assumed that Tryon was intending to give an order to change direction at some point. Captain Bourke of the *Victoria* asked Tryon twice if he should alter course. He was ignored by the admiral. When he asked a third time, Tryon told him irritably to put his engines astern. By then it was too late.

Camperdown rammed the *Victoria*, tearing a 12 feet (3.5m) gash below the water line. Just 13 minutes after the collision, the *Victoria* capsized and sank. *Camperdown* was also holed but she stayed afloat. Of *Victoria*'s crew, 357 were rescued and 358 died, including Tryon.

DEATH WALKER

On the day of the accident, Lady Tryon was holding a luncheon party at their London home. Several of the people present later swore that they saw Admiral Tryon walking down the stairs as if to join the party at about the time that he was drowning in the Mediterranean.

"It's all my fault."
Admiral Tryon's last words.

OTHER ILL-FATED ADMIRALS

Admiral John Byng (1704–1757)
Until 1756, when he was ordered to relieve the British garrison of Fort St Philip on Minorca, Admiral John Byng (right) had led a distinguished career in the British Royal Navy. On May 20, he attacked a French fleet, but by approaching in oblique order allowed his lead ships to be shot to pieces before his main force arrived. The French slipped away and Byng made no attempt either to follow them or to sail to Fort St Philip, which then surrendered to the French. Byng was court-martialled and found guilty of "not doing his utmost in battle". He was shot.

Admiral Zinovy Rozhdestvensky (1848–1909)
Admiral Zinovy Rozhdestvensky (left) was commander of the Russian Baltic Fleet when he was ordered to steam his ships halfway round the world to protect Port Arthur in eastern Siberia in the Russo-Japanese War that had just broken out. The voyage got off to a bad start in the North Sea when Rozhdestvensky opened fire on some British trawlers that he mistook for Japanese torpedo boats. On May 27, Rozhdestvensky was finally approaching Port Arthur when he steamed straight into a Japanese ambush. Unable to get his big gun battleships to open fire in time, Rozhdestvensky suffered an appalling defeat, losing 33 out of 45 ships.

Politics

"We must come to see that the end we
seek is a society at peace with itself, a society
that can live with its conscience."

Martin Luther King

MODERN POLITICAL REFORMER

Mohandas Gandhi (later known as Mahatma, meaning "great soul") was involved in many reforms, but he is best remembered for his campaign of civil disobedience against the British regime in India during the 1930s and 1940s.

Some credit him with gaining independence for India, though others blame him for the partition of the subcontinent into separate states for Hindus and Muslims.

Gandhi was born into a wealthy Indian family in 1869 and trained as a lawyer in London. He returned to India but his career as a lawyer did not flourish. He was on the point of becoming a teacher when in 1893 he got a job with a law firm in South Africa. While in South Africa he represented many Indians, and then embarked on a campaign against laws compelling Indians to carry identity cards. He promoted what he called *satyagraha*, a form of non-violent non-cooperation. After seven years of struggle, this method of campaigning led to a government climbdown.

> *He promoted what he called* satyagraha, *a form of non-violent non-cooperation.*

In 1915 Gandhi returned to India and at once threw himself into political agitation, championing the causes of the impoverished classes of India. At this time his campaigns were not always directed against the British,

MAHATMA GANDHI (1869–1948)

"I object to violence because when it appears to do good, the good is only temporary; the evil it does is permanent." Ghandi

but often against corrupt local officials or ruthless landlords. In 1921 he became leader of the Indian National Congress and transformed the organization into a mass movement aimed at social equality between the castes, as well as greater self-government for India. He organized boycotts of foreign-made goods in an effort to boost Indian industry and again advocated *satyagraha*. In 1930, Gandhi broke the law by making salt without a government licence. Many others followed his example and were imprisoned.

By 1936 he was working openly and actively for an independent

In 1930, Gandhi broke the law by making salt without a government licence.

and united India. The situation was complicated by the fact that large tracts of India were ruled by independent monarchs. There were also irreconcilable religious differences between the Hindu majority and the Muslim minority.

When World War II broke out in 1939, Gandhi thought the Indians should support Britain but not actively fight. Later he declared that India should not help a war being fought for democratic freedom while that freedom was denied to India itself. He called for Britain to leave India at once and was imprisoned until 1944.

In 1946 he opposed the British offer to grant independence to India as it contained clauses that he thought might lead to partition. He worked to calm the escalating disputes between India's religious communities but failed. India and Pakistan became separate states, both independent of Britain, in 1947, and Gandhi withdrew from public life in protest. On January 30, 1948, he was shot dead by a Hindu extremist .

THE ZULU REBELLION

In 1906, the British in South Africa went to war against the semi-independent Zulu kingdom. Gandhi saw the war as a chance for the Indians living in South Africa to prove their worth to the colonial authorities. He urged Indians to volunteer for the local armed forces and to join the fighting. When the army refused to allow Indians to serve as officers, Gandhi suggested that they should volunteer as medical staff and stretcher bearers. In all, 24 Indians served during the short campaign, but there was no noticeable improvement in the way the local authorities treated Indians.

OTHER "ARCHITECTS" OF POLITICAL CHANGE

Deng Xiaoping (1904–1997)
An early convert to Communism, Deng gradually emerged as the leader of China after Mao's death in 1976. By 1980 he was supreme, although he preferred to operate in the background. He set about transforming China by opening up the country to outside influences and unleashing an economic revolution based on breaking down state controls. He did, however, retain a tight grip on political power for the Communist Party. Deng retired from politics in 1992. His reforms have since gathered pace and transformed China into an economic powerhouse.

Boris Yeltsin (1931–2007)
Yeltsin was elected President of Russia in 1991 after hardline communists had launched an armed coup against the then president Gorbachev. It was Yeltsin who mobilized mass opposition to the coup and persuaded army units to join him in Moscow. Catapulted to power, Yeltsin introduced radical economic reforms to bring Russia into the capitalist world economy. These involved massive privatizations, enormous upheavals, and significant hardships, but they laid the foundations for later economic prosperity.

Margaret Thatcher (b.1925)
Margaret Thatcher was elected Prime Minister of Britain in 1979 on a manifesto that promised to deliver economic reforms. These reforms involved promoting a free market economy and selling many of the country's nationalized industries, as well as curbing the power of the trade unions. Britain's involvement in the Falklands War of 1982 ensured her popularity with many and she subsequently won two more general elections.

ANCIENT POLITICAL REFORMERS

The Gracchus brothers were two aristrocrats who instituted social and political reform in ancient Rome.

Although they ultimately failed in their reforms, the brothers had enormous influence on Roman government; they questioned the ineffective structure of the democratic republican system of the time and paved the way for the introduction of a more dictatorial, imperial rule.

Tiberius was the elder of the brothers, and Gaius the younger. The two young men became convinced that Rome was facing an economic and social crisis. They believed that the root cause of the problems was the decline in the numbers of self-employed citizens who had traditionally dominated elections and provided men to the army.

Vast wealth had poured into

THE GRACCHUS BROTHERS
Tiberius (c.168BC-133BC) & Gaius (c.159BC-121BC)

"Rome is the mob." Gaius Gracchus

THE TRIBUNE

The Gracchus brothers used the position of Tribune to push through their reforms. The office was established in 493BC and given the task of defending the rights of the poorer citizens against the richer noblemen. They had enormous power: they could call meetings of the assembly and control its agenda; they could veto any act by a government official; suspend meetings of the Senate; and imprison anyone they said disturbed the peace of the city. There were two Tribunes, elected annually. Both had to agree before they could take any action.

Rome during the conquest of neighbouring states, but this money had been taken by a relatively few noblemen. At the same time, an agricultural depression caused the bankruptcy of thousands of farmers. The result was that a few rich men used slaves to farm vast tracts of public land, while impoverished farmers and their families flocked to Rome to live off hand-outs from the government.

In 133BC, Tiberius was elected to the position of Tribune. He passed laws that limited the amount of land any one man could own. He then authorized government funds to be used to set up poor men as farmers on small holdings. When Tiberius stood for election that year, promising to continue his reforms, he was murdered by a gang of men hired by noblemen opposed to his reforms.

In 123BC, Gaius was elected Tribune, promising to complete his brother's reforms. Determined not to share Tiberius's fate, he took to being accompanied around Rome by a gang of his toughest supporters. He also pushed his powers to the limit,

They had shown that the path to political power lay through appealing to the poor citizens.

introducing constitutional reforms of doubtful legality, then having them ratified by his supporters in the popular assembly.

In 121BC, Gaius was opposed by a virtually unknown man named Marcus Livius Drusus. He used vast sums of cash to hire his own gang of guards and to bribe as many voters as he could, while promising to introduce reforms even more dramatic than those of Gaius.

Drusus won the election, but soon revealed himself to be a tool of the rich noblemen opposed to reform.

He began abolishing the reforms of the Gracchi. At the next meeting of the popular assembly, Gaius and his supporters challenged Drusus. A savage battle ensued on the streets of Rome, in which around 5,000 people were killed, including Gaius.

Although the brothers were dead, and their reforms were soon abolished, they had shown that the path to political power lay through appealing to the poor citizens. Gaius had shown that the republican constitution was vulnerable to abuse of power. Over the coming years many others followed the Gracchus brothers, though more often for personal ambition than a desire for social reform.

OTHER EARLY CONSTITUTIONAL REFORMERS

Solon (c.640BC–c.559BC)
The aristocratic poet Solon (below) was given dictatorial powers to draw up a new constitution for Athens in 594BC. He reformed the constitution to give poor citizens a vote in electing government officials, although only noblemen could stand for election. Economically, Solon introduced laws that encouraged trade.

Pericles (c.490BC–429BC)
Greek politician and general Pericles (left) was born into an aristocratic family but was a great champion of democracy. He reformed the constitution of Athens to give more power to the poorer citizens and was instrumental in increasing the size of the Athenian navy, founding overseas commercial colonies, and building public works, such as the Parthenon in Athens.

Lycurgus (fl.660BC)
Lycurgus (right) is recognized as the great law giver of Sparta, though whether he invented the laws or merely codified what already existed is unclear. He established the Spartan military system, which gave the Spartans the most-feared army in Greece. He divided political power between two kings, chosen from different families, a senate, and elected officials.

JOHN F KENNEDY (1917–1963)

"There are risks and costs to a programme of action. But they are far less than the long-range risks and costs of comfortable inaction." John F Kennedy

the USA had ever had. He had faced down the USSR over the Cuban missile crisis and was overseeing a range of social reforms as well as cracking down on organized crime. He decided to visit Dallas, Texas, at the invitation of Texas Governor John Connally in order to rebuild political fences in the run up to the opening of his campaign to be re-elected in 1964.

At 12.30pm on November 22, 1963, the open-topped car with President Kennedy, Governor Connally, and their wives entered Dealey Plaza and passed before the Texas Book Depository. A number of shots rang out and Kennedy slumped forward in his seat. He was later declared dead from massive head injuries, while Connally was partially paralyzed.

> *A number of shots rang out and Kennedy slumped forward in his seat.*

In Dealey Plaza, a bystander named Howard Brennan told police that he had seen a man with a rifle leaning out of a window of the Book Depository. The police raced to the window and found a Carcano M91/38 rifle. A quick head count revealed that one staff member, Lee Harvey Oswald, was missing. Oswald was cornered in a movie theatre, where he tried to shoot his way clear but he was arrested. Two days later, while being transferred from one jail to another, Oswald was shot dead by Jack Ruby, a nightclub owner.

The assassination of US President John Fitzgerald Kennedy has proved to be one of the most mysterious political killings of all time.

Officially, the murder was solved within days of the event, but discrepancies in the official account and suspicions of a conspiracy have meant that the mystery surrounding the killing has never been fully solved.

President Kennedy was, in 1963, one of the youngest and most glamorous presidents that

Questions began to be asked about evidence that contradicted the Commission's findings.

Investigations were swiftly launched by Dallas Police and the FBI but both were overtaken by the Warren Commission, set up by the new president, Lyndon Johnson. This concluded that Oswald had been responsible for firing three shots. One shot had missed. The second had wounded Kennedy and Connelly. The third had killed Kennedy. Oswald's rifle had fired three shots and most witnesses reported hearing three shots. It also concluded that it was most likely Oswald acted alone.

It was not long before questions began to be asked about evidence that contradicted the Commission's findings. One of the most important concerns an alleged second gunman standing on the "grassy knoll" that was beside the president's car when he was killed. Several people in the plaza thought they heard a shot fired from the knoll. Other ideas put forward suggest that Kennedy was shot by Russian spies, by Cuban agents, by the mafia, or by rogue elements of the US government. None of these ideas has been proven.

Harold Holt (1908–1967)
On December 17, 1967, Harold Holt, the Australian Prime Minister, drove with friends to Cheviot Beach on Point Nepean, near Melbourne. There was a strong wind and the surf was heavy but Holt was a powerful swimmer and so wasn't concerned. He plunged into the surf and was seen swimming strongly. Then he vanished from sight. The Navy's efforts to find him grew to become one of the largest coastal searches ever mounted in Australia, but no sign of Holt or his body was ever found.

Feng Yuxiang (1882–1948)
Feng Yuxiang followed his father into the imperial Chinese army. When the Chinese imperial government collapsed, Feng set himself up as a regional warlord. In 1945 he began clandestine meetings with both the Chinese Communist forces and the Soviet Union, while ostensibly pledging support to the US-backed Nationalist regime. In 1948 he was on board a ship on the Black Sea when a mysterious fire broke out. Feng was the only casualty of the blaze, which has never been properly explained.

LEE HARVEY OSWALD IN THE SOVIET UNION

Oswald was himself assassinated—by Jack Ruby—while being transferred to county jail by police after his arrest (left) for the killing of president Kennedy. After his death it was discovered that Oswald had lived in the Soviet Union from 1959 until 1962. He arrived in Moscow on a student visa but at once announced that he wanted to gain Soviet citizenship. He was welcomed with open arms by the Soviets. However, after a meeting with Oswald the Soviet government went off the idea and put him in a hospital for "observation". The KGB interviewed Oswald and recommended that he be expelled from the USSR, apparently because of concerns over his sanity. Instead, he was sent to live in Minsk and given a factory job. There he met teenager Marina Prusakova whom he married six weeks later and by whom he had a child. Oswald returned to the USA with his family in June 1962.

POLITICAL VISIONARY

Black American Baptist preacher Martin Luther King was a leader of the US Civil Rights Movement, sparking social and political reforms, the impacts of which are still being felt. His reputation as a political visionary was cemented by his great 1963 "I have a dream" speech.

King was born in Atlanta, Georgia, in 1929 and named in honour of Martin Luther, the German protestant religious leader of the 16th century. After attending school locally he moved to Boston University to obtain a doctorate of philosophy and in 1954 he became pastor of the Dexter Avenue Baptist Church in Montgomery, Alabama.

Two years later, King began his civil rights campaign when he organized a boycott of buses by black Americans in protest at Rosa Parks being forced to give up her seat to a white man according to bus company rules. The year-long campaign ended with a court ruling that ended racial segregation on public transport.

In 1957 King founded the Southern Christian Leadership Conference, an organization devoted to harnessing the power and solidarity of churches with black congregations to the cause of civil rights. Using this body and his contacts in the civil rights movement, King organized and led a succession of marches against racial segregation across the southern states of the USA.

MARTIN LUTHER KING (1929–1968)

"We must come to see that the end we seek is a society at peace with itself, a society that can live with its conscience. And that will be a day not of the white man, not of the black man. That will be the day of man as man." Martin Luther King

None were successful but the marches managed to publicize the existence of racial segregation and win over public opinion.

In April 1963, while serving a jail sentence in Birmingham City Jail for participating in a civil rights demonstration, he wrote:

"I submit that an individual who breaks a law that conscience tells him is unjust, and who willingly accepts the penalty of imprisonment in order to arouse the conscience of the community

King organized and led a succession of marches against racial segregation across the southern states of the USA.

over its injustice, is expressing the highest respect for the law."

Later that year, King helped organize the March on Washington for Jobs and Freedom to highlight the failure of the national government to legislate on racial issues. It was here that King made his "I have a dream" speech.

> The marches managed to publicize the existence of racial segregation and win over public opinion.

Two years later, he organized a mass march to the State Capitol in Alabama. The first march ended in violence and rioting when local whites attacked the marchers. A second march three weeks later was peaceful and saw King deliver his "How long, not long" speech.

By 1967, many of the demands of the civil rights movement had been met, though not always implemented. King moved on to supporting labour disputes involving black workers and other causes. He was shot dead on April 4, 1968, by James Earl Ray.

THE FBI AND KING

King came to the attention of the FBI when it became known that two of his close advisers were linked to the Communist Party USA. They could find no direct links to Communist agitators but uncovered evidence of extramarital affairs. The FBI bugged his phones and made various other attempts to undermine him. Six FBI agents were secretly watching King on the day he was shot.

Imre Nagy (1895–1958)

A committed Hungarian Marxist who envisaged a community of independent communist states, Nagy became increasingly disillusioned with Russia's harsh rule of Eastern Europe after 1945. He became Prime Minister of Hungary in 1956 and began to implement a policy of liberal communism. On November 1 he announced that Hungary was a neutral state and withdrew from the Warsaw Pact. A few days later columns of Soviet tanks rolled into Hungary. That led to bitter street fighting and thousands of casualties. Despite being given a promise of safe conduct out of Hungary, Nagy was arrested, tried for treason, and executed.

Vaclav Havel (b.1936)

Czech leader Vaclav Havel had his first play, *The Garden Party*, performed in 1963 to great critical acclaim. After this, Havel divided his time between work, writing, and calls for political reform that landed him in prison several times. By 1989 he was the undisputed leader of the Czechoslovak opposition to communist rule and so played a lead role in the "Velvet Revolution" that swept the communists from power. He was elected President of Czechoslovakia in 1989 and then of the Czech Republic in 1993. He held office until 2003, overseeing his nation's transformation into a democratic state.

Simón Bolívar (1783–1830)

Born into an old Spanish aristocratic family in Venezuala, Bolívar became convinced that the only way the colonies could achieve economic and social reform was if they became independent of Spain. He led an armed uprising in May 1813, the start of ten years of warfare, which led to the independence of present-day Bolivia, Colombia, Ecuador, Peru, and Venezuela. He died of tuberculosis in 1830.

BLACK RIGHTS LEADER

Nelson Mandela was the hero of the anti-apartheid movement in South Africa. His initial hard line opposition to the regime was later transformed into a desire for reconciliation and peace that helped to lead his country into the 21st century.

Mandela was born into the royal family of the Transkei—a part of South Africa—but he fled at the age of 20 to study and to avoid an arranged marriage.

He moved to Johannesburg where he had a succession of jobs before studying law. In 1948, the National Party (NP) won the general election and began introducing apartheid policies. Mandela was soon prominent in the African National Congress (ANC) campaign against the new laws, which distinguished between residents on the basis of race. He was arrested for treason in 1956 and although acquitted, this convinced him that the new government would not change its policies in response to debate.

> *He was arrested for treason in 1956.*

NELSON MANDELA (b.1918)

"I am not a saint, unless you think of a saint as a sinner who keeps on trying." Nelson Mandela

In 1961, he became leader of the newly formed armed wing of the ANC, the Umkhonto we Sizwe (MK). He began a campaign of sabotage against military and government targets, raised funds abroad, and arranged for volunteers to undergo military training in other African states.

The aim was to prepare for a guerrilla war, though the MK did not begin killing until after Mandela had ceased to lead it.

Nevertheless, the violent aims of the MK became known to the government and Mandela was arrested again in 1962. He was at first sentenced to five years in prison for organizing an illegal strike, but was later charged with sabotage of government property and of attempting to incite a foreign invasion of South Africa. Mandela admitted the sabotage but denied the invasion charge. He was found guilty of all charges and sentenced to life imprisonment.

Mandela was taken to prison on Robben Island, where he was to spend the next 18 years.

He was taken to the hard labour camp on Robben Island, where he was to spend the next 18 years. There, he used his influence within the ANC to train a new generation of activists. In 1982, he was moved to Pollsmoor Prison, where a series of clandestine meetings with the South African government began. In 1989 Frederik Willem de Klerk became President of South Africa and announced that Mandela would be set free. The ANC was declared to be legal and negotiations began to move South Africa towards multi-party elections. These took place in 1994.

The ANC won the elections and Mandela became President of South Africa. He set out on a policy of reconciliation by insisting there should be no policy of revenge for the years of apartheid. When South Africa hosted the Rugby World Cup in 1995, Mandela encouraged the whole country to support the team.

In 1999, Mandela stepped down as President, but is still highly respected in international politics.

MANDELA'S WIVES

Nelson Mandela's first wife was Evelyn Ntoko Mase. They broke up in 1957, after 13 years, largely due to his revolutionary activism which clashed with her faith as a Jehovah's Witness. He then married Winnie Madikizela. They parted due to the growing gulf between their political views. In 1998, he married Graça Machel, widow of Samora, the former Mozambican president.

Malcolm X (1925–1965)

Black American activist Macolm Little was born into a poor family. He passed through a variety of jobs as well as prison before he joined the Nation of Islam in 1952 and changed his surname to X. He devoted himself to militant black rights' movements, and the campaign for equality between blacks and whites. In 1964, he visited Mecca and converted to a more conventional form of Islam. On February 21, 1965, Malcolm was delivering a speech in New York when a fight began in the audience. Malcolm tried to intervene but he was shot 16 times and died.

Steve Biko (1946–1977)

Biko was one of the leaders of the South African Students' Organization (SASO), which opposed apartheid in South Africa. His activities led to him being "banned" by the government, meaning that he was not allowed to speak in public and could not travel to certain parts of the country. He nevertheless largely orchestrated the Soweto riots of 1976. On August 18, 1977, Biko was arrested and received severe head injuries while in police custody. He died four weeks later.

Colin Powell (b.1937)

Colin Powell is a former army officer who was US Secretary of State from 2001 to 2005, the first African American to hold that post. Powell joined the army in 1958 and served in Europe, Korea, Vietnam, and the USA, rising through the ranks to become a general. In 1987, he transferred to the government to serve as National Security Advisor but returned to the US Army in 1989 and became Commander-in-Chief. In 1993, he became the Chairman of the Joint Chiefs of Staff, at 52 the youngest man ever to hold that position.

MOST FAMOUS FEMALE SPY

MATA HARI (1876–1917)

For all her fame as a great spy, Mata Hari was not very successful. Indeed, it is not even certain that she was a spy at all.

RUMOURS AND GOSSIP

There have been many rumours about the execution of Mata Hari and the fate of her body. It is said that she blew a kiss to the men of the firing squad moments before her death, though another version has it that the kiss was intended for her lawyer—who was one of her many lovers. Her last words were said to have been, "Merci, monsieur", directed to the commander of the firing squad. Another version has it that her last words were, "Harlot, yes, but traitor, never". Her family did not claim her body and so it was used for medical study. Her head was embalmed and kept at the Museum of Anatomy in Paris, from where it was stolen by persons unknown.

Mata Hari's fame rests as much on her glamour and colourful life as on her espionage activities during World War I.

Born in the Netherlands as Margaretha Zelle, she adopted the stage name of Mata Hari when she began to win fame as an exotic dancer. Her routine was billed as being based on Indonesian temple dances, but in reality they were highly sexually charged. This blend of outward respectability and soft pornography ensured the success of her act. She had affairs with many politicians and military officers.

When World War I began, the Netherlands remained neutral so Mata Hari was free to continue travelling with her act. Her romantic links to senior officers continued. This soon attracted suspicion. She was questioned by the British in 1916, who concluded that she was a spy for the French and advised her to stay in the Netherlands. Instead, she went to France where she was arrested as a German spy, tried, and shot dead.

The charges against her were brought by a French spy named Georges Ladoux. He was later unmasked as a double agent himself, so there is considerable doubt as to Mata Hari's guilt. The French government has refused to release the record of her trial or the evidence of her guilt. Until they do so, the mystery will remain.

This blend of outward respectability and soft pornography ensured the success of her act.

Guy Burgess (1911–1963)
& Donald Maclean (1913–1983)

Guy Burgess (right) and Donald Maclean (far right) were members of the British establishment who became committed communists and spies for the Soviet Union. Their unmasking in 1951 seriously undermined faith in the British secret services but it was not until many years later that it emerged they were part of a much larger spy network—the Cambridge Five. Both Burgess and Maclean fled to the Soviet Union on May 26, 1951, after being warned by Kim Philby of the British secret service, also a Soviet spy who later defected to Russia. Of the two who remained in Britain, Blunt traded a confession for freedom from prosecution; Cairncross was never prosecuted and denied being the "Fifth Man".

Rose O'Neal Greenhow (c.1817–1864)

When the American Civil War broke out, Rose Greenhow was an attractive widow of some social standing living in Washington DC. She believed that states should have the right to secede from the Union and so chose to stay in Washington and use her contacts to collect information on the movements of the Unionist forces. She passed these on to the Confederate army and is credited with giving General PGT Beauregard the information he needed to win the First Battle of Bull Run. She was arrested in August 1861. After a short spell in prison, she was deported to Europe but drowned on her return.

John Walker (b.1937)

A US Navy officer, Walker (left) spied for the Soviet Union from 1968 to 1985. When he became heavily in debt, Walker contacted the Soviet Embassy and sold them a secret naval cipher card for several thousand dollars. In total, he is thought to have earned over $1 million dollars from the Soviets. He was eventually caught by the FBI and sentenced to life imprisonment.

Richard Sorge (1895–1944)

Considered to be one of the greatest spies of all time, Sorge (below), who was half Russian but grew up in Germany, worked for the Soviet Union until his death in 1944. He became a firm communist and in 1919 went to Russia where he agreed to spy for the new Soviet secret service. In 1933 he was ordered to Japan where his greatest triumph was to learn that the Japanese were going to attack the USA in December 1941. He was arrested and hanged by the Japanese when they realized he was working for the Soviets.

LEADING BRITISH SUFFRAGETTE

Today women's suffrage is considered a right and most countries allow women to vote and participate in politics on an equal footing with men.

This was largely a development of the 20th century. Until then, women had been banned or disqualified from voting. It was a combination of changing social attitudes and a campaign by a determined band of women—suffragettes—that changed this.

One of the most active of these was the British woman Emmeline Pankhurst. Aged 22, she married lawyer Richard Pankhurst who was already active in reform movements. In 1889 Mrs Pankhurst founded the Women's Franchise League which worked for changes to laws that discriminated against women.

Then, in 1903, she founded the Women's Social and Political Union (WSPU), which embarked on a much more radical agenda. With her daughters, Christabel and Sylvia, Mrs Pankhurst began

EMILY PANKHURST (1858–1928)

"We are here not because we are law-breakers; we are here in our efforts to become law-makers."
Emmeline Pankhurst

THE WOMEN'S PARTY

In November 1917 Emmeline Pankhurst founded a new political party—The Women's Party. At first its policies were purely patriotic and related to winning the war. At the 1918 general election, Christabel Pankhurst stood as the candidate for the Smethwick constituency in Staffordshire. She lost by just 778, less than five per cent of votes cast. After failing to make much impact at a subsequent by-election, the party was dissolved in 1919.

a campaign of vandalism and personal assault. Suffragettes were often arrested and put in prison for their acts.

When World War I broke out in 1914, Pankhurst suspended the campaign and urged women to do everything that they could for the war effort. When the war was over, the government realized that women had proved themselves equal to men in many jobs. In March 1918 limited voting rights were extended to women. Ten years later, women were given voting rights equal to men.

Suffragettes were often arrested and put in prison for their acts.

Katherine Sheppard
(1847—1934)

Kate Sheppard (left) was an anti-alcohol campaigner in New Zealand who, in 1886, turned her organizational talents to the campaign for women's suffrage. In 1891 she presented a vast public petition to Parliament and three years later a law giving women the right to vote on the same basis as men in New Zealand was passed.

Emily Davison (1872–1913)

Davison was a British suffragette who took part in some of the movement's more violent and illegal activities. She was sent to prison after she launched a violent attack on a man she mistook for a government minister. At the Epsom Derby, on June 4, 1913, she ran out on to the track in front of the King's horse carrying a banner. The horse struck her and she died four days later.

Lily Maxwell (b.1806)

Mrs Lily Maxwell earned herself a place in suffragette history when she became the first woman to vote at a British parliamentary election—in Manchester on November 26, 1867. At that time, the only people allowed to vote were those who owned property and paid rates above a fairly high value. Mrs Maxwell owned a shop and paid rates on it, so she registered to vote.

Susan Anthony (1820–1906)

One of the leading early suffragettes in the USA and a prominent human and women's rights campaigner, Susan Anthony (above) founded the National Women's Suffrage Association in 1869. In 1872 she tried to vote at the presidential elections but was arrested and imprisoned. Thereafter, she travelled the USA and Europe constantly, making speeches and agitating for change.

Emily Davison with the King's horse, Anmer, at the Epsom Derby in 1913.

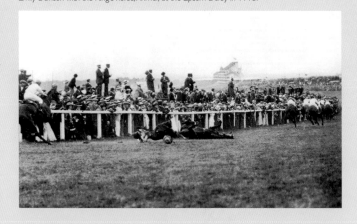

Emily Stowe (1831–1903)

Stowe was the first woman to practice as a doctor in Canada, and one of that nation's leading suffragettes. She worked as a teacher but when her husband fell ill she took up medicine and in 1867 qualified in the USA. It was not until 1880 that she gained a licence to practise medicine in Canada. In 1877 she founded the Toronto Women's Literary Guild, a reformist movement.

SCANDALOUS POLITICIAN

JOHN PROFUMO (1915–2006)

"To my very deep regret I have to admit that this was not true, and that I misled you and my colleagues and the House."
John Profumo in his resignation speech in 1963.

The British politician John Profumo was the focus of one of the greatest political scandals of recent British history. The scandal dragged on for months, included many society figures, and is credited with bringing down Harold Macmillan's government.

Profumo came from a noble Italian family that had been resident in Britain for generations. He served in the army with distinction in World War II, then entered politics and began a steady rise to become Secretary

Christine Keeler (right) and Mandy Rice-Davies.

of State for War by 1960. In January 1961, Profumo met the model Christine Keeler at a high society party hosted by society osteopath Stephen Ward at Lord Astor's Cliveden House. Profumo and Keeler began an affair which lasted for some weeks but was then ended by Profumo.

The following year, gossip about the affair became widespread, and was given added potency when it became known that Keeler had also been the lover of Yevgeny Ivanov, the senior naval attache at the Soviet Embassy. This revelation added a security risk to the affair. The Cold War was at its height at the time and any clandestine link between the Soviets and the defence secretary was political dynamite. When it emerged that Keeler and her friend Mandy Rice-Davies were linked to members of London's underworld, another dimension of scandal was added.

Eventually, a Member of Parliament raised the issue in the House of Commons. In March 1963 Profumo made a statement in which he said that there had been "no impropriety whatever" in his relationship with Keeler. The statement seemed to calm

The charges were not proven, but Stephen Ward committed suicide on the last day of the trial.

the scandal, but within weeks fresh allegations were made that showed the affair had been a sexual one. On June 5, Profumo resigned as a government minister and from other public positions.

> *Any clandestine link between the Soviets and the defence secretary was political dynamite.*

Meanwhile, Stephen Ward was under investigation for having lived off immoral earnings. The allegations, which were covered by laws on prostitution, were that he had introduced Keeler, Rice-Davies, and other young girls to rich men and taken a number of gifts as payment. The charges were not proven, but Ward committed suicide on the last day of the trial.

In September 1963, Macmillan resigned as Prime Minister and his Conservative Party lost the following general election.

AFTER THE SCANDAL

A few weeks after he resigned, Profumo went to work at Toynbee Hall, a charity in the impoverished East End of London. At his own request he began at the lowest level—cleaning toilets. He continued to work there for the rest of his life, gradually working his way up until he became the charity's chief fundraiser. In 1975, Profumo was made a Commander of the British Empire (CBE) for his charity work. He rarely appeared in public and made no attempt to return to politics.

Bill Clinton (b.1946)

As President of the USA from 1993 to 2001, Clinton was widely acknowledged to be a success, but his personal life came in for criticism. Rumours of an extramarital affair almost ruined his bid to become President but, with the support of his wife, he overcame these. Then, in 1998, new media reports linked him to Monica Lewinsky. The resulting investigation led to the impeachment of Clinton by the Republican-controlled House. He was acquitted by the Senate but the affair blighted his second term.

Richard Nixon (1913–1994)

Nixon was elected President of the USA in 1969, and re-elected in 1972. But within weeks it emerged that men working for his re-election campaign had broken into offices run by his Democratic rivals at the Watergate building. There then began a long-running saga of newspaper reports, government leaks, and briefings focusing on how much he had known about the break-in and to what extent he had tried to cover up the affair. Although little was proven, there were widespread suspicions about Nixon's actions. He resigned on August 9, 1974.

Édith Cresson (b.1934)

Cresson was a Commissioner of the European Union who resigned in 1999 amid questions over her behaviour. She had hired a close friend, Philippe Berthelot, to be a "visiting scientist", but instead he acted as a personal adviser, causing a degree of scandal. The Belgian police began an investigation but decided that no laws had been broken. The affair was believed to have eventually led to the collective resignation of the Commission.

SOCIAL REFORMER

In his short life, Arnold Toynbee managed to have a profound impact on the social conscience of Britain. He also assisted hundreds of working men to better themselves, and even found time to write history.

Born the son of a prosperous and famous physician, Arnold Toynbee was educated at good local schools in London before going to Oxford University, where he read political economy. In 1878, he graduated and took up a teaching post at Balliol College. It was there that Toynbee coined the phrase "Industrial Revolution" to describe the economic and social changes that had taken place across Britain in the previous century and a half, and which were then spreading across Europe, North America, and other continents.

Toynbee did far more at Balliol than come up with snappy phrases. He studied the history of the ebb and flow of economic prosperity and its causes. This led him to formulate ideas that were ground-breaking for their era and revolutionary in their impact. One of his key beliefs was that none of the generally accepted laws of economics were, in fact, laws at all. Toynbee believed that they were not universally true, as laws should be, but were only true under most circumstances.

The concept that free trade was always a good thing for the general economy in the long

ARNOLD TOYNBEE (1852–1883)

"It is a paradoxical but profoundly true and important principle of life that the most likely way to reach a goal is to be aiming not at that goal itself but at some more ambitious goal beyond it." Arnold Toynbee

run, although it could be bad for small sectors of the economy in the short run, was one of the ideas that Toynbee attacked most aggressively. He believed that free trade had generally been a good thing in the early 19th century because of the peculiar circumstances of that time, not because it was a good thing in itself. This brought him into direct confrontation not only with other economists, but also with numerous politicians.

He believed that factory owners would inevitably try to reduce wages to starvation point.

Toynbee also believed that untrammelled free competition was only a beneficial policy to follow in certain circumstances. He believed that government had a duty to interfere in trade "to prevent the weak being trampled underfoot". In particular, he believed that those who owned factories would inevitably try to reduce wages to starvation point and that they could be stopped only by trades unions or legislation.

He believed that government had a duty to interfere in trade.

When he could get away from Oxford, Toynbee set about putting his ideas into practical effect. He encouraged the founding of trades unions and worked to boost their membership. He established a public library in Whitechapel, a deprived area of London's East End, and agitated for more to be opened. One of his key messages to students at Oxford was that they should spend a part of their time aiding the poor. One such effort resulted in the founding of Toynbee Hall in 1884. Based in Whitechapel, it provided education to the locals as well as social aid, and it is still in existence today.

Toynbee died aged 30. His early death is often said to have been brought on by overwork.

OTHER CAMPAIGNERS FOR SOCIAL REFORM

William Wilberforce (1759–1833)

In 1785, the English social reformer William Wilberforce underwent a dramatic conversion to the evangelical form of Protestant Christianity and so decided to dedicate his life to the work of God. This he saw as the abolition of slavery, and his tireless campaigning is generally credited with having brought slavery to an end within the British Empire when it was abolished on March 25, 1807.

Dorothea Dix (1802–1887)

At the age of 38, Dorothea Dix decided to devote herself to campaigning for what she termed the "indigent insane"—people suffering mental health problems who had no family to care for them. She amassed evidence on the hardship these people suffered and her ideas and campaign finally won through. She is credited with having greatly improved the lot of those suffering mental health problems in the USA.

Horace Mann (1796–1859)

An educational reformer, Horace Mann is widely considered to be the father of the US education system as it exists today. Born into a poor family, he nonetheless graduated from Boston University in 1819 aged 23. He then became a teacher and in 1837 was appointed head of the Massachusetts Board of Education. In that position, Mann worked to establish a state-wide system of basic education for all.

Popular History

"*People thought me bad before, but if ever I should get free,
I'll let them know what bad means.*"

Billy the Kid during his trial

BOXING LEGEND

It was February 25, 1964, at Miami Beach when Cassius Clay became heavyweight champion of the world, defeating Sonny Liston by a technical knock-out.

Despite being the seven-to-one underdog, Clay was boxing confidently and had lived up to his promise to "float like a butterfly and sting like a bee". As the bell rang for round seven, the challenger stood ready, arms characteristically at his side. Then Clay threw his arms in the air and began to dance. Liston was unable to continue. Aged 22, the self-professed "greatest fighter that ever lived" was world champion.

Born in Louisville, Kentucky in 1942, Cassius Marcellus Clay Junior was 12 years old when at the Columbia Auditorium someone stole his bicycle. When Clay told a policeman he wanted to "whup" the thief, the cop, Joe Martin, told him he "better learn to box first"—and trained the boy for the next six years.

He trained very hard and it paid off. Aged just 18, he won gold at the 1960 Rome Olympics. On his return home, Clay went professional, hired the experienced Angelo Dundee as his trainer, and began to make his mark. Two qualities immediately set him apart from most fighters: first was his style. Heavyweights typically were slow and hit hard to body and head. The 6ft 3in (1.91m) tall Clay would dance around the ring,

MUHAMMAD ALI (b.1942)

"Champions are made from something they have deep inside them—a desire, a dream, a vision. They have to have last-minute stamina, they have to be a little faster… But the will must be stronger than the skill." Muhammad Ali

flicking out shots with incredible speed. Second, he knew the value of working up a crowd. Clay's non-stop patter, his shameless bravado, and his habit of insulting his opponents soon earned him as many enemies as friends.

The day after the Liston fight, Clay outraged the public when he joined the Nation of Islam and abandoned his "slave name" in favour of Muhammad Ali. It was the first sign of the fighter's interest and commitment to the

Clay would dance around the ring, flicking out shots with incredible speed.

politics of race and religion.

In 1967 Ali was drafted into the armed services to fight in Vietnam. He refused on religious grounds but famously added: "I ain't got no quarrel with them Vietcong…" Ali was stripped of his title, had his boxing licence suspended, and didn't fight again for three and a half years. He also faced a five-year prison term for draft dodging.

> "I ain't got no quarrel with them Vietcong…"

He lost to Joe Frazier in 1971 but a few months later won another battle when the Supreme Court dropped the charges against him. Then came a remarkable win in "The Rumble in the Jungle" fight against George Foreman. He was champion again.

Next followed what many critics rate as the best fight ever—the 1975 "Thrilla in Manila", where Ali beat Joe Frazier. Three years later, he lost to Leon Spinks. But in a dramatic rematch Ali beat Spinks to become the first fighter ever to win a world title three times.

STILL FIGHTING

In 1982 Ali had another battle on his hands when he was diagnosed with Parkinson's disease. He fought back, throwing himself into political and social campaigns. He also champions the causes of developing countries and fights world hunger. Among the many accolades he has received are the BBC's Sports Personality of the Century and the USA's Presidential Medal of Freedom.

Sugar Ray Robinson
(1921–1989)
Walker Smith became Sugar Ray Robinson after borrowing his friend's Amateur Athletics Union card so that he could fight before he was 16. His record was incredible: as an amateur he scored 85 wins without loss and as a professional he fought more than 200 opponents, lost only 19 times, and won 110 of his fights by knock-out.

Roberto Durán (b.1951)
Born in Guarare, Panama, Durán became one of the greatest fighters of the 20th century, winning world titles at four weights. Hugely popular with fight fans, Duran always lived up to his *Manos de Piedra*, "Hands of Stone", nickname. By the age of 21 Duran was world champion.

Sugar Ray Leonard (b.1956)
Ray Charles Leonard boasted the same trainer, Angelo Dundee, as Ali. He was also a three times Golden Gloves champion, twice National AAU champion, and he won the light welterweight gold at the 1976 Montreal Olympics. His amateur career was outstanding, with only 5 losses in 150 bouts. As a professional, he became the first fighter to win titles in five weights.

Joe Louis (1914–1981)
Known to boxing fans around the world as the "Brown Bomber", Joseph Louis Barrow became one of the undisputed all-time greats. In 1937, he defeated James Braddock to capture the world title having only suffered one defeat to the German Max Schmeling. Eager for revenge, in 1938 he won a rematch with Schmeling. He then began a 12-year reign as world champion.

TEENAGE GUNFIGHTER

BILLY THE KID (1859–1881)

*"People thought me bad before, but if ever I should get free,
I'll let them know what bad means."*
Billy the Kid during his trial.

Billy the Kid was born William Bonney in New York in 1859. His father died when he was young and his mother remarried, and by 1866 was running a boarding house in Silver City, New Mexico.

Billy waited on tables and helped his mother, but he spent most of his time learning card-sharping and how to handle a gun.

In 1871, when Billy was just 12, he killed a man. He fled and drifted into Arizona, then Mexico, doing odd jobs or gambling. By 1876 he was back in New Mexico leading a gang of rustlers.

When Billy arrived on the scene, the cattle business in New Mexico was split between John Chisum and Jim Murphy. Chisum owned a vast ranch while Murphy headed a consortium of smaller ranchers. Supporting Chisum was a banker, Alexander McSween, who had business links to some of the smaller ranchers. Among these ranchers was an Englishman named Tunstall. He was taken in by Tunstall, who persuaded Billy to give up rustling and become an honest cowboy.

> In 1871, when Billy was just 12, he killed a man.

But then Tunstall was shot dead by Murphy, and Billy went on the rampage. Over the next few months he led a group of Tunstall cowboys on a bloody revenge that saw them ambush and murder dozens of men linked to the killing of Tunstall. By the time the killings came to an end, Murphy had died in hospital and most of his men were dead.

In April 1879, Billy the Kid was arrested by the famous lawman, Pat Garrett, who knew Billy well. The Kid was convicted of murder and sentenced to death. On April 17, Billy slipped his hands out of his handcuffs, grabbed a gun, and shot dead the two lawmen who were guarding him. Stealing a horse, he went on the run.

The outlaw went back to his traditional past-times of cattle

Billy was careful never to rob from those linked to those who knew him.

rustling and card-sharping, using his undoubted charm to keep one step ahead of the lawmen. He was careful never to rob from those linked to anyone who knew him and so was assured of a friendly welcome in many places. Among his regular haunts was the Maxwell Ranch just outside Fort Sumner.

On July 13, 1881, Pat Garrett was in Fort Sumner when he heard that Billy was in town. Guessing that he would head for the Maxwell Ranch, Garrett rode out there. He arrived before dark and sat in darkness to wait. A few hours later the door opened and a figure appeared.

"Quien es?" [Who's there] called out a Mexican voice. Garrett fired a single shot that hit Billy in the heart and killed him instantly. He was just 21.

THE BODY COUNT

Billy the Kid is usually credited with 21 killings, one for each year of his short, eventful life. In fact, he was convicted of only four murders, plus the two lawmen he shot while escaping in 1879. Billy is thought to have killed about ten other men, plus an unknown number of Mexicans during his years south of the border.

OTHER WESTERN GUNSLINGERS

Butch Cassidy (fl.1890)
Born Robert LeRoy Parker, Cassidy (below) led a gang known as the Wild Bunch or the Hole in the Wall Gang. It included Kid Curry and the Sundance Kid as well as up to a dozen others. The gang held up numerous banks and trains during the 1890s, taking over $200,000 in loot. Two American bandits were killed in Bolivia in 1904, but it is unclear if these were Cassidy and Sundance.

Sam Bass (1851–1878)
The cowboy Sam Bass (above) was an outlaw for barely a year but his bold exploits made him a legend. In 1877, he was stranded in the Dakotas. With three others, Bass decided to hold up a train to pay his way back to Texas. He then recruited a larger gang, held up the Weatherford Stage and two more trains, each time taking a huge haul of cash. When he tried to rob the bank at Round Rock in July 1878, Bass was shot.

Henry Plummer
(1832–1864)
Plummer (below) arrived in Montana in the 1860s when rustlers were a major problem. He volunteered as sheriff and within six months all rustlers had either been jailed or had left the area. But Plummer failed to catch a gang of ruthless outlaws who held up stagecoaches—because he himself was leader of the gang by night. He was eventually recognized and hanged.

ROYAL REBEL

Known to history as Bonnie Prince Charlie, Charles Edward Stuart was born in 1720. His father was Prince James Edward Stuart, the son of the ousted Catholic King James II of Britain.

Young Prince Charles was brought up in the firm belief that he was the legitimate King of Britain and that the Hanoverian dynasty that then occupied the throne were usurpers. It was a belief that dominated his life.

In 1715, those in Britain who supported the Stuart dynasty organized an uprising that ended in defeat at the battles of Sheriffmuir in Scotland and Preston in England. Prince James had been in Scotland during the uprising and came away convinced that the Stuarts lacked the support to regain the throne. He advised his two sons to find careers for themselves in Europe. His younger son, Henry, became a Cardinal but Charles always retained hopes of becoming king one day. He trained to be an army officer, fighting bravely at the siege of Gaeta in 1734.

Charles was then summoned to Paris by King Louis XV of France who wanted to use him to give legitimacy to a French invasion of England. Louis then engaged in diplomacy and threats against King George II. Charles was told that Louis was awaiting a suitable opportunity, but he decided to take matters into his own hands, believing that if he could get a

BONNIE PRINCE CHARLIE (1720–1788)

"I have come home." Bonnie Prince Charles on being told by Alexander MacDonald of Boisdale to abandon the rebellion and go home.

pro-Stuart rebellion started, Louis would send an army to help him.

On July 23, 1745, Prince Charles landed at Eriskay in the Hebrides. The local clans refused to join him so he moved to the mainland. There was then an anxious wait at Glenfinnan until 700 men of the Clan Cameron came marching in. The rebellion was underway.

Charles marched south to Edinburgh with about 2,500 highlanders. He was met outside the city at Prestonpans by a British army of 2,300 led by Sir John Cope. The Battle of Prestonpans ended in victory for Charles and most of Scotland surrendered to him. He recruited more men to double the size of his army.

He found that he had an army of just 5,000 men, while English armies of 50,000 marched against him.

Charles marched to capture Carlisle and invade England. From Carlisle he headed south to Derby. He had expected English Catholics to rally to his cause, but they stayed at home. He found that he had an army of just 5,000 men, while English armies of 50,000 marched against him.

> *He had expected English Catholics to rally to his cause, but they stayed at home.*

He wanted to make a dash for London but his clan commanders opted for a return to Scotland to find more recruits. The march back north was interrupted at Falkirk when an army of 10,000 English and Scots was defeated, but the retreat went on to Inverness.

On April 16, 1746 Charles faced the combined armies of England and lowland Scotland, plus the highland clans hostile to him, at the Battle of Culloden. He lost the battle and fled. After several months on the run, he boarded a French ship for the continent.

PRINCE IN EXILE

After his rebellion, Charles lived under assumed names for 18 years and travelled widely, once even visiting London. He later lived in Rome, sinking heavily into alcoholism. In the 1770s, the British colonies in America rebelled and declared themselves independent. There was a move to make Charles the new King of America, but they came to nothing. He died in 1788.

Spartacus (d.71BC)
Spartacus was a gladiator in ancient Rome who led a rebellion of slaves and gladiators in 73BC. He led a force of more than 100,000 north to escape Roman territory. His followers, however, thought they could defeat the Roman army and turned south. They were defeated on the banks of the Silarus in 71BC by an army led by Crassus. Spartacus was crucified, along with thousands of his men.

Louis Riel (1844–1885)
Louis Riel was leader of the Métis, a people of Indian and European mixed race who lived in the Northwest Territories of Canada. In 1869 they rebelled against the incorporation of the Territories into Canada, leading to the formation of the province of Manitoba. Hostilities continued and Riel fled to the USA. He returned in 1885 to lead a rebellion in Saskatchewan. It was crushed and Riel executed for treason.

William Wallace (c.1272–1305)
Wallace began his attacks on English garrisons in 1297. His small force grew rapidly to become an army and in September his 25,000 men defeated the main English army at Stirling Bridge. Wallace was proclaimed Protector of Scotland and launched a great raid into northern England. On July 22, 1298, he was defeated at Falkirk by King Edward I of England. He was captured by the English in 1305 and hanged.

FEMALE POISONER

The great Renaissance princess Lucrezia Borgia has gone down in history as one of the most prolific and heartless poisoners of men on record, as well as being a wanton seductress.

In fact, it is not entirely clear how guilty Lucrezia was of the crimes alleged against her, or whether she was a mere tool in the hands of her overbearing male relatives.

The Borgia family moved from Spain to Italy when Alfonso Borgia became a cardinal. In 1492, Alfonso's nephew Rodrigo bribed his way to becoming Pope, taking the name Alexander VI—and he was the father of Lucrezia. It was a bad time for the papacy. Over the previous century or so, corruption and turmoil had torn Italy apart. Alexander made it his mission to regain for the papacy all its lost lands and revenues, and to siphon off some of those to enrich his own family.

LUCREZIA BORGIA (1480–1519)

"They are forever with God." Lucrezia Borgia when asked about her brother Cesare and father Alexander.

ENVENOMING RING

Lucrezia was said to have a big jewelled ring in which was hidden a small compartment that contained poison. It was believed that she used her beauty and sexual desires to gain the confidence of a man marked for death by Cesare or Alexander. She would be quite happy to bed the intended victim if she had to, but otherwise would take whatever opportunity she could to position the ring over his food or drink and release the poison.

While still under the age of 10, Lucrezia was engaged to two Italian noblemen, but Alexander broke off both engagements when they ceased to be politically advantageous. At the age of 12, Lucrezia was married to Giovanni Sforza, a son of the mighty Sforza family that ruled Milan. Giovanni moved to live in Rome, but the marriage had not been consummated before Alexander no longer needed Sforza's support for his intrigues. Lucrezia told Giovanni that Alexander planned to murder him, prompting the young man to flee. When he was offered an annulment and a cash payment, he accepted.

Lucrezia told Giovanni that Alexander planned to murder him, prompting the young man to flee.

Lucrezia, meanwhile, became pregnant in 1497. She was packed off to a convent to give birth in secrecy. Many alleged the father was Lucrezia's brother, Cesare.

At the age of 12, Lucrezia was married to Giovanni Sforza.

In 1498, Lucrezia was married to Alfonso of Aragon, nephew of the King of Naples. Only 18 months later, Cesare allied himself to a French family who claimed the Kingdom of Naples, making Lucrezia's marriage to Alfonso inconvenient. Alfonso died with convenient suddenness. Whether he was poisoned by Lucrezia or strangled by Cesare is unclear.

In 1501, Lucrezia married the Prince of Ferrara. She left Rome and so escaped the machinations of her brother and father. After the deaths of Alexander in 1503, and Cesare in 1507, depending on which source you believe, Lucrezia either continued her immoral career or became a model Renaissance duchess.

OTHER "FEMME FATALES"

Catherine Deshayes
(c.1640–1680)
Deshayes, who was known as "La Voisin" during her career as a sorceress and poisoner, earned a living as a fortune teller to the noble ladies of Paris. She is known for her involvement in the *Affair des Poisons* scandal, which disgraced the reign of Louis XIV. She was convicted of witchcraft and burned in public.

Vera Renczi (b.1903)
Born into a noble Romanian family, Vera Renczi married a wealthy businessman and had a son. In 1925, she suspected her husband of being unfaithful so she murdered him by putting arsenic into his wine. The body was buried in the cellar, while Renczi told friends that he had run off with another woman. A second husband was also poisoned for the same reason after less than a year of marriage. Renczi then embarked on a string of affairs with men, some married and some not, several of whom vanished or left on mysterious errands from which they did not return. Police were called when the wife of one of the men named Renczi as the last person to see her husband alive. A search of the house revealed 35 bodies, all men.

Mary Ann Cotton
(1832–1873)
Cotton was a notorious female serial killer in Victorian England. It is thought that she poisoned up to 20 people using arsenic, but her success at covering her tracks make her total tally uncertain. Her first victim was her husband William Mowbray in 1865. She was eventually caught by a suspicious coroner.

WARRIOR QUEEN

Of all the queens who have ruled in their own right, none can match the warrior reputation of Boadicea, or Boudicca, who ruled the Iceni of eastern Britain in the 1st century AD.

Riding in her war chariot, she led her tribe against the Roman invaders of Britain, inflicting massive damage on their armies before her eventual defeat.

When the Romans invaded Britain in AD43, King Prasutagus of the Iceni chose to ally himself to Rome in return for being allowed to retain his kingdom. Around AD58 Prasutagus died, leaving his kingdom and wealth jointly to the Roman emperor Claudius and his two daughters. This was a common ruse among client rulers to ensure a smooth handover. This time it didn't work, perhaps because Roman law did not recognize daughters as heirs.

The Roman authorities moved in to annex the kingdom. When Prasutagus' widow, Boadicea, objected, she and her daughters were seized. Boadicea was flogged, and her daughters raped. Province procurator, Catus Decianus, had hoped this would shame them in the eyes of their warriors. In fact, it outraged the Iceni, who mustered for war. Warriors poured in from neighbouring tribes and Boadicea soon had a vast army behind her.

She moved first against the Roman colony of Camulodunum,

BOADICEA (d.AD60)

"In height she was very tall, her appearance was terrifying, the look in her eye was very fierce, and her voice was hard; a great mass of red-gold hair fell to her hips."
Dio Cassius

now Colchester. She stormed the city and took the last bastion of the fortified Temple of Claudius after a siege of two days. All Romans were put to the sword and the city burnt to the ground. A detachment of the IX Legion was marching south under Quintus Petilius Cerialis from Lincoln. Boadicea ambushed the column in dense woodland somewhere near Newark. The Roman infantry were annihilated. Cerialis got away with a few cavalry and fled back

All Romans were put to the sword and the city burnt to the ground.

to Lincoln, which he barricaded against attack. But Boadicea turned south, not north. She captured London, slaughtered its inhabitants, and destroyed it utterly.

> *Boadicea ambushed the column in dense woodland somewhere near Newark.*

The Roman governor of Britain, Gaius Suetonius Paulinus, had been campaigning in what is now north Wales when the war began. He came marching down Watling Street, now the A5, leading the XIV and XX Legions, plus some auxiliaries. Boadicea set off northwest to meet him. Exactly where they met is not now known but it may have been in Warwickshire. Suetonius took up a defensive position in a valley with his flanks covered by woods. Boadicea attacked but Suetonius was ready for her. The disciplined Romans defeated the Celts, killing 80,000 to their own loss of 400.

Boadicea survived the battle, but is said to have committed suicide rather than surrender.

BOADICEA IN FICTION

The warrior queen has been the subject of a feature film, *Boadicea* in 1928, and of a TV film *Warrior Queen* in 2003. In 1978 she was the topic of a British children's TV series. She has also been the subject of novels by writers such as Rosemary Sutcliff, Manda Scott, Alan Gold, and David Wishart. On the stage she featured in Henry Purcell's 1695 musical *Bonduca, or The British Heroine*.

Zenobia of Palmyra (fl.267–273)

Zenobia of Palmyra became Queen of Palmyra, in modern Syria, in 267. Palmyra was already a powerful state, but Zenobia set out to make it a great empire. The Roman Empire at this time was weakened by civil wars, so Zenobia announced that she wanted to protect the eastern provinces. In fact, she invaded them, riding at the head of her army. Within four years she had acquired Egypt, Syria, Asia Minor, Palestine, and Lebanon. In 273 the Roman Emperor Aurelian demanded that Zenobia hand over the provinces; she refused and Aurelian invaded. He defeated Zenobia at Antioch. Zenobia was sent to Rome as an honoured prisoner.

Artemisia of Halicarnossos (fl.480BC)

Artemisia of Halicarnossos inherited the Kingdom of Caria in Asia Minor from her father Lygdamis, ruling it as a subject ruler of the Persian Empire. In 480BC she was ordered by Xerxes of Persia to send five warships to join his invasion of Greece. She chose to lead them herself and became one of Xerxes' leading naval advisors. At the Battle of Salamis in 480BC she fought so well that Xerxes stated, "My men have become women, my women have become men". The battle ended in defeat for Persia and the invasion was called off. Artemisia then returned to her kingdom, which she ruled until her death.

Cartimandua (fl. AD44–69)

Cartimandua was Queen of the Brigantes tribe of central Britain when the Romans invaded in AD43. She formed an alliance with Rome against the traditional enemies of her tribe, the Catuvellauni, and was rewarded by being made an ally of Rome. When King Caractacus of the Catuvellauni ventured into her territory she had him arrested and sent to Rome in chains. In 57 she divorced her husband Venutius, a Brigantes nobleman, in favour of his armour bearer. This led to civil war among the Brigantes, a conflict which Cartimandua won with Roman aid. In 69 Venutius allied himself to northern tribes and invaded Brigantes territory. He swept to victory, ousting Cartimandua who fled to Rome.

CELEBRATED "DANDY"

Beau Brummell was born George Bryan Brummell, the son of a secretary to Lord North. From such humble beginnings, Brummell rose to be the most fashionable man in Europe, exerting an influence on male fashion that persists to this day.

Brummell was educated at Eton and Oxford, where he became better known for his good looks and adventurous social life than for his academic talent. His father arranged for him to become an officer in the 10th Dragoons in 1790 and he seemed set on course for a solid military career. However, this path led him to meet Prince George, eldest son and heir to King George III. When Brummell's father died, he inherited a fortune, gave up his army career, and moved to London to begin a new career as a gentleman of leisure.

He rented a house in the fashionable Mayfair area and quickly joined the elite group of companions around Prince George. Brummell's wit, humourous remarks, and good looks won him many friends, but it was his dress that really marked him out. He took a bath every day, then an unheard of luxury, and had his shirt and underwear washed every day. His appearance was immaculate.

Brummell began a revolution in men's fashion. He abandoned the stuffy formality of court dress, with

BEAU BRUMMELL (1778–1840)

"This can be said of Brummell, that he dictated the main lines of male fashion to the whole of Europe for the next hundred years."
Hardy Amies

its knee-breeches and abundance of silk and embroidery. In its place he introduced the clothes of a country squire, but produced in beautiful cloth and cut with exquisite skill. His day suits were three-piece affairs with coat, trousers, and waistcoat all made from the same woollen cloth and devoid of decoration. One glaring innovation was that Brummell had his sleeves cut so that they hung in front of the jacket and were slightly bent—the way arms would

He took a bath every day, then an unheard of luxury, and had his shirt and underwear washed every day.

naturally rest when riding. Modern business suits are derived from those introduced by Brummell for gentlemen in the city.

> Brummell began a revolution in men's fashion.

For eveningwear, Brummell preferred a plain black suit worn over a white shirt and white tie. This oufit was the ancestor of modern-day, formal, white-tie eveningwear. He established a code of good dress that could be aspired to by almost any reasonably affluent man. Simplicity, elegance, and comfort were his watchwords. Unfortunately, Brummell came to rely on his friendship with the Prince and high aristocracy to avoid paying his bills. When he fell out with the Prince, he found his debts were called in; he could not pay them. Brummell fled to France to avoid bankruptcy. He died in 1840, apparently from syphilis.

PARTING REMARK

Brummell's fall from favour was sudden and complete. He had a minor disagreement with the Prince of Wales in 1815, as a result of which the prince snubbed him at a social event in front of friends. This angered Brummell. When the two men next met, the Prince was accompanied by Lord Alvanley. Brummell accosted the pair and said: "Alvanley, who's your fat friend?" The Prince ostracized Brummell and never spoke to him again.

OTHER FAMOUS FASHIONISTAS

Edward VII (1841–1910)
As Prince of Wales, Edward (below) came to dominate British male dress, until by 1890 he was the arbiter of sartorial dress across Europe. When he went to the spa for his spring break, tailors from all over Europe flocked there to take note of his latest style. Among his innovations were the Homburg hat and Norfolk jacket.

Richard Nash (1674–1762)
Nash (above) earned his nickname "The Beau" from his elegant dress and impeccable manners; he played a leading role in making Bath the most fashionable resort in 18th-century England, supervising the construction of public buildings, houses for rent, and theatres. He also encouraged a new informality in manners.

Yves St Laurent (1936–2008)
St Laurent (below) moved to Paris from Algeria aged 17 to work for Christian Dior. When Dior died in 1957, St Laurent became chief designer. After a brief spell in the army he started his own label. St Laurent established the ready-to-wear side of couture fashion and popularized numerous trends such as the beatnik and the safari look. He retired in 2002.

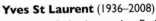

ECCENTRIC LORD

Lord Byron is best known today for his moving and romantic poetry, but in his own day he was as famous for his scandalous and highly eccentric personal behaviour. His assorted pranks, scandals, and loves kept British society agog with interest and fascinated most of Europe.

LORD BYRON (1788–1824)

"Mad, bad, and dangerous to know."
Lady Caroline Lamb speaking about Lord Byron.

Throughout his life, George Byron, 6th Baron Byron, managed to show a charismatic personality that captivated or repulsed all who met him. Nobody, it seems, was indifferent to his dazzling wit and outrageous behaviour. When at college in Cambridge Byron was told he was not allowed to bring his pet dog into Trinity College, so he went out and bought a pet bear instead. When the bear died, he acquired a fox.

In 1809, Byron left on a tour of foreign countries, then considered a normal part of an education for a young gentleman. Due to the war with Napoleon, Byron went to the Mediterranean, visiting Spain, Albania, and Greece—then part of the Ottoman Empire. What was not considered normal was the passionate gay affair that Byron indulged in in Athens and the fact that he began writing his first major work, *Childe Harold's Pilgrimage*.

On his return in 1812, Byron considered entering politics and went to Westminster to take up his place in the House of Lords, where he was a strong advocate of social reform. At the same time, he embarked on an affair of great intensity and scandal with Lady Caroline Lamb.

While still involved with Lady Caroline, Byron caused further scandal when his divorced half-sister Augusta produced a daughter. Byron was known to have a deeply emotional relationship with Augusta and it was suspected at the time that the child was Byron's. In 1814, Byron ditched Lady Caroline in favour of her cousin, Lady Anne, whom he married the following

Byron caused further scandal when his divorced half-sister Augusta produced a daughter.

year. Byron treated his wife poorly and was unfaithful more than once. One month after the birth of their baby daughter in 1815, she left him.

Byron then left Britain, travelling up the Rhine and renting a house in Geneva. There he met the fellow poet Percy Shelley, his wife Mary, and her sister, Claire Clairmont, with whom Byron had an affair and a daughter. In 1817, Byron moved on to Venice, then to Rome. All this time Byron was writing his poetry, and sending it home to be published to much acclaim and commercial success.

In 1821, he moved to Genoa where he met Greek exiles and became embroiled in the campaign for Greek independence from Ottoman rule. He travelled to Greece and donated £4,000 ($8,000) to refit the Greek fleet. He also took command of a part of the army and joined the attack on the Ottoman fortress of Lepanto in 1824. He then fell ill and despite a partial recovery died on April 19 of that year.

OTHER UNCONVENTIONAL LORDS

Mad Jack Mytton (1796–1834)

At the age of two, Jack Mytton (right) inherited the rank of Squire of Halston Hall, Shropshire, and a fortune. He was expelled from every school he attended, arrived at Cambridge University with 2,000 bottles of port, was elected to Parliament but only attended once, and liked fox hunting naked. His most famous exploit was to arrive at a dinner party riding a bear. He died in prison for debt.

3rd Earl of Lucan (1800–1888)

In 1826, George Bingham (left) became commander of the famous 17th Lancers. During the Crimean War he commanded the British cavalry, during which time he grew increasingly ill-tempered. His behaviour is held to have contributed to the disastrous but heroic Charge of the Light Brigade in 1854.

4th Earl of Bristol (1730–1803)

Frederick Augustus Hervey was clever, well-educated, and highly eccentric. He trained to enter the Church but went to Rome to study art. Later, he became Bishop of Derry. He inflicted a range of odd rules on his clergy but was beloved by them. They coined a saying: "God created men, women, and Herveys".

MAD ROMAN EMPEROR

Caligula was the third Emperor of Rome, and the first to be undeniably mad. But his career hadn't started out that way.

At first, Caligula seemed to be a promising, highly talented successor to his grandfather, Tiberius, and great grandfather Augustus.

Born Gaius Julius Caesar Germanicus on August 31, AD12, the boy spent much of his childhood on campaign with his father, the successful general Germanicus. At the age of two he was given a miniature soldier's outfit, which he wore as he tramped around the legionary camps as a child. He became popular with the soldiers. They gave him the nickname of Caligula, meaning "Little Boot".

When Tiberius died on March 16, AD37, Caligula took over and began well. He made a tactful speech to the Senate, promising to respect the forms and procedures of the Roman Republic. Then, in September of that year, Caligula collapsed. It's not clear what afflicted him, but

CALIGULA (AD12–41)

When Tiberius died on 16 March, AD37, Caligula took over and began well. He made a tactful speech to the Senate promising to respect the forms and procedures of the Roman Republic.

HORSE PLAY

Caligula is famous for his friendship with Incitatus, a successful chariot-racing horse. Caligula had the horse stabled in the palace with a marble stall, ivory manger, and purple blankets. Incitatus was a frequent guest at banquets and on occasion invitations were issued in his name. In fact, if a senator failed to invite Incitatus, he could fall from favour and lose his government position.

his doctors thought it was tied to his epilepsy. The malady confined him to bed for two months.

When Caligula recovered, he was a changed man, plagued by insomnia and nightmares, and convinced that he had been poisoned. He had his 15-year-old cousin, Gemellus, murdered along with Macro, the general who had smoothed his rise to power. The killings shocked Roman society; the new emperor was revealed as a man capable of sudden

The new emperor was revealed as a man capable of sudden and unpredictable violence.

and unpredictable violence.

Nevertheless, Caligula settled down to the business of government, although he was lavish in his expenditures. Caligula's one weakness in his official duties was spectacle. He couldn't get enough of shows and chariot-racing. Vast sums of money were spent on public events and the treasury was gradually depleted.

> *Caligula's one weakness in his official duties was spectacle.*

Caligula married four times. His first wife died in childbirth. He then "stole" his next wife on the day of her wedding, only to divorce her two months later. His third wife, Lollia Paulina, was divorced within weeks. He then married his mistress, Milonia Caesonia and the philandering came to an end.

Meanwhile, public debt was reaching serious levels and the Senate was not happy. Caligula began to confiscate a slice of the legacies left by rich men. He then introduced new taxes, including one on prostitution.

In AD40 Caligula led a failed attack on Britain. Frustrated and bitter, he ordered his men to collect seashells on the beach and celebrate a triumph over the sea. On returning to Rome he then declared himself a god.

The random killings, frequent acts of madness, and a neglect of government proved too much for some senators, who had Caligula murdered on January 24, AD41.

Nero (AD37-68)
Like his uncle Caligula, Nero began well but soon went off the rails. He came to power after his mother murdered the emperor Claudius in October AD54. In AD59, he murdered his mother and took control. He then ordered the murder of his wife so that he could marry Poppaea Sabina, who he eventually killed in a fit of anger. Nero's main love, however, was the arts. When soldiers came to kill him, he declared, "Oh, what an artist the world is losing".

Commodus (161–192)
The son and heir of the popular and capable emperor Marcus Aurelius, Commodus became emperor at the age of 19 and at once began to neglect his official duties. He soon had a harem of 300 women and 300 boys who were used in debauched orgies. He enjoyed displaying his skills as a swordsman in exhibition bouts with leading gladiators and when he tired of that, took to killing condemned prisoners in the arena for fun. On December 31, AD192 he was poisoned by his mistress, Marcia, and then strangled by the athlete Narcissus.

Elagabalus (203–222)
Inheriting the imperial power at the age of just 15, Elagabalus was the nephew of the emperor Caracalla, and was put in power by the army. But Elagabalus was no soldier. When he arrived in Rome he installed a cult statue of the Syrian sun god whose name he bore. Every day at dawn he summoned the Senate to watch him sacrifice a dozen cattle to his god. He then spent the rest of the day indulging his sexual desires and humiliating politicians in public. He was killed by mutineering Praetorian Guards.

In oceano Vulgo Prasma

FAMOUS WOMANIZER

Undoubtedly the most well-known seducer in history, Giacomo Casanova owes his fame as much to his writings as to his amorous escapades.

Giovanni Giacomo Casanova was born in Venice in 1725 as the son of actress Zanetta Farussi, though whether his father was actually her husband or local nobleman Michele Grimani was never clear. He excelled at academic study and attended the University of Padua. He lost his virginity, by his own account, at the age of 16 in a night of passion with two sisters who had seduced him. That same year he became a Doctor of Law, later graduating as a physician.

By 1740, he was back in Venice where he set up as a lawyer. Instead of working, he ingratiated himself with the elderly, rich Alvise Malipiero, who introduced him to society. After a scandal of some kind, Casanova joined the army, which sent him to join the Venetian garrison of Corfu.

> *Instead of working, he ingratiated himself with the elderly, rich Alvise Malipiero.*

GIACOMO CASANOVA (1725–1798)

"I am writing My Life to laugh at myself, and I am succeeding." Giacomo Casanova

He found Corfu boring so became a theatrical violinist back in Venice. Then he saved the life of the wealthy Signor Bragadin, who rewarded him with an endowment good enough for him to give up working and become a gentleman of leisure.

After being falsely accused of rape, Casanova spent the next few years travelling in Europe. When he returned to Venice in 1753, he was arrested on charges of witchcraft. He was sentenced to five years in prison but escaped and went on the run.

Back in Paris, Casanova was appointed as a trustee of the state lottery, and used the position to milk funds into his own pocket. He also established a silk factory where he embarked on a series of affairs with his young female employees. At one point he had 20 mistresses, each occupying a separate apartment at his expense. The costs were enormous.

At one point he had 20 mistresses, each occupying a separate apartment at his expense.

By 1760, he was using the bogus title Chevalier de Seingalt, sometimes upgrading himself to Count de Farussi. Using these false names and his astonishing ability to charm himself into the favour of rich old men, he womanized his way around Europe.

In 1774, he went back to Venice, but was expelled for writing satirical verses about public figures. After more years of travel, adventure, and seductions, he met Marianne de Charpillon in London in 1784. She was intelligent, witty, beautiful, and 16 years old—but for once Casanova had met his match. Charpillon had been brought to London by her family in the hope of becoming the mistress of a rich nobleman who would keep all of them in comfort. She was not going to throw herself away on an adventurer of limited means. For some months Casanova pursued her, but he got nowhere. He finally gave up and sank into despair and depression.

Casanova fled London to Dux, in Bohemia, where he ingratiated himself into the employment of Count Joseph von Waldstein. He became librarian to the count and spent the last 16 years of his life studying and writing his memoirs.

CASANOVA'S NOBLE CONNECTIONS

During his many travels around Europe, Casanova got to meet and know an astonishing number of leading figures including: Pope Clement XIII, Catherine the Great of Russia, Frederick the Great of Prussia (who allegedly tried to seduce him), Madame de Pompadour, Mozart, and Voltaire.

OTHER NOTORIOUS LADYKILLERS

King Charles II (1630–1685)
King Charles II of England (left) was known as the "Merry Monarch" for his fun-loving ways—and the chasing of women was prime among them. He began early, taking his first mistress as a 16-year-old prince living in exile. This woman, Lucy Walter, had a son who was later created Duke of Monmouth. As king after 1660, Charles's most famous mistress was Nell Gwynn, the most popular comedy actress of her time. She gave the king two sons. He is thought to have had more than a dozen illegitimate children in total.

Tom Jones (b. 1940)
The great Welsh singer Tom Jones (right) has been married to his wife for 50 years, but that has not stopped a string of claims about affairs with other women. In 1974, he was linked to the USA's ex-Miss World, Marjorie Wallace. In 1987 he is said to have had an affair with 24-year-old model Katherine Berkery, which produced a son in the form of Jonathan Berkery. Jones did not recognize the boy as his, but Berkery has nevertheless gone on to forge a career in the music business.

"GREAT" QUEEN

Catherine II of Russia began her life as Sophie, a daughter of the minor German ruler Prince Christian August of Anhalt-Zerbst.

She was chosen as wife of Peter, heir to the Russian throne for complex diplomatic reasons, which deemed a junior princess of a Prussia-friendly state as the best wife for the future Tsar.

Arriving in Russia at the age of 15, Catherine decided to do everything necessary to be fit to sit on the throne. She learned Russian, took the more Russian name of Catherine, and embraced the Orthodox faith. However, she soon found that her husband was not as keen on her as she was on Russia. He virtually ignored her while dallying with a mistress and indulging his tastes for games. Catherine took her own lovers, while making contact with politicians hostile to her husband and learning statecraft.

In 1762, Peter became Tsar Peter III, and at once plunged Russia into an unpopular Scandinavian war. The war went badly and on July 13 the imperial bodyguard revolted, deposed Peter, and proclaimed Catherine the new ruler of Russia. Three days later, Peter was murdered by Alexei Orlov of the guard. Exactly how far Catherine herself had planned the coup is unclear, but at the very least she had known about it and given her permission to the plotters to rise up.

CATHERINE THE GREAT (1729–1796)

"I shall be an autocrat: that's my trade. And the good Lord will forgive me: that's his." Catherine the Great

Catherine had no real right to power in Russia, but that did not stop her. She maintained a firm grip by skilfully playing off factions within the Russian nobility against each other. Favourites were raised up, some being taken to Catherine's bed, then cast down and others selected from rival factions. Through all these intrigues Catherine kept a tight control over everything and ensured that power and wealth came from her alone.

In 1764, Catherine put Stanislaw Poniatowski, her former lover, on the throne of Poland, securing her western border. In 1768, she

Three days later, Peter was murdered by Alexei Orlov of the guard.

went to war against the Ottoman Empire. Victory in the six-year conflict made Russia the dominant power around the Black Sea and incorporated the Ukraine into the Russian Empire. The Crimea was annexed in 1783 and four years later the Ottomans attacked Russia, starting a five-year war that again ended in Russian victory.

> *Catherine put Stanislaw Poniatowski, her former lover, on the throne of Poland.*

In 1788, Russia was attacked by Sweden but Catherine formed an alliance with Denmark and peace returned. She sought to extend Russian influence by acting as arbiter in international disputes. In 1779, she brought an end to the War of the Bavarian Succession between Prussia and Austria.

At home, Catherine sought to develop the arts and education to bring the state more into line with Germany and France. She likened herself to a philosopher-monarch. She died in 1796 after suffering a stroke in the bath.

CATHERINE'S LOVE LIFE

Throughout her 34-year reign, Catherine enjoyed a succession of lovers, though nobody is certain how many. Her favourite seems to have been Grigori Alexandrovich Potemkin, whom she rewarded with vast estates. After the affair cooled, Potemkin would select young noblemen who he thought might interest Catherine and instruct them in the duties of being the imperial lover.

Alfred the Great (849–899)

Alfred became King of the English kingdom of Wessex in 871 at a time when Viking raids were tearing into Britain and western Europe. In 878, Alfred mustered his army and crushed the Vikings at the Battle of Edington and in 886 captured London, forcing the Vikings to agree to a divided England. He put a great deal of effort into improving learning and literacy in England. His successors became kings of all England and the British Queen Elizabeth II is a direct descendant.

Constantine the Great (c.274–337)

Constantine I became joint Roman Emperor in 306 when his father died at York, north east England, preparing a campaign against the Picts. In 312, Constantine marched south over the Alps and defeated his colleague Maxentius at the Milvian Bridge near Rome. As sole emperor of the western part of the empire, Constantine rooted out corruption and attacked the Germans. In 324, he defeated Licinius, emperor in the East, and became undisputed master of the Roman Empire. Constantine then made Christianity the state religion and in 325 called the Council of Nicaea at which he forced the bishops to agree on matters of theology.

Frederick the Great (1712–1786)

Frederick II became King of Prussia in 1740. He proved to be capable of sound administration and enlightened despotism, introducing policies that favoured trade and boosted prosperity. All of this financed a huge army of 200,000 men with which he fought a succession of wars. He invaded Austria to seize Silesia, then attacked Poland to grab territory, and made war on a succession of German states. By the time he died, Prussia had doubled in size.

SPAIN'S MOST LEGENDARY OUTLAW

Diego Corrientes was born in Utrera in southern Spain in 1757 at a time when the local noblemen owned most of the land, controlled the justice system and administered the taxation system.

As a teenager, Corrientes fell foul of one such local nobleman and found himself accused of crimes he did not commit. Abandoning his farm, Corrientes formed a gang of like-minded young men and set about wreaking revenge on the aristocratic landowners.

His speciality at first was the theft of horses, which he drove over the mountains into Portugal to sell. Later, he turned to cattle theft, which proved to be more profitable. Corrientes was always careful to distribute some of his money to the peasants whose lands he passed through in order to obtain their support and help.

By 1780 he was leading a sizeable gang, not all of whose members operated under his control. Several of his men began

DIEGO CORRIENTES (1757–1781)

Corrientes was always careful to distribute some of his money to the peasants whose lands he passed through in order to obtain their support and help.

DIEGO IN THE MOVIES

The story of Spain's most famous bandit has been filmed several times, most notably in 1937 and in 1959. The 1937 movie was directed by Ignacio Iquino and starred Goyita Herrero and Pedro Terol. It is rarely shown these days, even in Spain. Rather more accessible is the 1959 epic (above) directed by Antonio Isasi Isasmendi and starring José Suárez, Marisa de Leza, and José Marco.

attacking the houses of the rich, using violence to get their hands on whatever loot they could find.

Such bloodthirsty actions lost Corrientes the support he had enjoyed from the local Andalusian people. With a sizeable reward on his head of 1,500 reales if dead (and double that amount if alive), he was soon arrested in 1781, taken to Seville, and hanged. His body was subsequently carved up and exposed to public view. His career has since become the subject of many legends, stories, songs, and, later, movies.

His career has since become the subject of many legends, stories, songs, and, later, movies.

Eustachio Borsa (fl.1850)

Borsa was a notorious Sicilian bandit who captured an English clergyman. Borsa demanded a ransom of £5,000. No money was paid, so Borsa sliced off the man's left ear and posted it to his wife. Still no ransom was paid, so the right ear was cut off. In the end, the British consul paid the ransom, then sent the bill to the Italian government.

Salvatore Giuliano (1922–1950)

Giuliano was a Sicilian peasant who became a bandit and separatist. He first took to crime as a black marketeer during World War II, and then headed for the mountains of eastern Sicily where he began a reign of benevolent terror over the locals. So tight did his grip become that he was nicknamed "King of the Mountains".

Emiliano Zapata (1879–1919)

Born into a peasant family in the Mexican state of Morelos, Emiliano Zapata (right) was elected by his village as mayor or headman in 1909. He pressed for land reforms but when the new Mexican President, Victoriano Huerta, dragged his feet, Zapata raised a rebellion and gathered a force of several thousand men under the title of Liberation Army of the South. Always flashily dressed in ostentatious Mexican costume, Zapata used his army to loot and extort on a grand scale, as well as to push for political reforms. He and his army then became embroiled in the Mexican civil war, with Zapata effectively ruling large areas of the south. He was shot dead on April 10, 1919.

Tsekouras (fl.1890)

Tsekouras was a Greek brigand operating in northern Greece during the 1890s. So serious did his crimes become that the Greek government offered a reward of 40,000 drachmas for his capture. The local army commander took his men into the mountains and the battle that followed lasted 17 hours.

Doroteo Arango Arámbula (1877–1923)

Far better known as Pancho Villa, many of the details about the life of Doroteo Arango Arámbula (left & right) are obscure and controversial. Born in 1877, Villa campaigned tirelessly for land reform to favour the peasants of his home state of Chihuahua in Mexico. He also campaigned to enrich himself, building up a force of armed men that he called an army but others viewed as a bandit gang. The size and mineral wealth of Chihuahua, which he came to rule made him a powerful man while his armed raid on Columbus in 1916 brought him forcibly to the attention of the outside world.

VICTORIAN HEROINE

Putting out to sea in a lifeboat to rescue shipwrecked sailors from a tempestuous sea is not a job for the fainthearted.

So it may come as a surprise to learn that one of the most celebrated lifeboat rescues of all time was undertaken by a 23-year-old woman in a rowing boat.

Grace Darling was born in Bamburgh, Northumberland, in 1815. Her father was a lighthouse keeper, dividing his time between two lighthouses—Longstone on Outer Farne Island and Coquet Island. The Darling family were at Longstone on September 6, 1838, when a severe storm blew in.

A short time after midnight, Grace looked out of her bedroom window to see a ship ashore on Harcar Island, a few hundred yards from Outer Farne Island. The ship turned out to be the SS *Forfarshire*, a coastal steamer with 31 passengers and 29 crew on board. The pounding waves and high seas would soon reduce the ship to wreckage, while low-lying Harcar Island would offer no shelter to survivors.

Grace ran to alert her father, who believed that the waves were so great that the nearest lifeboat, based at Bamburgh, would be unable to put to sea to cross the straits out to the Farnes. The only hope for the people on board the *Forfarshire* was if Darling could get across to them in the 21 foot (6.4m) rowing boat that was used to ferry back and

GRACE DARLING (1815–1842)

"In terms of carrying out a single feat of bravery, she is probably Britain's greatest heroine and this is the premier award for an act which did not only make an impression in this country but also abroad." Edward Playfair of Sothebys, at the sale of her Gold Medal of Bravery Award in 1999.

forth from the lighthouse to the mainland. It was clear that Darling could not handle the boat by himself in such heavy seas and so Grace volunteered to help.

Together the father and daughter rowed for over a mile (1.7km) across the raging seas to the wreck. They picked up four survivors, then rowed back to the lighthouse. Grace took the rescued people ashore and into

Together the father and daughter rowed for over a mile (1.7km) across the raging seas to the wreck.

the lighthouse while her father and one of the stronger rescued sailors returned to the wreck to rescue five more. The *Forfarshire* broke up before a third trip could be made. Nine other people got away in a lifeboat and were picked up by a passing merchant ship.

> *Darling could not handle the boat by himself in such heavy seas and so Grace volunteered to help.*

The events of that night made Grace Darling a national heroine, but her fame was short-lived. She died of tuberculosis four years later and is buried at Bamburgh. A memorial was built for her in the churchyard there, while a second one stands on Great Farne Island.

EXCERPT FROM *GRACE DARLING* BY WILLIAM WORDSWORTH

And would that some immortal Voice—a Voice

Fitly attuned to all that gratitude

Breathes out from floor or couch, through pallid lips

Of the survivors—to the clouds might bear—

Blended with praise of that parental love,

Beneath whose watchful eye the Maiden grew

Pious and pure, modest and yet so brave,

Though young so wise, though meek so resolute—

Might carry to the clouds and to the stars,

Yea, to celestial Choirs, GRACE DARLING'S name!

Dorus Rijkers (1847–1928)

Dorus Rijkers became a Dutch volunteer lifeboatman in 1872 when he saved the 25 crew of a wrecked Australian merchant ship. Over the following 30 years he rescued 487 people from shipwrecks during 38 rescue operations. In 1888, King William III of the Netherlands awarded Rijkers a gold medal of honour. He retired in 1911 and died in 1928.

Sir William Hillary (1771–1847)

Looming bankruptcy forced Sir William Hillary to seek a quiet life on the Isle of Man in 1808. Realizing how dangerous the coast was for ships lacking a pilot with local knowledge, he drew up plans for a lifeboat service manned by trained crews. In February 1823, his work caught the eye of Thomas Wilson, MP for Southwark, who helped him found the National Institution for the Preservation of Life from Shipwreck in 1824, a service entirely dependent on charity donations. In 1854, the name was changed to the Royal National Lifeboat Institution (RNLI).

Henry Blogg (1876–1954)

Henry Blogg (seen here, on the right) became one of the greatest lifeboatmen in the history of the RNLI. He won the gold medal of the RNLI three times, the George Cross, the British Empire Medal, and other awards. He was a crab fisherman, and in the summer ran a deckchair hire business. His greatest rescue came in 1941 when the *English Trader* ran aground off Happisburgh. As his lifeboat approached the ship, a wave rolled it over and five men, including Blogg, were thrown into the sea. None died, but the lifeboat had to turn back to port. Next morning they put to sea again. This time they succeeded in rescuing all 44 men on board the ship.

"THE KINGMAKER"

Richard Neville, 16th Earl of Warwick, was born in 1428 to one of the most influential families in England. At a young age he inherited vast estates, both in his own right and through his wife, which made him the richest nobleman in England.

In 1453, King Henry VI went temporarily insane and Warwick's support was instrumental in making the Duke of York the Protector of England. York ousted the corrupt courtiers, who clustered around the Queen, Margaret of Anjou, and cut off her money supplies from government coffers, thus earning her enmity.

When Henry regained his sanity, York was dismissed but in 1460 made a bid for renewed power. York was at first successful at the Battle of Northampton, but Warwick hesitated to join an open rebellion. At the Battle of Wakefield, York and several of Warwick's relatives were killed by government loyalists.

Warwick now came out in support of York's eldest son, Edward. Edward claimed the throne as Edward IV on the grounds that his bloodline was closer to the original Plantagenet dynasty than was that of Henry VI.

In 1461, Warwick and Edward defeated Henry's supporters at the Battle of Towton, the largest medieval battle fought in Britain. Henry fled to Scotland and

EARL OF WARWICK (1428–1471)

Older and more experienced, Warwick effectively ran the government for Edward, and did so with great skill and ability.

Edward became King of England. Warwick became known by the people as "the Kingmaker".

Older and more experienced, Warwick effectively ran the government for Edward, and with great skill and ability. But after a few years Edward began to take over the reins of power. Warwick did not care for being pushed aside, so he changed sides to free Henry from prison and restore him to power in 1470. Edward fled overseas but returned in 1471 to kill Warwick at the Battle of Barnet and regain power.

In 1461, Warwick and Edward defeated Henry's supporters at the Battle of Towton.

Samuel (fl. c.1000BC)

Samuel was a prophet living in Israel. The people asked him to choose which man should be the first King of Israel, the nation having previously been ruled by noblemen and judges. Samuel chose a brave warrior named Saul who ruled as king. Then Samuel and Saul fell out, so Samuel anointed a boy named David as king instead.

Marcus Antonius

(c.83BC–30BC)

In 42BC, Mark Anthony, was given the eastern provinces of the Roman Empire to administer. He married Cleopatra VII of Egypt. He crowned Cleopatra's son as Pharaoh, then he crowned his children by her to be King Alexander of Media, Queen Cleopatra of Libya, and King Ptolemy of Syria and Macedonia.

Rodrigo Díaz de Vivar

(c.1044–1099)

Better known as El Cid, meaning "the boss", Rodrigo Diaz was in 1072 the most famous nobleman and warrior of the Spanish kingdom of Castile. In that year, King Sancho died and El Cid helped Prince Alfonso become king. For nine years El Cid led the armies against the Moslems in Spain but he then fell out with Alfonso and went into exile. He later recruited an army of 10,000 mercenaries, seized Valencia from the Moslems, and set himself up as ruler—though he continued to pay formal homage to Castile.

Agrippina (c.AD15–59)

Agrippina married her uncle, Emperor Claudius of Rome, and persuaded him to adopt her son Nero as his own. This made him heir to supreme power in Rome. After ensuring that the leading noblemen and generals were willing to accept Nero as emperor, she murdered Claudius.

Stepan Stambulov

(1854–1895)

Stambulov became President of the Bulgarian Council and helped Prince Alexander of Battenberg to become King of Bulgaria. In 1886, Alexander was forced to abdicate and Stambulov persuaded the Council to elect Ferdinand of Saxe-Coburg-Goth as the new king.

Zoe Romanus (c.978–1050)

Zoe Romanus (left) was the daughter of Constantine VIII, Emperor of Byzantium. Her father married her to general Romanus, and the pair jointly inherited the throne in 1028. Six years later, Zoe murdered her husband and married her lover, who then became joint emperor as Michael IV. When Michael died, Zoe elevated a nephew to joint power. Michael V had her imprisoned but she escaped and recruited an army of supporters to march on the capital. Michael was strangled and Zoe returned to power, taking a new husband in the shape of Constantine IX.

INFAMOUS LAWMAN

Of all the men to pin on a lawman's badge in the Old West, none was as famous, as successful, or as controversial as Wyatt Earp, remembered today for his role in the Gunfight at the OK Corral.

In his day, however, Wyatt Earp was as well known for other exploits—not all of them law-abiding or respectable.

Born into a farming family in Illinois, Earp moved west to California with the rest of his family in 1864. He then spent three years as a teamster, driving freight wagons across the western territories and states. He began his career as a lawman in Missouri in 1870 but after his wife died, Wyatt seems to have taken to drink, and in 1871 was charged both with failing to fulfil his duties and with stealing a horse. Wyatt went on the run and his movements over the next three years are unclear.

> *After his wife died, Wyatt seems to have taken to drink.*

In 1874, he arrived in Wichita, Kansas, where he was hired as a law officer in the city marshal's office. The main task of the marshal's office was to keep order among the hard-drinking cowboys who delivered cattle from Texas. By 1876, the cattle trade had moved on to Dodge City, so Wyatt moved with it to become Assistant Marshal. It was

WYATT EARP (1848–1929)

"Fast is fine, but accuracy is everything."
Wyatt Earp talking about the skills needed for gunfighting.

there that he met the professional gambler "Doc" Holliday who became a long-term friend.

In 1879, he moved on to Tombstone, Arizona, where his younger brother Virgil was Marshal. Wyatt was hired as sheriff for the rural areas around the town. Two other brothers,

Morgan and Warren, arrived and so did Doc Holliday. In February 1881, Wyatt found a stolen horse in the possession of local cattle rancher and suspected rustler, Ike Clanton. Clanton handed over the horse, saying he had bought it in good faith, but the incident set in motion the ill feeling between the

Soon a gunfight had started. It lasted barely 30 seconds but cost the lives of three gunmen.

Earps and the Clantons, plus their friends the McLaury brothers.

On October 26, 1881, Frank and Tom McLaury, Billy Claiborne, and Ike and Billy Clanton met at the OK Corral in Tombstone to discuss unspecified business. They were armed, contrary to local laws. The Earps and Holliday went to arrest them. Virgil called on the cowboys to throw down their guns but they did not, so Holliday drew his gun. Soon a gunfight had started. It lasted barely 30 seconds but cost the lives of Billy Clanton and Frank and Tom McLaury.

After the gunfight, Morgan Earp was murdered by men loyal to the Clantons, causing Wyatt to begin the so-called "Earp Vendetta Ride", during which he and Holliday shot dead all those involved in the murder. The gunfight and the killings that followed marked the end of Wyatt's career as a law officer.

WYATT EARP IN HOLLYWOOD

In his old age, Wyatt Earp moved to Hollywood where he earned money advising film directors and actors on the Old West. Movie legend John Wayne met Earp several times when he was a young actor, and later said that he modelled his cowboy persona on Earp.

OTHER WESTERN LAWMEN

Pat Garrett (1850–1908)

Buffalo hunter and cowboy, Pat Garrett was hired in 1880 as a Sheriff in New Mexico on the strength of his accuracy with a gun. He won instant fame when he shot dead Billy the Kid and broke up the outlaw's gang (below). Garrett then joined the Texas Rangers, returning to New Mexico in 1897 to work on a difficult murder case. The culprits

were three deputy sheriffs, who Garrett caught after a prolonged gun battle. He then went back to Texas where he had worked for the government. He was shot dead by Jesse Brazel during an argument over grazing rights on land Garrett was renting.

Wild Bill Hickock (1837–1876)

Born James Butler Hickock in Illinois, Wild Bill Hickock fought in the Civil War. He became so famous for his courage and marksmanship that he was hired by the army to act as a scout in the Indian wars that followed. In 1869, Wild Bill was hired as a sheriff in Kansas. He solved a local crime wave by the simple expedient of shooting dead the gang leader. He then moved on to the cattle town of Abilene, the mining town of Deadwood, and other trouble spots. How many men he killed is unknown, but he curbed crime and disorder wherever he went. On August 2, 1876, he was playing poker in Deadwood when the cowboy Jack McCall got up and shot him in the back of the head.

PLOTTING DUKE

Exactly how culpable the Duc d'Enghien was for the intrigues and conspiracies that swirled around him has never been entirely proved. Certainly he gained far more fame through his death than he had ever done when alive.

Louis-Antoine-Henri de Bourbon-Condé was born in 1772 as a member of the French nobility. In 1788, he joined the army, and when the French Revolution broke out he fled the country to help organize a military force of French exiles to fight against the revolution. He took part in several campaigns, fighting as part of the Austrian army, but in 1801 he retired from the force to marry and live on his estates in Germany.

The French secret service did not believe he had given up politics and watched him closely. They reported that he was meeting with Charles Pichegru and Charles Dumouriez, both of whom were known to be plotting a coup to overthrow Napoleon Bonaparte, who by that date was ruling France.

> *The French secret service did not believe he had given up politics.*

Napoleon ordered his arrest. He sent a regiment of cavalry over the Rhine into neutral territory to seize him by force and drag him back to France. Once Enghien

DUC D'ENGHIEN (1772–1804)

"It [the execution of Enghien] was worse than a crime; it was a mistake."
French diplomat Charles Maurice de Talleyrand.

was under arrest, it became clear that the men he had been meeting were not Pichegru and Dumouriez but other noblemen living in exile. Napoleon could not afford to admit a mistake, so Enghien was instead charged with treason against France for his

role in the Austrian army. Others who had done the same received prison sentences but Napoleon ordered that Enghien be executed. He was shot on March 21, 1804. It has since emerged that he was involved with clandestine moves of some sort but how is unclear.

Napoleon could not afford to admit a mistake, so Enghien was instead charged with treason.

George Villiers (1628–1687)

Villiers, 2nd Duke of Buckingham, was a boyhood friend of King Charles II of England and politician. He fought valiantly in the English Civil War, then followed Charles into exile. In 1657, he returned to England to marry but was thrown into prison on suspicion of treason. He escaped in time to welcome Charles back as king, then threw himself into a cycle of political intrigue and womanizing. In 1675, he retired from public life.

George, 1st Duke of Clarence (1864–1892)

George was the younger brother of England's King Edward IV, but he was also the son-in-law of the Earl of Warwick and so joint-heir to his wealth. When Warwick rebelled against Edward in 1470, George backed him. A few months later he betrayed Warwick and backed Edward. In the end, nobody trusted him. He was found dead in 1478 having drowned in a barrel of wine.

Francis Egerton (1736–1803)

Egerton (left) became 3rd Duke of Bridgewater in 1746 at the age of 12. At 21, he became engaged to the beautiful Duchess of Hamilton. When she broke it off, he was distraught. He became obsessed with canals and began by building a canal from a coal mine he owned to Manchester, and thereby made a fortune. By the time of his death in 1803, Egerton had built up a canal and coal mining empire that was worth over £2 million.

Prince Albert, Duke of Clarence (1864–1892)

In 1889, police raided a male brothel in London and found the name of Albert, Duke of Clarence (right) mentioned in some documents; the Duke was heir to the throne. He was later blackmailed by two female prostitutes, fathered an illegitimate child, and was mixed up in the Jack the Ripper investigations. In the event, he died before his father and so did not become king

Elizabeth, Duchess of Kingston-upon-Hull (1720-1788)

Elizabeth Chudleigh was the daughter of an impoverished army officer. In August 1744, she married Augustus Hervey, who went to sea. She then married the elderly, very rich 2nd Duke of Kingston-upon-Hull who died four years later, leaving her a rich widow. But in 1775, Hervey, back from sea, inherited great wealth and sought a divorce from Elizabeth. Elizabeth was tried in the Westminster Hall for bigamy, found guilty and ordered to relinquish her fortune.

CONTROVERSIAL CULT FIGURE

Nathan Bedford Forrest was the first national leader of the Ku Klux Klan. Although he attempted to put a positive face on the organization, it was under his leadership that the KKK carried out its 1,000th lynching.

When the US Civil War broke out, Forrest was one of the richest men in Tennessee. He offered to raise and equip a regiment of cavalry for Tennessee to use in the Civil War. The offer was eagerly taken so Forrest was commissioned as a colonel. He soon displayed a talent for fast-moving cavalry raids across long distances behind enemy lines, as well as for the more conventional uses of cavalry on the battlefield, and he ended the war as a Lieutenant General.

> *He soon displayed a talent for fast-moving cavalry raids.*

The years after the war were hard for the defeated southern states, particularly for ex-soldiers. Far from aiding the impoverished areas, the Unionist government allowed speculative investors and businessmen to head south to buy up land and assets at knock-down prices. These men became known and detested as "carpetbaggers" from the type of travelling case they carried.

In December 1865, a group of Confederate war veterans in Pulaski, Tennessee, organized a

NATHAN BEDFORD FORREST (1821–1877)

"That is a damned fine idea."
Forrest on being told of the formation of the Ku Klux Klan.

secret society dedicated to mutual self-help among southern families that had lost out as a result of the war and its aftermath. The group was named the Ku Klux Klan (KKK) and its members wore white robes and masks. The idea of the KKK spread rapidly throughout the southern states and soon each town and village had its own group. Some concentrated on mutual assistance, but many became dominated by violent veterans intent on destroying the carpetbaggers and attacking the freed slaves who supported them. Lynchings took place and arson claimed several lives.

Some concentrated on mutual assistance but many became dominated by violent veterans.

In 1867, KKK leaders from across the South were summoned to a meeting to try and bring some sort of order and discipline to the organization. Forrest, who had voiced support for the movement, was elected leader with the title of Grand Wizard.

He claimed that the KKK had 550,000 members and that he could summon 40,000 armed men. However, many local groups refused to accept orders from Forrest, claiming that he was a figure-head only.

For the next two years, Forrest struggled to impose his authority on the KKK. He repeatedly claimed it was a peaceful organization, even as the total of KKK lynchings grew to hundreds every month. How far Forrest condoned the violence or whether he excused it in an attempt to control the KKK is unclear. In 1869, he left the KKK and, as conditions in the South improved, its membership declined. In 1871, the KKK was made an illegal organization and after a few high-profile prosecutions it began to collapse.

FORT PILLOW

Forrest has often been accused by Federal sources of committing a war crime at the Battle of Fort Pillow, though exactly what happened is a matter of dispute. On April 12, 1864, Forrest attacked Fort Pillow, garrisoned by 700 Unionist soldiers, almost half of whom were African American. Forrest's men overwhelmed the fortifications and killed 470 of the defenders.

David Koresh (1959–1993)

David Koresh (right) became leader of the Branch Davidian cult in 1986 and began preaching that he was the Son of God. He also began sleeping with many of his female followers, some of them as young as 12. On February 28, 1993, the authorities raided Koresh's compound near Waco, Texas, leading to a siege that lasted 51 days. The FBI then stormed the building, which caught fire and 76 cult members, including Koresh, died.

Shoko Asahara (b.1955)

In 1987, Japanese acupuncturist Shoko Asahara (left) began preaching the doctrine of Aum Shinrikyo. He rapidly built up a following of several hundred. On March 20, 1995, members of the cult released sarin gas on the Tokyo underground railway system, killing 12 and injuring thousands. The reasons for the attack are unclear.

Jim Jones (1931–1978)

Jones founded the People's Temple in the 1950s, then moved his church to "Jonestown" in Guyana. In November 1978, US Congressman Leo Ryan visited to investigate reports of ill treatment. He was shot dead by cult members. Jones then ordered his followers to commit suicide. Most willingly drank poison and more than 900, including Jones, died.

Marshall Applewhite (1931–1997)

Professional musician Applewhite founded Heaven's Gate in 1974. In 1997, he announced that the approaching Hale-Bopp comet was being escorted by a large UFO that was coming to collect the cult members. On March 26, he gathered 38 members at his ranch in Santa Fe, California, and together they committed suicide by drinking cyanide.

CELEBRATED DIARIST

Anne Frank was a young Jewish girl who had the misfortune to be caught up in the terrible events of the Holocaust, the attempt by the Nazi regime to exterminate all of Europe's Jews.

Throughout her traumatic experience, Frank kept a diary that was discovered and published in 1947, after World War II had ended.

Anne was born in Germany in 1929 but her family moved to the Netherlands in 1933 after the Nazis were elected to power in Germany. The Frank family settled in Amsterdam where Anne's father, Otto, worked at a chemical company, Opekta. Anne and her sister Margot attended local schools. In 1940, the Netherlands were invaded and conquered by Germany as part of Adolf Hitler's drive to conquer France and subdue Britain.

In 1940, the Netherlands were invaded and conquered by Germany.

The Germans set about stripping the land of goods that could help their war effort, and imposing Nazi rule on the Dutch people. As part of this programme, repressive measures against the Jewish population were imposed. Anne and Margot were forced to attend special Jewish schools.

In July 1942, Margot was told that she was to be forcibly moved to a labour camp where she would work manufacturing goods for the German armed forces. Rather than submit to this, Otto Frank decided to take his entire family into hiding. Otto had for some weeks been preparing for the move and had blocked off a number of rooms at his workplace to form a secret apartment. The family would be fed and cared for by a few trusted friends, while a story was put about that they had gone to live with relatives elsewhere.

Soon after going into hiding the family were joined by the van

ANNE FRANK (1929–1945)

"One of the wisest and most moving commentaries on war and its impact on human beings that I have ever read."
Eleanor Roosevelt

Otto had blocked off a number of rooms at his workplace to form a secret apartment.

Pels. Some months later a family friend Fritz Pfeffer also moved in. The small, secret apartment was rather cramped, particularly as the residents could not move around during the daytime in case they were heard. Gradually, the nerves of the inhabitants began to fray and petty disputes became common. Anne began a romance with Peter van Pels, then broke it off.

Through all this she kept her private diary. She kept an accurate record of events and her feelings, which showed that she never lost her passion for life or her hopes.

On August 4, 1944, a squad of German police arrived at the works and quickly discovered the hidden door to the apartment. They had received a tip-off, though who from has never been discovered. All the inhabitants were arrested and later sent to concentration camps. Only Otto Frank survived. When he returned to Amsterdam after the war, he was given Anne's diary, which had been found on the floor after the police had left.

RUMOURS OF FRAUD

Since the diary was published, there have been accusations that it was written by an adult or it had been heavily edited. When he died in 1980, Otto Frank left the original diary to the Netherlands Institute for War Documentation. It was then subjected to detailed examinations which concluded that the handwriting was that of Anne Frank and that the diary had not been tampered with in any way.

Samuel Pepys (1633–1703)
British politician and naval administrator Samuel Pepys drastically reformed the Royal Navy to make it a bastion of professionalism. He kept a detailed diary from 1660 to 1669 that he wrote in a form of shorthand and which is now recognized as of great importance to social history. Most of the work is taken up with his personal life, but contains much detail of life in London at the time, covering such events as the Great Plague.

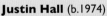

Alan Clarke (1928–1999)
Alan Clarke was a British Conservative politician, diarist, and military historian. He was an outspoken, flamboyant man with right-wing views on a diverse range of subjects. He kept a candid diary that chronicled his views of events and fellow Tories in a highly entertaining, satirical, and sometimes offensive manner.

Justin Hall (b.1974)
Born in Chicago in 1974, Amercian Justin Hall is a freelance journalist. In 1994, Hall began writing an online diary. At first this related to his opinions of websites and console games, but gradually it came to focus more on his own life. He is widely credited as being the founding father of blogging—a "blog" being an online diary, the word being derived from "web log".

GREAT AMERICAN INDIAN WARRIOR

Geronimo had a long and respectable career as a warrior behind him before he came to the notice of the US army campaign in Arizona. He was born in 1829 into the Chiricahua Apache and given the name of Goyathlay ("the yawner").

Geronimo (Jerome) was the name given to him by the Mexicans. His early life was peaceful but that changed on March 5, 1851. Geronimo was among a band of Apache who went into the Mexican town of Janos to trade, leaving their families in a camp outside. The camp was attacked by 400 Mexican soldiers from Sonora led by Colonel Jose Maria Carrasco. Among the dead were Geronimo's wife, children, and mother. Geronimo swore revenge and became a noted war leader among the Apache. His years of war against the Mexicans were poorly documented but he is known to have led many raids.

By 1875 Geronimo had remarried and settled on the Ojo Caliente Reservation in Arizona. In 1876, he and his family were forcibly moved to the San Carlos Reservation. Conditions there were harsh and so Geronimo left in 1876 taking with him most of the Chiricahua. They headed south into Mexico to join up with other Apache groups living under Chiricahuans Chato and Nachite.

General George Crook was sent to recapture the Apache, and

GERONIMO (1829–1909)

"The next white man who sees my face will be a dead white man." Geronimo after the death of his family.

he had permission to operate in Mexico as well as in the USA. He finally caught up with Geronimo in May 1883 in the Sierra Madre. Crook captured them all and took them back to San Carlos, having promised them better treatment. For two years Geronimo stayed on the reservation but then the Indian Department in Washington sent a different agent who, again, treated the Apache badly. Geronimo left, this time with a smaller band of followers.

In 1886, Crook talked many of the Apache into returning to the reservation, but then resigned his command in protest at orders to

Among the dead were Geronimo's wife, children, and mother. Geronimo swore revenge.

impose unconditional surrender on Geronimo. His place was taken by General Nelson Miles who had 5,000 men and 500 tribal auxiliaries to command. By this date Geronimo had only 18 warriors with him, plus a handful of women and children. At one point Miles had Geronimo cornered; the Apache fled into a cave and the soldiers sat down to starve him out. Days passed and then a report came that Geronimo had been spotted many miles away. Nobody has yet found the exit used by Geronimo and his men.

> *Days passed and then a report came that Geronimo had been spotted many miles away.*

The campaign turned when Miles decided to post his men to guard every known waterhole. The lack of water and free movement finally compelled Geronimo to surrender on September 3, 1886. The last of the free tribes had capitulated. Geronimo later made a living appearing at fairs. He died on February 17, 1909, aged 80.

GERONIMO'S SKULL

Geronimo was buried in the Apache Indian Prisoner of War Cemetery at Fort Sill, Oklahoma. In 1918, his grave was desecrated and his skull and other bones removed. The culprits were possibly three members of the Yale University secret society "Skull and Bones". One of them was Prescott Bush, grandfather of George W Bush. The bones are allegedly still in their clubhouse at Yale.

Sitting Bull (c.1831–1890)

Sitting Bull (right, with Buffalo Bill) was chief of the Unkpapa Sioux, driven from their reservation by miners in 1876. He took up arms, refusing to be transported to the Indian territory, and defeated General Custer. He died in 1890 as police tried to arrest him on Indian Agency lands.

Crazy Horse (c.1842–1877)

Crazy Horse was the war chief of the Ogalala Sioux. His bravery and skill made him a natural choice for Sitting Bull to appoint as war leader in 1876 when the Sioux and Cheyenne fought the white intruders. In 1877, he and his starving band of Ogalala surrendered to US troops.

Chief Joseph (c.1840–1904)

Joseph (right) was chief of the Wallowa band of Nez Percé tribe. In 1877, faced with settlement in a reservation, he led 800 of his people in a dramatic escape to Canada. Finally, with 200 of his people dead from exposure, he surrendered to General Miles; he was 40 miles from the border.

Vernon Bellecourt (1931–2007)

Bellecourt was a member of the White Earth Band of Ojibwe. After a successful career as a hairdresser, Bellecourt retired to lead the American Indian Movement, campaigning for the rights of First Nation peoples. In 1973, he took part in the occupation of Wounded Knee.

Metacom (c.1639–1676)

Also known as King Philip, Metacom (right) was chief of the Wampanoag tribe. He led the most costly and bloodiest of Indian wars in New England history, known as King Philip's War (1675–76). He was killed fighting in 1676 and his tribe was broken up.

MURDEROUS KING

King Henry VIII of England came to the throne in 1509 knowing that there were several noblemen in England and abroad who had a claim to the throne every bit as good as his own.

At first, he was secure in power due to popular policies, victorious foreign wars, and domestic largesse, but suspicion slowly took hold and he turned to violence.

The first victim of Henry's growing paranoia was the Duke of Buckingham, who was arguably closer to the royal bloodline than Henry. In 1510, he found out that Henry was having an affair with his sister. Buckingham packed his sister off to a remote convent and was openly critical of the King. In 1521, Henry ordered his arrest on spurious charges of witchcraft and treason. The hapless duke was tried by a panel of 17 lords hand-picked by Henry. He was found guilty and executed—only after his death did Henry bother with the legal niceties.

> *Henry ordered his arrest on spurious charges of witchcraft and treason.*

HENRY VIII (1491–1547)

"You have sent me a Flanders mare."
Henry to Cromwell, speaking about Anne of Cleves.

Next to go was Thomas Wolsey, Henry's Chancellor, who had risen through hard work and talent to become not only the most important minister in government, but also a cardinal in the Church. However, he fell out with Henry when the King demanded a divorce from Katherine of Aragon. The Pope refused the request and Wolsey was torn between loyalty to his King and to his church. He was arrested on charges of treason in 1530 and a rigged court convened to find him guilty, but he died before he was executed.

The lawyer and scholar Sir Thomas More replaced Wolsey as Chancellor. In 1534, Henry announced that he, and not the Pope, was now the spiritual head of the English Church. More refused to accept this and resigned. That was not enough for Henry who was determined

The hapless duke was tried by a panel of 17 lords hand-picked by Henry. He was found guilty and executed.

to enforce his grip on the church. More was tried for treason, found guilty, and executed in 1535.

By now Henry had acquired a taste for judicial murder. When his new wife Anne Boleyn failed to give him a son and heir, Henry had her arrested on a charge of having committed adultery with her own brother and four others. The Duke of Norfolk was chosen to preside over the court and was instructed by Henry to find them all guilty. And the court did. In 1536, Queen Anne and the five men were all executed.

More's replacement, Thomas Cromwell, fared no better. Having rigidly enforced Henry's rule over the Church of England, he persuaded Henry to marry Anne of Cleves for diplomatic reasons. But Henry found Anne repulsive and divorced her. Henry had Cromwell arrested for treason and executed without trial.

Henry's fifth wife, pretty Catherine Howard, was executed for adultery because of an affair she had had in her youth. Only his sixth wife, Catherine Parr, survived Henry, who died, overweight and cantankerous, aged 48.

HENRY'S WIVES

Henry VIII married six times: Katherine of Aragon was accused of not being a virgin and divorced. Anne Boleyn was executed on charges of adultery. Jane Seymour died after giving birth to a son. Anne of Cleves was divorced and sent to live away from court. Catherine Howard was executed for adultery, and Catherine Parr survived him.

Richard III
(1452–1485)

Richard III has long had a reputation as England's most bloodthirsty monarch. He fought beside his brother, Edward IV, in the Wars of the Roses. But when Edward died, Richard had Edward's two young sons put in the Tower of London.

Whether Richard had the boys killed or not isn't known, but he did take the throne from them. Just days later, Richard accused Lord Hastings of treason and had him beheaded without trial. Richard was killed in battle in 1485 by his rival for power, Henry VII.

Pedro the Cruel
(1334–1369)

Pedro became King of Castile in 1350 as the only legitimate son of the former king, Alfonso XI. His first act was to order the murder of all his illegitimate brothers. Only one of these escaped, Henry of Trastámara. In 1369, Henry judged the time was ripe to return to Castile to exploit the discontent against Pedro's brutal rule. The nobles abandoned Pedro (above right), who was defeated and executed by Henry.

Shaka (c.1787–1828)

Shaka became leader of the small Zulu tribe of southern Africa in 1812. He reformed the army, then conquered a vast empire. When his mother died in 1827, he was stricken by grief and ordered the killing of hundreds who he thought had shown insufficient grief for her death. Believing Shaka had gone mad, which he may have done, his two half-brothers killed him.

RENOWNED GAMBLER

POPULAR HISTORY

Perhaps the most famous gambler of all time, Doc Holliday also gained fame as a gunfighter during his time in the American West. What makes his career more surprising is that he was born into a genteel Georgia family in 1851, given a classical education, and trained as a dentist.

In 1873, however, John Holliday was diagnosed as suffering from TB and given only a few months to live. He believed that the hot, dry climate of the southwestern states might improve his health so he moved to Dallas, Texas, where he opened a new dental practice. In Dallas he realized that he had a real talent for gambling.

In the following months, Holliday moved through Denver, Deadwood, and Cheyenne, always seeking places where gambling was legal and funds plentiful. As time passed, Holliday acquired the nickname of "Doc" for his medical degree. He also began drinking whisky to suppress his TB cough, and this contributed to his notorious temper.

He perfected his shooting, becoming both accurate and fast on the draw. Holliday knew that he had to be able to back up his gaming disputes with violence and, in any case, he counted his days as numbered by disease, which made him careless with his own life.

In 1877, Holliday met Wyatt

DOC HOLLIDAY (1851–1887)

"Doc was a dentist whom necessity had made a gambler; a gentleman whom disease had made a frontier vagabond... and at the same time the most skilful gambler and the nerviest, speediest, deadliest man with a gun that I ever knew." Wyatt Earp

Earp and in 1878, both men were in Dodge City. Holliday was again working as a dentist, though he joined Earp on many gambling forays. By September, Holliday had given up dentistry for good and bought a bar. When Earp got into an argument with a group of armed cowboys, Holliday appeared, wielding a shotgun and so cemented the friendship between the two men.

The following year found Holliday in New Mexico playing

He began drinking whisky to suppress his TB cough, and this contributed to his notorious temper.

cards in a saloon when a former soldier named Mike Gordon began abusing one of the saloon girls. Holliday intervened. At which point Gordon pulled a gun, and Holliday shot him dead.

It was the only one of his many shootings that ended in him facing trial. Holliday was acquitted and in 1880 moved on to Tombstone, Arizona, where he found his old friend Wyatt Earp was town marshal. Earp and his brothers were engaged in a feud with a cattle ranching family named the Clantons. The feud ended in the famous Gunfight at the OK Corral in October 1881 where Holliday killed at least one man. Holliday then moved on to Colorado, by now addicted to laudanum, as well as whisky. In 1887, he moved to Glenwood Springs where he became seriously ill. He took to his bed and died on November 8.

HOLLIDAY ON FILM

Doc Holliday has been a popular character with film-makers, though his appearances have had little to do with reality. Among the actors to have played him are: Cesar Romero, Victor Mature, Kirk Douglas, Douglas Fowley, Gerald Mohr, Peter Breck, Arthur Kennedy, Jason Robards, Sam Gilman (in a *Star Trek* episode), Dennis Hopper, Willie Nelson, Val Kilmer, and Adam West.

OTHER SUCCESSFUL CARD SHARPS

Joseph Jagger (1830–1892)
Jagger was a British engineer who realized that if a roulette wheel were not regularly serviced it might begin to favour a particular set of numbers. In 1873, he hired six men to watch the roulette wheels in Monte Carlo and discovered the numbers that one of them favoured. In July 1875, he entered the casino for the first time himself and over three days he won a massive £60,000 ($120,000).

Scene from The Man Who Broke the Bank in Monte Carlo (1935), *based on Jagger's story.*

John, 4th Earl of Sandwich (1718–1792)
John Montagu, 4th Earl of Sandwich (above), was a British nobleman and politician who was also a successful card player. He was so keen to stay at the gaming tables that in the 1760s he instructed his cook to come up with a tasty, nutritious snack that could be eaten without interrupting card play. The cook put a slice of beef between two slices of bread and butter, and named the snack "the sandwich".

Nick Dandalos (1893–1966)
Nick "The Greek" Dandalos (below) was born in Crete but moved to the USA in his early twenties. He began gambling on the horses and won a considerable sum using inside information. In 1919, he was involved in a match-fixing scandal in baseball, then moved on to poker. He moved from New York to Hollywood and by the 1940s was a frequent star of movie gossip columns.

HARRY HOUDINI (1874–1926)

"My brain is the key that sets my mind free." Harry Houdini

wearing a straightjacket and handcuffs, or locked naked inside a high-security prison cell, the great Houdini would always get free.

The high drama of his acts, spiced with the frisson of failure, packed theatre houses the world over. All who witnessed his marvellous feats were left pondering how he performed the impossible. Was he peculiarly double-jointed? Could he dislocate his limbs? Like all good magicians, Houdini kept everyone guessing.

> Houdini built his whole career on his uncanny ability to escape.

Born Erik Weisz on March 24, 1874 in Budapest, Hungary, Houdini's family moved to America when he was just four years old. Times were tough at the turn of the century, and the young Ehrich Weiss, as he was called then, took whatever jobs he could get. But after seeing the travelling magician, Dr Lynn, Ehrich set his heart on becoming a magician and he was soon performing simple tricks in sideshows and dime museums.

Having adopted the stage name Houdini, inspired by the French illusionist Jean Eugène Robert-Houdin, he tried every kind of magic for five years. His most successful act at the time was the 'needle trick' in which he would swallow a number of needles followed by a piece of cotton, and then regurgitate the needles, all neatly threaded together. But success proved

"Ladies and Gentlemen... introducing my original invention: the Water Torture Cell..."

With these words, recorded in 1914, Harry Houdini introduced the illusion that defined his genius. Into this water-filled, glass-fronted cell, Houdini was lowered head-

first, his hands cuffed, his feet locked in wooden stocks. Once submerged, he only had minutes to free himself before effectively drowning in front of his audience. It was a virtuoso feat of escapology that he performed until his death.

Houdini built his whole career on his uncanny ability to escape. Whether hung from a crane,

The high drama of his acts, spiced with the frisson of failure, packed theatre houses the world over.

elusive, and at one point Houdini even put all his equipment up for sale. Finding no takers, however, he carried on and in 1893, while performing at Coney Island, he met his wife and partner to be, Wilhelmina Beatrice Rahner.

Houdini's fortunes began to pick up in 1898, when he specialized in escaping from handcuffs, brought to his shows by the audience. Houdini later elaborated this winning concept by challenging police forces in the towns he visited to lock him in their jails. Year by year, his stunts became more flamboyant. He was put inside riveted milk churns, locked inside mailbags, sewn inside a huge football, and even chained up Jonah-like in the belly of a whale.

On October 31, 1926, Harry Houdini died due to peritonitis following a burst appendix. Had he sought medical advice sooner, his life could almost certainly have been saved.

THE AFTERLIFE AND CONAN DOYLE

When Houdini's mother died in 1913, he tried to contact her through spiritualist mediums. He soon realized, however, that many so-called psychics were just illusionists like himself and began a life-long campaign to debunk the fraudsters. While in London, he became close friends with Sir Arthur Conan Doyle, author of *Sherlock Holmes* and also an active proponent of spiritualism. The two fell out when Conan Doyle claimed that Houdini was himself a medium.

David Blaine (b.1973)

Many parallels exist between Blaine and Houdini. Both men began as magicians but became famous as escapologists. Blaine is best-known for being buried alive for seven days, and for spending 35 hours on a 105 feet (27m) pole, more than 63 hours inside a block of ice, and 44 days in a Plexiglass box (right). But it was with his act Drowned Alive that he attempted to eclipse Houdini, and hold his breath underwater for a record 8 minutes 58 seconds, while escaping from chains and handcuffs—all after being submerged for seven days. Although he failed to beat the record, he achieved a remarkable 7 minutes 8 seconds.

Derren Brown (b.1971)

Derren Brown's act revolves around predicting and controlling human behaviour in a way that baffles and bewilders his audiences. But Brown doesn't claim to possess prescient powers; instead, he describes his show as "a mixture of magic, suggestion, psychology, misdirection, and showmanship". In 2004, he paralleled Houdini when he introduced seances into his act and exposed the methods used by so-called psychics, such as "cold reading". This technique uses gleaned information about a person from their body-language, appearance, and speech together with their answers to leading questions.

David Copperfield (b.1956)

Aged only 12, David Copperfield was the youngest ever person to be admitted to the Society of American Magicians. The *Guinness World Records* book lists Copperfield as having the highest ticket sales of any solo performer, and as being the most awarded magician in history. As well as his fabulous illusions and story-based performances, in 1991 Copperfield also established the International Museum and Library of the Conjuring Arts, in Las Vegas.

LEGENDARY BUSHRANGER

NED KELLY (1855–1880)

"A man would be a nice sort of dingo to run out on his mates."
Ned Kelly at his trial when asked why he had not fled
from the police at Glenrowan.

then turned to horse theft, for which he was arrested and briefly imprisoned. His early run-ins with the police came to a head in 1877 when a group of policemen called at the Kelly farm. The Kellys felt they were being victimized. An argument broke out, which ended with Kelly's mother being arrested and young Ned fleeing the scene.

Four policemen gave chase, tracking Kelly for a few days until they reached Stringybark Creek. Meanwhile, Kelly had teamed up with some friends and doubled back. The fugitives opened fire, killing three of the policemen. Kelly was now an outlaw, with a price of £2,000 on his head.

In 1978, Kelly and his gang rode into Euroa with a closed horse and buggy. They walked into the bank and held up the staff at gunpoint while the vault was emptied. The staff were then loaded into the buggy and driven off to a remote location before being released.

Ned Kelly has become the hero of books, films and television shows. One of the last of the great Australian bushrangers— outlaws who rode the Australian bush, robbing banks, farms, and wagons.

Edward Kelly was born into a family of petty thieves and was only 14 when he was arrested for the first time after a fight with a local Chinese shopkeeper. Kelly

Kelly's fame rests as much on the astonishing bulletproof armour that he wore during raids.

A bullet found a chink in his armour, Kelly went down, and was quickly overpowered.

The reward was put up to £4,000, and the police rounded up family members of Kelly and his gang. When the prisoners were neither released nor charged with a crime, Kelly wrote a letter to Donald Cameron MP accepting the blame for his crimes, pointing out that his family were innocent, and asking for them to be released. The letter made him a hero to the many Australians who felt themselves to have been wronged by the government.

In 1880, Kelly had suits of bulletproof armour made for himself and his men. He planned to lure the police to a farm called Glenrowan, ambush them, and then ride off to raid local banks. However, the police approached Glenrowan by a different route and soon Kelly and his gang were under siege. A bullet found a chink in his armour, Kelly went down, and was quickly overpowered.

Despite a petition of mercy signed by 60,000 Australians, Ned Kelly was hanged in Melbourne prison in 1880.

THE JERILDERIE LETTER

When the Kelly gang raided Jerilderie in 1879 (pushing their reward money up to £8,000), they left behind an 8,300-word letter that they asked to be printed in the local newspaper. The editor handed it to the police. It was not until more than 20 years after Kelly's death that the full text was released. The letter gave the gang's version of events, seeking to justify the crimes by claiming they had been victimized by the police without cause.

Daniel Morgan (c.1830–1865)
Better known as "Mad Dan" because of the savage glee he took in using violence against anyone who resisted him, Morgan preferred to attack remote farms and homesteads. On April 8, he held up a farm at Peechelba. When a baby began crying, Morgan let the maid go to care for it. She got a message to a farmhand who shot Morgan dead.

"Mad Dan's" body—gun in hand—was put on display after his death.

Frank Gardiner (c.1830–c.1904)
Gardiner won enduring fame when, on June 15, 1862, he led a gang that held up a wagon train carrying gold from the gold mines of Forbes. The gang got away with an estimated £12,000 in gold. By this point Gardiner had been a bushranger for eight years, but he then went straight.

Andrew Scott (c.1845–1880)
In 1869 Andrew George Scott, a lay preacher, decided to solve his money troubles by robbing his local bank—adopting the name of "Captain Moonlight" when engaged in criminal activity. He was sentenced to 18 months for forgery in 1871 and on his release returned to bushranging. He was eventually captured and hanged in 1880.

Scott's capture by police after holding up Wantabadgery Station in November 1879.

Fred Ward (1836–1870)
After escaping from prison in 1863, Fred Ward (right) took to bushranging, accompanied by his half-Aborigine wife. The pair never killed or took money from women, which, together with their habitual singing, made them rather romantic heroes. Ward became known as "Captain Thunderbolt" and is thought to have stolen around £20,000 in total.

MISSING LORD

Richard Bingham the 7th Earl of Lucan led a hedonistic lifestyle that ended with a mystery that has never been solved.

Born in 1934, Richard Bingham was the eldest son of the 6th Earl of Lucan. He went to Eton College, then joined the Coldstream Guards as an officer—a conventional enough youth for the heir to one of Britain's premier aristocratic titles. He was, however, already suffering ill-defined emotional problems.

By the mid-1960s, Lucan had become a professional gambler. He was highly skilled at poker, backgammon, and bridge, games through which he made a considerable amount of money.

> By the mid-1960s, Lucan had become a professional gambler.

In 1964, soon after his marriage to the society beauty Veronica Duncan (right), Lucan began frequenting the Clermont Club. This up-market gambling club had a highly exclusive membership based on personal wealth.

In 1973, the couple separated and Lady Lucan gained custody of the couple's three children. She hired a nanny, Mrs Sandra Rivett, to live in with her and care for the children. A divorce began and Lucan asked for custody of the children, alleging that his wife was mentally unstable. Meanwhile, his financial position was getting worse as his gambling losses mounted and he began to find it difficult to meet his legal fees.

On the night of November 7, 1974, Lucan's life took a dramatic and mysterious turn. Mrs Rivett was attacked by an intruder when she went downstairs at Lady Lucan's house in Lower Belgrave Street, London. She was battered to death and her killer was starting to bundle her body into a sack when Lady Lucan came down to investigate. She too was attacked by the intruder, but fought him off.

When the lights went on she found herself confronted by Lord

LORD LUCAN (b.1934)

On the night of November 7, 1974, Lord Lucan's life took a dramatic and mysterious turn.

He had then panicked and fled, but the question was, where had he gone?

Lucan, while Mrs Rivett's dead body lay on the floor. Lady Lucan later claimed that her husband had admitted killing the nanny, before breaking down and leaving the room to wash off the blood.

Lady Lucan ran out of the house to the local pub where she poured out her story. The police were called but Lucan had fled by the time they arrived. Later that night he called on a friend, Mrs Maxwell-Scott, to whom he told his version of events. Lucan claimed that he had been passing when he saw a fight taking place in the house. He said that he had broken in and fought off the intruder. After telling his story, Lucan left and hasn't been seen since. His car was found abandoned at Newhaven port.

It is generally believed that Lucan did break into the house to murder his wife, but had killed the nanny by mistake. He had then panicked and fled, but the question was, where had he gone?

THE TRAIL GOES COLD

Since Lucan's disappearance there have been many alleged sightings. One turned out to be another fugitive Briton, John Stonehouse. A string of sightings in South Africa in the 1990s turned out to be a quite different man who resembled Lucan. In 2003, press reports identified an Englishman who had died in Goa under the name of Barry Halpin as Lucan, but this turned out to be false. Some believe he committed suicide the day after the killing. In 1999, Lucan was officially declared to be dead.

Anthony Ashley-Cooper
(1938–2004)

Anthony Ashley-Cooper, 10th Earl of Shaftesbury, led an unconventional life by any standards, but it was his dramatic death that hit the headlines. He inherited the earldom in 1961 along with a substantial fortune. In 2002, he married Jamila Ben M'Barek, a Parisian nightclub hostess of Tunisian origin. In January 2005, the earl went missing and a month later Jamila and her brother Mohammed were arrested by French police. In April, the earl's body was found in the Alps, whereupon Jamila and Mohammed were charged with murder. It emerged that the earl had been considering a divorce; he had been killed after an argument over the divorce terms.

Hugh Hefner (b.1926)

Hugh Hefner's reputation as a playboy rests on his ownership, editing, and creative control of *Playboy* magazine, and on his self-proclaimed determination to live his life according to the precepts of the magazine. Born in 1926, Hefner served in the army during World War II and went through a variety of publishing jobs before, in 1953, borrowing $8,000 to start the magazine. After his divorce in 1959, Hefner began a well-publicized series of relationships with glamorous women. He married again in 1989, but his hectic lifestyle showed no sign of slowing down and he remains active in supervising the *Playboy* business empire.

DASHING BUCCANEER

HARRY MORGAN (c.1635–1688)

"These robbers are as courteous as if they were Spanish."
Unnamed Spanish lady during Morgan's occupation of Panama.

The differences between a pirate, a buccaneer, and a privateer are not always well understood. But Harry Morgan understood them, and was always careful to remain a buccaneer—a fact which saved his life.

Morgan was born into a Welsh farming family of some wealth and as a teenager went to live in Bermuda. In 1655, Jamaica was conquered by the English and Morgan moved there to join the local garrison as an officer.

In 1664, he received a commission as a privateer from the governor. A privateer was an unpaid auxiliary to the armed forces of a nation at war who was expected to attack only the enemy and abide by the rules of war. He was, however, free to loot as much as he liked in order to recompense himself and his men. But if he attacked anyone else or acted with undue savagery he would become a pirate and be liable to be hanged.

Morgan's first voyage lasted from 1664 to 1666 and made him a fortune, which he invested wisely. He specialized in capturing Spanish colonial towns, then extorting cash from the residents to stop his men burning the town to the ground.

> *He specialized in capturing Spanish colonial towns, then extorting cash from the residents.*

In 1668 the British governor of Jamaica, Thomas Modyford, put Morgan in charge of all the English buccaneers and gave him orders to attack the Spanish to forestall a planned invasion of Jamaica. Morgan recruited French buccaneers from Tortuga and sacked Puerto Príncipe on Cuba, then Puerto Bello on the mainland. He and his men returned with a vast haul of 250,000 pesos in gold and silver. Morgan bought a couple of sugar plantations, got married, and entered colonial society.

In August 1670, Morgan was given a new commission and mustered 2,000 buccaneers—

Morgan's first voyage lasted from 1664 to 1666 and made him a fortune, which he invested wisely.

the largest such force ever assembled—and led them to attack the large Spanish city of Panama. Sailing to the mainland, then marching overland, Morgan arrived to find a Spanish army 1,600 strong drawn up to defend the city. A charge by the buccaneers broke the Spanish, who retreated back to the city walls. The Spanish managed to get most of the city's wealth away by sea, then abandoned Panama. The buccaneers stayed for two months, but did not find as much plunder as they had expected and went home disappointed.

Meanwhile, Spain had accepted the legality of Britain's colony in Jamaica. As a price they exacted a promise that all pirates would be executed. A new governor, Thomas Lynch, arrested Morgan and sent him to Britain to stand trial. At his trial, Morgan was able to show that he had never strayed over the line to become a pirate and was acquitted of all charges. A smiling King Charles II knighted Morgan, then sent him back to Jamaica to live on his plantations.

BEYOND THE LINE

An agreement between Spain and Portugal, the 1494 Treaty of Tordesillas, agreed a line down the centre of the Atlantic, to the west of which all newly discovered lands belonged to Spain. Protestant nations, such as England, refused to recognize the agreement and began setting up colonies west of "the line". The Spanish claimed these colonies were illegal and began attacking them.

Sir Christopher Myngs (1625–1666)

Sir Christopher Myngs was a British naval officer sent to Jamaica in 1656 to defend the island against the Spanish. Myngs soon realised that his 44-gun ship was not strong enough, so he recruited buccaneers to join his force. His greatest success came in 1658 when he raided the coasts of Venezuela and Colombia, destroying Spanish warships and forts. He returned to England in 1665, leaving Jamaica reasonably secure from attack.

Michel de Grammont (fl.1670–1686)

Michel de Grammont first entered buccaneering history when he commanded a French ship attacking Spanish colonies in the Caribbean in 1674. In June 1678 he had risen to command a force of six ships and 800 men on a raid along the Venezuelan coast that resulted in a good haul. In 1683 he led a joint French-Dutch force to capture the city of Vera Cruz in Mexico, moving on to the Campeche, which was occupied for three months. In April 1686 he left Tortuga Island to attack Florida but never returned. It is assumed he was shipwrecked.

Jean L'Ollonais (c.1635–1668)

Jean L'Ollonais was a French buccaneer who strayed over the line into piracy in spectacular fashion. He arrived in the Caribbean in 1650 and soon became the commander of a buccaneer ship operating out of Tortuga. Every Spaniard he captured was killed, often with dreadful cruelty, and so L'Ollonais was deemed a pirate. He was killed and probably eaten by local tribesmen when he was shipwrecked in the Gulf of Darién.

HISTORICAL PROPHET

Over the years, many people have claimed the ability to see into the future. Some have momentary flashes of events that happen some time later and often experience such a revelation only once.

Others claim the ability to predict the future or prophecy on a regular basis and almost to order. One of the most famous prophets of all time was the Frenchman Michel de Notredame, known by the latinized version of his surname, Nostradamus. His great fame today rests principally on his book *Les Propheties*, which was published in 1555.

Nostradamus was born in southern France the son of a corn merchant. He studied to be a doctor at the University of Montpellier but was expelled before finishing his studies. He set himself up as a healer and produced a special "rose pill" said to be able to prevent the plague. Ironically, his wife and children died of the plague in 1534.

NOSTRADAMUS (1503–1566)

"Some of the prophets predicted great and marvellous things to come. For myself, I in no way claim such a title for myself."
Letter to King Henry II of France, 1558.

Epinal print of Nostradamus from the 1800s.

Nostradamus then abandoned his home and set off to travel around Europe. He returned in 1547 to marry a second, wealthy wife with whom he had six children.

It was at this point that he began to claim powers of prophecy learned on his travels.

In 1550, he wrote an almanac containing prophecies for the coming year as well as more mundane facts such as the date of Easter. The book sold well, and he produced one a year for the next 11 years. The prophecies in the books proved to be reasonably accurate and soon local noble families were asking him to cast

So obscure were the verses that some people thought Nostradamus had gone insane.

horoscopes for them. His efforts at astrology were not particularly successful and so he turned to writing prophecies in verse form.

The result was a book of one thousand four-line verse prophecies written in a mixture of French, Latin, Italian, and Greek. The verses were written to include plenty of symbolism and euphemisms. The language changed mid-sentence, making it notoriously difficult to interpret. Some suspect that Nostradamus deliberately adopted this obscure format so that his prophecies could be ambiguous. Certainly, his habit of not inserting dates or, more often than not, names would tend to make them so.

So obscure were the verses that some people thought Nostradamus had gone insane; others held him to be divinely inspired. His fame was assured when the Queen, Catherine de Médicis, summoned him to Paris to discuss his prophecies. and made him the royal doctor.

In 1566, having predicted his own death, Nostradamus died, apparently of oedema.

OTHER REPUTED SOOTHSAYERS

Mother Shipton
(c.1488–1561)
English soothsayer Mother Shipton was born in Yorkshire. She told fortunes and made prophecies. Some of these, about events such as the Great Fire of London, were remarkably accurate. Her least-accurate prophecy was: "The world to an end shall come/In eighteen hundred and eighty-one."

Nakayama Miki
(1798–1887)
Nakayama Miki was born into a farming family at Nara, Japan. She wanted to become a Buddhist nun, but her family forced her into an arranged marriage. When her husband died in 1838, Miki had a revelation from a deity that told her, "I am the general of Heaven. The Divine King of Heavenly Reason". After this she claimed to have acquired the power of prophecy and, with her daughter, embarked on a life dedicated to charity and the performance of spiritual dances. The faith she developed became known as "Tenrikyo", and shows features of Shinto, Buddhism, and shamanism, as well as some original ideas.

Jeane Dixon (1904–1997)
Born in Wisconsin, Dixon set herself up as a psychic in the 1950s. In 1956, she famously wrote in a magazine article that "the 1960 presidential election would be won by a Democrat who would then go on to be assassinated or die in office". She was later to give advice to Nancy Reagan during the presidency of Ronald Reagan.

GRIGORI RASPUTIN (1869–1916)

"Rasputin—the evil genius of Russia."
Politician Vladimir Purishkevich, 1916.

miraculous powers. He then fell in with a secretive, banned sect, the Khlysty, rumoured to indulge in sexual acts as part of their rituals. Rasputin quickly left the group and went to live with a hermit monk named Makariy. He then returned home and, outwardly, settled down. He married, had three children, and began farming. But in 1901, he left home to begin his ministry, and by 1905, had established a firm reputation as a preacher and miracle worker.

> *He then returned home and, outwardly, settled down.*

He was approached by a noble lady who asked if he could cure haemophilia. Rasputin was led to a small boy suffering huge internal bleeding from a bruise. The boy was Alexei, son and heir to Tsar Nicholas II of Russia. Rasputin led the boy in prayer and insisted that he was given total bed rest. The

The Russian mystic Grigori Rasputin has been reviled throughout most of the 20th century as a religious charlatan and trickster, though during his lifetime he was hailed as an almost saintly figure by many who knew him.

Rasputin was born into a peasant family at Pokrovskoye in Siberia. He was an unruly boy and when a teenager his family sent him to spend three months at the Verkhoturye Monastery to learn some discipline. Instead, he had a vision of the Virgin Mary which convinced him that he had

LIFE AFTER DEATH

According to Prince Yusupov, on the night Rasputin died, he survived being poisoned, hit over the head, and shot four times. His attackers finally killed him by drowning him in the Neva River. This account of Rasputin's apparent invulnerability was widespread when, in 1917, Communist revolutionaries tore open his grave and threw his body on to a fire. Legend has it that, as the horrified revolutionaries watched, the body sat up in the flames and Rasputin's face turned towards them. The body then collapsed into ashes.

He had a voracious sexual appetite and drank to excess most nights.

bleeding stopped. Thereafter, the Tsarina Alexandra insisted that Rasputin should stay nearby. She came to believe that God spoke to her through Rasputin.

Others at the Imperial court were not so convinced by Rasputin's claims to sanctity. It soon became known that he had a voracious sexual appetite and that he drank to excess most nights. The fact that he gradually came to have some degree of political influence over Alexandra, and through her over the Tsar, angered and disturbed government officials while senior figures in the church disliked his unorthodox preaching.

When World War I began, the Tsar left his wife in charge of domestic policy. Soon, opposition to her poorly thought-out policies began to centre on Rasputin. One of those in opposition, Prince Felix Yusupov, decided that Rasputin had to die. Rasputin went to attend a dinner at his house and was found dead three days later floating in the Neva River.

Rasputin surrounded by his admirers, 1914.

OTHER DUBIOUS HOLYMEN

Hong Xiuquan (1814-1864)

Hong was a brilliant young scholar from southern China who suffered a nervous breakdown, during which he claimed that he had been to heaven where he was told to purify China of demons. By 1850, he had around 30,000 followers in his sect, which preached a mix of Christianity and traditional Chinese religion. The imperial government tried to put the sect down by force, but Hong defeated the army and founded the "Heavenly Kingdom of Transcendent Peace" (Taiping) with himself as its king, ruling most of southern China. The imperial government finally reconquered the region in 1864 and Hong committed suicide.

Simon Magus (fl. 1st century AD)

Magus was a religious leader in Samaria from about AD25. The biblical accounts are vague, but he seems to have led a cult based upon his ability to talk to the pagan gods of the Samaritans. In about AD40 he converted to Christianity. He then travelled to Jerusalem where he offered a huge sum of money to St Peter in return for a share in the power given to him by Christ. Peter refused, saying that the powers were not for sale. This event has given rise to the word "simony", which means the buying and selling of ecclesiastical office.

RUTHLESS REVOLUTIONARY

MAXMILIEN ROBESPIERRE (1758–1794)

"Terror is only justice prompt, severe, and inflexible; it is then an emanation of virtue."

Robespierre speaking in February 1794 to justify the high number of executions.

Maximilien Robespierre was largely responsible for unleashing the "Reign of Terror" during the French Revolution. He became the most feared, most powerful man in France.

Robespierre was born into a poor family in Arras, and followed the family tradition by becoming a criminal lawyer in 1781. As well as running a successful practice, he wrote a number of academic papers on the law and

constitutional matters. When the Estates General was summoned in 1788, Robespierre was a natural choice to be elected to represent Arras. He went to Paris as the French Revolution began.

In Paris, Robespierre quickly established himself as a spokesman of the extreme left. He joined the Jacobin Club, a hotbed of radical debate, and began delivering a series of inflammatory speeches to the crowds of poor citizens. He became known by his supporters as "The Incorruptible".

> *He joined the Jacobin Club, a hotbed of radical debate.*

Food shortages followed a poor harvest, and ideological splits developed among the revolutionaries calling for reform. In the elections of 1792, Robespierre was elected to represent Paris. He formed his radical supporters into a group that sat on the upper benches of the Convention, and in December 1792 he led calls for the King to be tried and executed for his crimes against the French people.

When the king was executed, the powers of Robespierre and his key ally Danton were almost unlimited. A mob of their supporters stormed the Convention to arrest 32 moderate deputies who had opposed the execution. In July 1793 the radicals formed the nine-member Committee of Public Safety, under Robespierre, which had almost unlimited powers to ensure

Then began "The Terror", a period of executions, arbitrary imprisonment, and widespread fear.

the success of the Revolution. Then began "The Terror", a period of executions, arbitrary imprisonment, and widespread fear. The purge of moderate deputies begun by the mob in the spring now proceeded to trials for treason and executions by the guillotine. When Danton protested about the judicial violence, he was arrested, tried for treason, and executed on April 5. Robespierre persuaded the Convention to pass a law setting up a Revolutionary Court, able to condemn enemies of the revolution to imprisonment or death on the mere grounds of accusation. The court sent 1,300 to the guillotine in the following weeks. Robespierre claimed this brutal action was necessary but his popularity began to wain and on July 28, 1794, he was arrested after being wounded by a bullet to the jaw. The following day, he was executed without trial.

OTHER BRUTAL INSURGENTS

Lenin (1870–1924)

Born into the minor aristocracy, Vladimir Ilyich Ulyanov became a lawyer, but was secretly organizing Communist agitation. In 1900, he fled abroad and from exile, Lenin reorganized the Russian Communist Party around a small core of professional activists. In 1917, he returned to Russia to lead the Communist Revolution and take power as dictator, in the name of the workers. Russia was plunged into civil war as he enforced a Communist revolution on farming and industry. He died in 1924 with the revolution incomplete.

Mao Zedong (1893–1976)

Mao led the Chinese Communist revolutionary forces through the protracted civil war that saw them seize power in 1949. Once ruling, Mao launched China into massive upheavals as land ownership was reformed and anti-Communist groups liquidated. In 1958, he began the Great Leap Forward, a programme of economic reforms that led to widespread famine and around 4 million deaths. In 1966, Mao launched the Cultural Revolution, a ruthless purge of political enemies. Thereafter, his grip on power was absolute until his death.

MODERN GOOD SAMARITAN

Known throughout the world as Mother Teresa, the nun who did so much good work in the Indian slums was born in Albania with the name Agnes Gonxha Bojaxhiu.

Agnes had a conventional enough upbringing, though she showed an interest in religion throughout her childhood. In 1928, she left home to join the Catholic order, the Sisters of Loreto, and never saw her family again. After a year in Ireland learning English, she was sent to India to be a teacher. She took her final vows in 1937, by which time she was working in Calcutta. On taking these vows, she adopted the name of Teresa in homage to St Thérèse de Lisieux, the patron saint of missionaries.

In 1946, Mother Teresa underwent a spiritual experience; she felt that she was spoken to by God who gave her a new and arduous mission. Speaking of the event later, she said: "I was to leave the convent and help the poor while living among them. It was an order. To fail would have been to break the faith."

> *In 1946, Mother Teresa underwent a spiritual experience.*

She left the Sisters of Loreto to work on her own, ministering to the homeless and the starving. At first she had no money, and had to beg for supplies. Then, in 1950, she received papal blessing

MOTHER TERESA (1910–1997)

*"Our Lord wants me to be a 'free nun',
covered with the poverty of the cross."*
Mother Teresa in her diary, 1949.

to start her own congregation: the Missionaries of Charity. With official backing she found raising funds easier and soon the order had 13 members in Calcutta.

In 1952 Mother Teresa was given a plot of land by the Calcutta town council and opened a

home for the terminally ill. A second similar institution soon followed and was made available to all people regardless of their faith. A third home was opened, dedicated to those suffering from leprosy. Meanwhile, orphans and abandoned children were

In 1979 Mother Teresa won the Nobel Peace Prize for her humanitarian work.

approaching the homes for food, so a fourth home was opened.

In 1965 the first overseas house was opened in Venezuela, followed by homes in Italy, Austria, the USA, and several African countries. In 1979 she won the Nobel Peace Prize for her humanitarian work.

By the 1980s she was involved in more dangerous activities, braving the guns and bombs of the Lebanese civil war to secure the evacuation of 37 children from a hospital on the front line. In 1991, she opened a home in her native Albania, and soon had homes across Eastern Europe.

In 1983, Mother Teresa suffered a heart attack, and a second in 1989. She offered to resign as head of the Missionaries of Charity, but the members refused and she continued with her work despite declining health. In 1996, she finally stepped§ down. At the time of her death, the Missionaries of Charity included 4,000 nuns, an associated order of 300 monks, and around 100,000 lay members, operating a total of 610 missions in 123 countries.

THE BEATIFICATION OF MOTHER TERESA

Almost as soon as she died, there were moves to have Mother Teresa declared a saint. The first step is to be beatified—to be recognized as being a holy person. For this it is conventional for at least one miracle to be performed through the intercession of the person. She was beatified in 2003 following a 2002 miracle when an Indian woman was cured of a cancerous growth after she put a locket containing Mother Teresa's picture on her stomach.

OTHER WELL-KNOWN PHILANTHROPISTS

Jane Addams (1860–1935)
Born into a wealthy Illinois family, Addams (below) helped found Hull House in Chicago, one of the first centres in the USA to provide services and educational opportunities for the poor. In 1915, she founded the Women's International League for Peace and Freedom.

John D Rockefeller
(1839–1937)
Industrialist Rockefeller (left) earned a colossal fortune through his ownership of Standard Oil. Throughout his life he believed he should donate ten per cent of his income to good causes. He donated some $550 million to charity.

Andrew Carnegie
(1835–1919)
Carnegie (right) earned a vast fortune through steel and rail interests but in 1901, at the age of 66, sold up to devote himself to good works. By the time of his death he had given away $35 million, while his remaining $30 million was distributed after his death via the terms of his will.

"If I have seen further, it is by standing on
the shoulders of giants."

Isaac Newton

SCIENCE

ANCIENT MATHEMATICIAN

The great Greek inventor, and gifted mathematician, Archimedes of Syracuse is best known today for his scientific works, but in his lifetime he was more admired as an inventor of the most deadly weapons of his age.

Archimedes was born in Syracuse, then a wealthy Greek colony on the island of Sicily, to a noble family that was probably related to the kings of the city. As a young man he travelled to Alexandria in Egypt, then the centre of intellectual activity in the Greek world and site of the famous library of Alexandria. At Alexandria, Archimedes won great fame for working out how to calculate the volume of a cone—something that had so far eluded even the finest mathematicians. He went on to develop what became known as the "Archimedes Screw", a simple pumping device for water.

Returning to Syracuse, Archimedes was hired by the Romans to devise a reliable apparatus for measuring distances along roads. He produced a cart that had mounted on it a complex system of gears that turned an indicator dial once for every mile the cart travelled. This device was used to erect milestones on Roman roads across Europe and was still in use 300 years later.

In 215BC, King Hieron of Syracuse was succeeded by his son Gelon who went to war

ARCHIMEDES (c.287BC–c.210BC)

"Give me somewhere to stand and I can move the Earth."
Archimedes in a lecture on levers, c.230BC.

against Rome. The Romans began a siege of Syracuse but found themselves held off by a series of weapons invented by Archimedes. One of these was a catapult that had an automatic loading system, allowing it to shoot three times as quickly as a conventional weapon. A second was a system of mirrors

that could concentrate the rays of the sun and set fire to a ship's sails 300 yards (274m) away.

The most impressive of his machines, however, was the dreaded "Claw". This device consisted of a massive wooden beam that could be pushed out over the top of the city walls.

Archimedes won great fame for working out how to calculate the volume of a cone.

From the outer end dangled strong cables attached to a claw-shaped grappling hook. Inside the city was a complex system of pulleys and levers. Once the hook caught on a Roman ship, the pulleys were worked by teams of oxen to pull the beam down and lift the ship up out of the water. When the ship had been pulled up far enough, it was suddenly let go to crash back into the sea with terrific force, sinking the ship. Prudently, the Romans decided to pull back from the harbour.

> *The most impressive of his machines, however, was the dreaded "Claw".*

Finally, in 210BC, they managed to break through the city walls. The Roman commander, Marcellus, gave orders that Archimedes was to be spared. But when the Roman soldiers burst into his house and ordered him to follow them, Archimedes was so engrossed in a mathematical problem that he ignored them. The angry soldiers killed him.

EUREKA!

King Hieron of Syracuse gave a jeweller a block of pure gold to make a crown. The crown weighed the same as the gold block, but Hieron suspected he had replaced some of the gold with brass. Archimedes wrestled with the problem until one day, getting into his bath and seeing the water rise, he realized the answer. He then ran naked down the street shouting Eureka ("I have got it") to tell the King.

Euclid (fl.300BC)

Probably the best-known and most read mathematical book of all time is *Elements*, a 13-volume epic devoted to geometry. It was written by Euclid, about whom little is known, and first published in Alexandria, a largely Greek-populated city in Egypt, in around 300BC. This work is the earliest important mathematical work to have survived intact. Euclid also wrote on astronomy, music, and optics but these works have been lost.

Pythagoras (fl.6th century BC)

Born on Samos, Pythagoras later moved to Crotona in Italy. There, he founded a religious community devoted to ascetic living and frequent ritual purifications. While the beliefs of his religion have been lost, his mathematics have not. He made discoveries relating to the musical scale of notes, the relationship between numbers and fractions, and, most famously, the theorem of triangles that bears his name.

Leonardo Fibonacci (c.1170–c.1250)

Fibonacci is also known as Leonard of Pisa. His main contribution to mathematics was to adopt and popularize the system of numerology that we currently employ, replacing the cumbersome Roman numerals that had no easy way to represent zero. His chief work, *Liber Abaci*, was published in 1202 and explained at some length and with many examples the advantages of the new numbers.

MARIE CURIE (1867–1934)

"One never notices what has been done; one can only see what remains to be done." Marie Curie

"A poor student, haunted by dreams," was how Eve Curie once perceptively described her mother, one of the greatest scientists who ever lived.

But her observation captures something of the personality of this tiny, self-effacing woman whose discoveries transformed our understanding of the world.

Born Marya Sklodowska, Curie grew up in Warsaw the fifth child in a family of teachers. Incredibly bright, she could read by the age of four. But her home life was hard. She lost her mother when she was only 11 and her father was not good with money. At the age of 18 Curie took a job as a governess to help fund her sister Bronia through university. Then in 1891 she signed on at the Sorbonne in Paris, changing her name to Marie. Despite her poverty, in 1893 she came first in her class, and a year later received a masters degree in mathematics.

Eager to pursue a career in scientific research she was looking for laboratory space when she met Professor of Physics, Pierre Curie. Recognizing each other as kindred spirits, they were married within a year.

Working in a dirt-floor shed, Marie Curie began to explore the strange rays produced by uranium, which Becquerel had reported in 1896. Her first important observation was how the strength of the rays appeared directly proportional to the quantity of uranium in her sample. She also noted that whether she heated, cooled, or mixed uranium with other substances, these rays appeared unaffected. To Curie this could only mean that these mysterious rays, which she called radioactivity, had to come from the very atoms of the element.

When she subsequently found higher levels of radioactivity in a sample of pitchblende she concluded that other elements must be involved. This was exciting, groundbreaking research and in 1898, Pierre Curie joined his wife in the lab. It was backbreaking work, as to extract even the tiniest trace

Finally the Curies found what they were looking for—a new element, which Marie named polonium.

of radioactive material required the processing of many tonnes of pitchblende. But finally the Curies found what they were looking for—a new element, which Marie named polonium. Shortly afterwards they found another, more radioactive element—this they called radium.

In 1898, Pierre Curie joined his wife in the lab.

With this success Marie became the first woman in Europe to be awarded a doctorate in physics. It would be followed by a string of "firsts" including, in 1903, becoming the first woman to win a Nobel Prize, and the Sorbonne's first woman faculty member when she took over her husband's professorship, following his tragic death in a road accident.

Desperate to isolate pure samples of polonium and radium, Curie drove herself on. Her triumph won her a Nobel Prize for Chemistry in 1911, as well as fame for being the first person ever to win two Nobel Prizes.

THE RADIUM GIRLS

After World War I, watches and clocks made luminous by radium rapidly became all the rage. Factories opened, and many young women were employed to paint this magic mineral onto numerals and dials. When their camel hair brushes lost shape, the girls were advised to suck them. By the time the cancerous effects of radiation were understood, for many of these girls it was already too late.

Henri Becquerel (1852–1908)
In 1903, French physicist Henri Becquerel shared the 1903 Nobel Prize for Physics with Pierre and Marie Curie for the discovery of radiation. Becquerel had been investigating the fluorescence of uranium salts when he noted that his photographic plates became fogged even when not exposed to sunlight. But it wasn't until the Curies found polonium and radium, that the significance of his discovery was appreciated.

Wilhelm Röntgen (1845–1923)
In 1895, while experimenting with a cathode ray device, German physicist Röntgen noticed a flickering image some distance from his equipment. He realized that he was dealing with a new kind of radiation. Within a fortnight, Röntgen had taken the first X-ray photograph. In 1901, he was awarded the first-ever Nobel Prize in Physics.

Ernest Rutherford (1871–1937)
New Zealander Ernest Rutherford is considered by many to be the father of atomic physics. He not only explained what radiation is, coining the terms alpha, beta, and gamma radiation, he also noted how the intensity of an element's radiation fell off over time—a period he termed its "half-life". From his understanding of radioactive particles, Rutherford then unravelled the mysteries of the atom itself, until finally, in 1917, he split the atom.

EVOLUTIONARY SCIENTIST

Few individuals have contributed so much to our understanding of the natural world, and our place in it, as this modest Victorian gentleman, who explained the mechanism by which life evolves.

Born in 1809 in Shrewsbury, Shropshire into a wealthy family, Charles Darwin lost his mother when he was aged just eight. His father, a successful physician, sent him to boarding school, and then to Edinburgh to study medicine, with a view to his son joining the family practice.

But it was not to be. Appalled by the brutality of operations without anaesthetic, Darwin gave up his medical studies, persuading his father that the Church would be a respectable alternative. So, in 1827, he joined Christ's College Cambridge to study theology.

Darwin had always been interested in natural history. At Cambridge, this interest became a passion as he spent most of his spare time collecting beetles and studying with professor of botany, and lifelong friend, JS Henslow.

Darwin had always been interested in natural history.

It was Henslow who suggested that Darwin join Captain Robert FitzRoy's expedition to South America as a naturalist aboard HMS Beagle. It was an incredible opportunity and Darwin seized it with enthusiasm. The voyage

CHARLES DARWIN (1809–1882)

"It is not the strongest of the species that survives, nor the most intelligent that survives. It is the one that is the most adaptable to change." Charles Darwin

lasted five years, during which time Darwin studied the flora, fauna, and geology of the places visited, writing them up meticulously in his journals, later published as *The Voyage of the Beagle*.

On the long ocean passages, Darwin had plenty of time to read

and he was greatly influenced by the natural history writing of Alexander von Humboldt and Charles Lyell's *Principles of Geology*. Lyell believed that the present is the key to understanding the past, and Darwin became a firm believer in this new world view.

With painstaking care and rigour he catalogued all his finds, frequently seeking expert opinion.

As well as collecting samples of the plants and animals he encountered, Darwin also unearthed many fossils, and noted their similarities with, or differences to living species of the same regions. But it would be years after Darwin's return to England before his ideas would begin to coalesce into anything resembling a theory. With painstaking care and rigour he catalogued all his finds, frequently seeking expert opinion on their significance.

One of several misconceptions surrounding Darwin is that he "invented" the concept of evolution. What Darwin did was synthesize the many new ideas of his time with his own observations and propose a truly viable mechanism for how change might occur: he coined it "survival of the fittest".

Although *The Origin of Species* is Darwin's seminal work, in many ways his *The Descent of Man* and *The Expression of the Emotions in Man and Animals* were more controversial. In these works Darwin took mankind down off its pedestal and argued that the difference between *Homo Sapiens* and other animals was simply one of degree and not of kind.

THE HAND OF GOD

Darwin never completely relinquished his religious beliefs. Fundamentally, he believed in creation and that the creator had established natural laws that it was for mankind to discover—and discovery was what Darwin devoted his life to.

Jean-Baptiste Lamarck (1744–1829)

Darwin was one of those who praised Lamarck (right) as a great zoologist. He was first to coin the term "invertebrate" and he did much to advance the science of taxonomy. Although he is often derided for his idea that acquired traits could be inherited, he made valuable contributions to the evolution debate—he believed that the Earth was very old, so allowing for the possibility of slow, steady change.

Georges Cuvier (1769–1832)

One of the greatest thinkers of his time, Cuvier (left) developed the science of vertebrate palaeontology, and in the process established beyond reasonable doubt that species from the past had indeed become extinct—contradicting the church's belief in the permanence of life. But he did not believe in evolution—he saw organisms as the sum of their parts, and thought that a change to any one part would render them unable to survive.

Thomas Malthus (1766–1834)

Malthus was a political economist who believed that the rising population in 19th-century England was the direct cause of a worsening in living standards. He also believed that overpopulation would lead to famine, and that this was God's way of keeping mankind in check. However, it was his observations that plants and animals produce more offspring than survive that were an influence on the work of both Darwin and Wallace.

Alfred Russel Wallace (1823–1913)

Wallace (left) shared Darwin's passion for nature. In 1858, he produced the work for which he is today best remembered, an essay entitled: *On the Law Which Has Regulated the Introduction of New Species*. Having stated his belief in evolution, he then went on to theorize further, in parallel with Darwin, connecting the work of Malthus to a theory of the "survival of the fittest".

MODERN INVENTOR

Few people have influenced modern life as profoundly as the inventor Thomas Alva Edison.

He almost single-handedly ushered in the Hollywood Age of "Lights! Camera! Action!", by inventing the light bulb, phonograph, and movie camera, and then provided the alkaline batteries to power them.

More than 75 years after his death, Edison's name remains synonymous with invention, and his total of 1,093 US patents unmatched. Despite his incredible success, however, Edison started out with little in the way of formal education. His mother taught him to read and add up, and the rest he learned himself.

Having sold newspapers on the local railway for two years, at the age of 15 he learned how to use a telegraph, and by 1868 he knew he could improve and expand the capabilities of telegraphy.

Edison started out with little in the way of formal education.

A year later Edison received $40,000 for his telegraph-based Universal Stock Printer. This gave him the funds he needed to set up his first proper workshop in New Jersey. Five years later, he moved to Menlo Park, south of New York.

At Menlo Park in 1876, Edison set up a research and development laboratory the like of which the world had never

THOMAS EDISON (1847–1931)

"The reason a lot of people do not recognize opportunity is because it usually goes around wearing overalls looking like hard work." Thomas A Edison

seen. After a short gestation, his "invention factory" duly delivered. Edison's foil phonograph was the first machine that could both record and reproduce sound. Edison later confided that it was his all-time favourite invention.

But Edison didn't always invent

—often he improved, as he did with the electric light bulb. Having bought Henry Woodward and Matthew Evans' 1875 patent, Edison began improving the device's longevity and reliability. In less than two years he had developed a carbon filament bulb

Edison's foil phonograph was the first machine that could both record and reproduce sound.

that lasted 40 hours. Before long his bulbs could last 1,500 hours.

In 1882, his first commercial power station came on line, and soon a square mile of New York had electric light. The electric age had dawned. Edison wasn't infallible, however. During the 1890s he almost went bankrupt, but he soon bounced back with what would prove to be his most profitable invention of all. Edison believed that electric vehicles would win out over steam or petrol, provided a better battery could be invented. Ten years later he succeeded in this—but by that time petrol-powered cars had come out on top. Fortunately, there were numerous other markets for his alkaline battery and his investment was repaid many times over.

In 1928, the US Congress awarded Edison a special Medal of Honour. When he died, the nation dimmed its lights in honour of one of its brightest stars.

OTHER GREAT SCIENTIFIC INNOVATORS

Robert Bunsen (1811–1899)

Although familiar to science students everywhere as the inventor of the eponymous Bunsen burner, German chemist and physicist Robert Bunsen (left) was a scientist of far greater renown. Together with Gustav Kirchhoff, he helped invent the science of spectroscopy, using his famous burner to vapourize chemicals. This breakthrough in chemical analysis, not only led to the discovery of new elements, it also allowed scientists to study the very composition of the universe.

Alexander Graham Bell (1847–1922)

Born in Edinburgh, Scotland, Graham Bell (right) grew up in a family fascinated by speech. Affected by his mother's progressive loss of hearing, Bell became a teacher for the deaf before beginning to explore the nature of the vibrations we hear as sound. In 1876, he succeeded in transmitting his voice using his "electrical speech machine". Within two years, Bell had set up the first telephone exchange.

Nikola Tesla (1856–1943)

Nikola Tesla was a scientist captivated by the beauty and mystery of electricity. Widely regarded as a genius, ideas such as that for an induction motor, seemed to come to him fully formed. He also took X-rays concurrently with Röntgen and designed a radio before Marconi.

EMINENT PHYSICIST

Few scientists have permeated popular culture as deeply as Albert Einstein. More than 50 years after his death, this wild-haired genius remains one of the most recognized people on the planet.

But the images of Einstein that everyone recognizes today come from the autumn of the great scientist's life. That he did all of his really great work when he was a young man is often overlooked.

He was born in Ulm, Germany and went to school first in Munich and later Zurich. The young Einstein's performance gave few clues to his future genius. In 1895, he failed an exam to study electrical engineering. Keen to pursue this route he attended a secondary school at Aarau.

In 1900, Einstein graduated as a teacher of maths and physics; in 1902, he secured a job in the Bern patent office where he worked until 1909.

The young Einstein's performance gave few clues to his future genius.

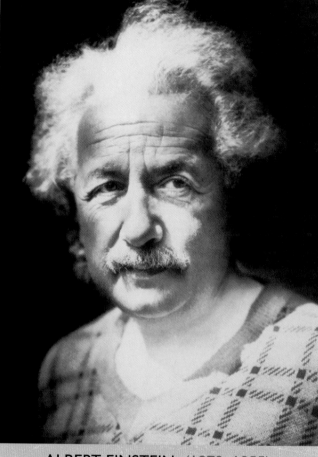

ALBERT EINSTEIN (1879–1955)

"We should take care not to make the intellect our god; it has, of course, powerful muscles, but no personality." Albert Einstein

This was a golden period for Einstein. He used his free time to produce a series of theoretical physics papers. The first was on photo electrics, and explored how light can cause metals to produce an electric current. It was incredible work for which he received a Nobel Prize in 1921.

But it was his second paper that made him famous. This dealt with his special theory of relativity and contained the equation $e = mc^2$. In this equation, Einstein sought to demonstrate a relationship between energy (e), matter (m), and the speed of light (c). But perhaps more intriguing was his idea that time was not a constant. Einstein claimed that if you could travel on a spaceship at or near the speed of light you would perceive time differently to the people left back on Earth. These ideas struck a chord in an age fascinated by science and eager to look beyond the Earth.

In 1915, Einstein wrote the general theory of relativity, to try to reconcile the effects of gravity.

Although his special theory of relativity had been a stroke of genius, it was not without flaws. After much mental wrangling, in 1915, Einstein wrote the general theory of relativity in an attempt to reconcile the effects of gravity.

At first sight his ideas seemed like science fiction. Einstein suggested that both time and space would bend around massive objects, due to the effects of gravity. The maths was complex and the ideas revolutionary.

Not everyone believed him—but Einstein was ready to prove his sceptics wrong. He suggested that his theory could be tested by making observations during a solar eclipse. Conveniently, an eclipse was due in 1919 and astronomers confirmed his theories.

Einstein was in California when World War II broke out, and he never returned to Germany. His next goal was to develop a unified field theory—also known as the "theory of everything"—but now past his prime, this holy grail would elude even his genius.

BRAIN BOX

Before he died, Einstein gave permission for his brain to be studied, provided the findings were kept secret. To date, tests carried out by three laboratories have revealed that the part of his brain used for mathematical thinking was a little larger than average, and because it lacked a groove normally found in this area, Einstein may have benefited from superior neuron communication.

Wolfgang Amadeus Mozart (1756–1791)

Mozart is widely regarded as the greatest musical genius of all time. The son of a musician, Mozart was born in Salzburg, Austria in 1756. He began composing minuets at the age of five, had written his first symphony by the age of nine, and his first opera by the age of 12. By the time he died, aged only 35, he had composed more than 600 works.

Stephen Hawking (b.1942)

British theoretical physicist, mathematician, and cosmologist Stephen Hawking has become one of the best-known scientists of current times. Despite his disabilities, he has spent much of his life grappling with the laws that govern our universe. His *A Brief History of Time* spent over four years on the bestseller list, and made the scientist a household name.

Kim Peek (b.1951)

Immortalized in the film *Rain Man,* Peek is a highly gifted savant—although not autistic—possessed of a remarkable photographic memory. Peek was born with brain abnormalities, chief of which was the absence of nerves linking the two hemispheres of his brain. From the age of 16–20 months, he could read whole books in an hour, and remember almost every word. Incredibly, he can name the day of the week for almost any date in history.

Daniel Tammet (b.1979)

Daniel Tammet (left) is an autistic savant and possibly one of this century's most gifted people. His special facilities focus on mathematics and language learning. Seeing numbers as colours, he can do complex calculations in his head. What makes Tammet particularly special to scientists studying genius is his ability to articulate his experience.

SCIENCE

ALEXANDER FLEMING (1881–1955)

*"I did not invent penicillin. Nature did that.
I only discovered it by accident."* Alexander Fleming

Alexander Fleming's discovery of penicillin was one of the most important breakthroughs of the 20th century, and elevated this son of a Scottish farmer to the very highest echelon of the medical pantheon.

But almost as marvellous as the miracle drug itself, is the serendipitous path that led to its discovery in September 1928.

Fleming's first lucky break came in 1901 with a small inheritance. He was 20 years old and had been working as a clerk in a shipping office for four years.

Fleming used his windfall to enroll at St Mary's Hospital London to study medicine.

Five years later, he graduated with such distinction that it seemed likely he would become a surgeon. But the captain of the St Mary's rifle club, eager not to lose Fleming from his team, suggested that he take up a research post at the hospital. And so Fleming became a bacteriologist, working as assistant to Sir Almroth Wright, a pioneer in the field of immunization.

> *He worked hard to discover a new and effective anti-bacterial agent.*

During World War 1 Fleming had seen first hand the insidious and deadly effects of infection, and so when he returned to St Mary's in 1918 he worked hard to discover a new and effective anti-bacterial agent.

Fleming's laboratory was never the tidiest, and when he went away for his summer holiday in 1928, he left a petrie dish with a culture of bacteria uncovered on his bench. He had been exploring the effects of mucus on cultures of Staphylococci bacteria.

The culture in the dish, however, had become contaminated with a yellow-green mould, around which was a clear circular space. Fleming knew that many moulds practise a form of chemical warfare, creating substances that kill or inhibit the growth of bacteria, and his curiosity was

Diseases that had once killed indiscriminately could now be cured almost instantly.

aroused. Consulting a colleague, Fleming discovered that the mould was called Penicillium notatum—a relative of the common bread mould.

Fleming called the mould's antibiotic "penicillin". He reported his discovery in the 1929 *British Journal of Experimental Pathology*. However, isolating the mould's active ingredient was beyond the Scotsman's skill and in 1939 a sample was passed to a team of chemists at Oxford University, led by Howard Florey and Ernst Boris Chain.

This team of crack chemists extracted and purified enough of the active ingredient to begin trials on mice infected with lethal doses of bacteria. Within a year their findings were published in *The Lancet*, and the world took notice. Diseases that had once killed indiscriminately could now be cured almost instantly, and within a decade penicillin had saved millions of lives.

In 1945, Fleming, Florey, and Chain received the Nobel Prize for Physiology or Medicine.

SUPERBUGS

As early as 1945, Fleming was wise to penicillin's Achilles heel. Used too sparingly, or for too short a time, it not only fails to kill its target bacteria, it encourages them to become resistant to the drug's effect. We now live in a world infested by antibiotic-resistant "superbugs". And among the most feared is Staphylococcus aureus—the bacteria Fleming was originally experimenting on.

Edward Jenner (1749–1823)

English doctor Edward Jenner was the father of immunology and saviour of countless lives through his discovery of the smallpox vaccine at a time when smallpox was one of the biggest killers. Jenner had noticed that people who had been sick with the relatively harmless disease cowpox did not contract smallpox. In 1796, he inoculated a young boy with cowpox pus. The boy caught cowpox but had immunity to smallpox afterwards.

John Snow (1813–1858)

Based on his work identifying the cause of a cholera outbreak in 1854, British physician John Snow is regarded as one of the fathers of epidemiology. At the time, it was thought that cholera was the result of breathing "foul air"—but Snow traced and identified a public water pump as the source of the disease. He was also one of the first to experiment with ether and chloroform to produce safer anaesthetics.

Louis Pasteur (1822–1895)

Pasteur was the French chemist and microbiologist who not only proved the germ theory of disease but showed how heat could be used to make food and water safer. While working for a drinks company when he was a professor of chemistry at the University of Lille, Pasteur discovered that sour wine and beer were produced by bacteria—and that it could be prevented by boiling, a process we now call pasteurization.

ANCIENT ASTRONOMER

GALILEO (1564–1642)

"And yet it does move."
Galileo's muttered aside after publicly announcing
that the Earth was fixed and immovable.

Galileo Galilei was an Italian astronomer and mathematician who gradually came to believe that the world view that was then accepted by both the Church and all scientists was wrong.

The persecution that he subsequently suffered has made him a symbol of martyred truth.

Galileo was born in Pisa, attended the university there, and rose to be professor of mathematics. In 1583, he made his first major discovery when he watched a heavy lamp swinging from a long chain in Pisa Cathedral. He realized that the time taken for each swing was identical, and later proved that the time taken depended on the length of the chain and weight of the lamp. In so doing, he formulated the study of pendulums and made possible the construction of highly accurate clocks for the first time.

He then went on to discover that objects of different weights fell at precisely the same speed—unless they were interrupted by air resistance or other factors. He proved this by dropping iron balls of assorted sizes off the Leaning Tower of Pisa. This led him on to study density and specific gravity.

> *He proved this by dropping iron balls of assorted sizes off the Leaning Tower of Pisa.*

Galileo was then invited to Florence to give talks to the household of the Grand Duke of Tuscany, and from there moved on to Padua to the position of professor of mathematics. There, he perfected the refracting telescope. With this, he embarked on his astronomical studies, making discoveries such as the four moons of Jupiter. In 1612, he announced that the evidence he had found convinced him that the Sun was the centre of the universe and that the Earth rotated around it.

This announcement led him into trouble. The Church and all other scientists believed that

The Church and all other scientists believed that the Earth was the centre of the universe.

the Earth was the centre of the universe. They based their view not only on the fact that nobody could feel the Earth moving, but also on words from the Bible.

In 1616, Galileo was summoned to Rome to explain his theories. He was ordered to stop teaching his ideas, dubbed heliocentric. Galileo complied, but in fact was amassing evidence for his ideas in secret. In 1633, he published *Dialogue Concerning the Two Chief World Systems*, which presented all the evidence he had collected.

The Inquisition arrested Galileo and tried him for heresy. He was convicted and sentenced to life imprisonment, later reduced to permanent house arrest at his villa near Florence. Although going blind, Galileo continued his work.

BURIAL DISPUTES

When Galileo died, the Grand Duke of Tuscany wanted to bury him next to his father in the Basilica of Santa Croce. Pope Urban VIII forbade the burial, so instead he was buried in a corridor off the main church. It was not until 1737 that his body was permitted to be moved to lie next to that of his father.

OTHER EMINENT EARLY STARGAZERS

Tycho Brae (1546–1601)
Brae (above) was the greatest practical astronomer of the pre-telescope age. Astronomer to the Danish king, for 20 years from 1576 he observed the heavens full time, cataloguing the positions of 777 stars with such accuracy that his tables remained standard for generations.

Nicolas Copernicus (1473–1543)
Polish astronomer Nicolas Copernicus (right) was the first astronomer seriously to challenge the view that the Earth was the centre of the universe. He worked on his theory that the sun was the centre of the universe in secret.

Johannes Kepler
(1571–1630)
Assistant to Brahe for some years, Johannes Kepler later became the court astronomer to the Holy Roman Emperor Rudolf II. He adopted the heliocentric ideas of Galileo, but avoided publishing them in an easy-to-understand format to avoid controversy. Instead he published data and theories in Latin in a form that only other astronomers could understand. His key discovery, among many others, was the Third Law of Astronomy.

Claudius Ptolemaeus
(c.90–c.168)
Better known as Ptolemy, Ptolomaeus (above) was a Greek scientist living in Alexandria, Egypt, during the Roman rule. His books are the only ancient works on astronomy to have survived the fall of the Roman Empire, though it is thought that he was more a writer and codifier of others' work than a practical astronomer himself. Ptolemy recorded the theory that the Earth is fixed and that the stars, sun, and planets revolve around it. Though the premise was later proved wrong, his mathematical methods were ground-breaking.

HIPPOCRATES (c.460BC–c.377BC)

*"Life is short, the art of medicine is long; the occasion fleeting,
experience deceitful and judgement difficult"*
First aphorism of Hippocrates.

the Persian Empire. At a young age, Hippocrates went to train as a doctor with his grandfather Nebrus, one of the most respected physicians in the area.

Hippocrates was determined to be the best healer there was. He grew disillusioned with the traditional methods used by his grandfather and others, and at about the age of 25 devised what was then a revolutionary method. Instead of relying on what other physicians taught him, Hippocrates thought that the best way of discovering how to cure diseases was to learn from examples.

> *Hippocrates was determined to be the best healer.*

Fortunately for him, the local temple of Asclepius had a unique library of reference material. It had been the custom for centuries that those who had been cured of disease should donate to the temple a tablet on which the symptoms of the disease and the steps taken to cure it were inscribed. Hippocrates set himself the vast task of reading each and every tablet, sorting them out into categories of disease, and then compiling a list of the treatments that seemed to have worked best. It is difficult to appreciate just how revolutionary this idea was at the time.

Around 430BC, a plague broke out in Athens and the city authorities sent for Hippocrates. The doctor arrived in the city armed with his books and lists

It was an act of abstract thought that was to make the Greek physician Hippocrates of Kos the greatest medical doctor of the ancient world.

It is unfortunate that Hippocrates was so highly regarded in ancient Greece that almost every medical innovation was, at one time or another, credited to him. It is difficult now to know how much can truly be ascribed to him.

Hippocrates was born on the island of Kos, just off the coast of what is now Turkey, at a time when this area was under the control of

His treatments were quickly distributed throughout the city and the plague was defeated.

of symptoms and cures. He took a group of 42 patients, isolated them and set to work. He first studied their symptoms, then cross checked these with his records and prescribed treatment. Of the 42 only 17 survived but this was a much lower death rate than untreated citizens were suffering. His treatments were quickly distributed throughout the city and the plague was defeated. The Athenians made him a citizen of Athens and paid him a handsome fee in gold.

Returning to Kos, Hippocrates decided to take his second unprecedented step. He published his cures, treatments, and failures to make his knowledge freely available to other doctors. Before long, Kos had become the centre of the medical profession as students flocked to the island to learn from Hippocrates and to swap accounts of successes and failures. Hippocrates never again left Kos, but instead corresponded with other physicians to amass a vast library that he left to future generations of doctors.

HIPPOCRATIC OATH

Ancient doctors took an oath on the completion of their training that has been attributed to Hippocrates or one of his students. It laid out a series of ethical covenants. A version of the Hippocratic Oath is still used today in many medical schools, and includes rules such as sharing of knowledge, patient privacy and, above all, to do everything in the doctor's power to save life.

Socrates (c.469BC–399BC)

Socrates left no writings and founded no school—and yet his influence on later Western thought has been profound. His key move was to shift from earlier speculation about the natural world to the study of ethics and conceptual analysis. Rather than teach, he would hold conversations in which he asked questions and posed problems to tease out the opinions of others and expose the truth.

Eratosthenes (c.276BC–194BC)

Eratosthenes was the Master Librarian of the vast Library of Alexandria and was widely recognized as the greatest all-round scholar of his age. Among other feats he calculated the circumference of the Earth, measured its axial tilt, and invented a method for calculating prime numbers that still bears his name.

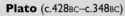

Plato (c.428BC–c.348BC)

Plato was probably the greatest philosopher of all time, laying the foundations for Western philosophy. When Socrates was executed, Plato fled into exile before returning to Athens to found the Academy. He produced 30 books in the form of dialogues and a series of letters, writing about an idealized political system and exploring, among others, the concepts of courage and morality.

Diogenes of Sinope (c.410BC–c.320BC)

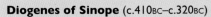

The Greek philosopher Diogenes of Sinope founded the cynic school of philosophy that held domestic comforts and social etiquette to be mere ostentatious fripperies. He made virtue of extreme poverty and lived in a barrel or large pot "like a dog"—which is "cynic" in Greek. He was accustomed to wandering through Athens in broad daylight holding up a lantern saying that he was "searching for an honest man".

SCIENTIFIC FRAUDSTER

For many years Soviet science was in the grip of Trofim Lysenko, a man who owed his power and influence more to his political contacts than to any scientific ability.

The study of genetics and agricultural science in the Soviet Union under Lysenko went down many dead ends, and numerous scientists had their careers ruined for contradicting his erroneous ideas.

Lysenko was born into a Ukrainian peasant family, earning a place at the Kiev Agricultural Institute through his academic ability. In 1929, he managed to grow a winter crop of peas in Azerbaijan. The success assured his rapid promotion. At the time it was hailed as spelling the end to the periodic starvation of livestock during the winter when fodder was scarce. However, nobody was able to repeat his success and suspicions grew that the results may have been faked.

TROFIM LYSENKO (1898–1976)

"He is responsible for the shameful backwardness of Soviet biology, and of genetics in particular, for the dissemination of pseudo-scientific views…for the degradation of learning…"
Physicist Andrei Sakharov speaking of Lysenko in 1964.

LYSENKO'S THEORIES

Lysenko based his work on a form of Lamarckism, which taught that an individual plant or animal could pass on to offspring characteristics it acquired while alive. This was contradicted by the idea that genes are inherited and passed on intact. His ideas, backed up by his supposed successes and political contacts, became orthodox in the Soviet Union although they had been largely abandoned elsewhere.

Lysenko went to Moscow. There he worked assiduously to make himself popular with top Soviet Communist leaders, including Stalin who was looking for ways to reform Soviet agriculture after the failed innovation of collectivization. With his peasant background, Lysenko had a credibility with the peasants that the Soviet leaders lacked. He was successful in persuading them to accept collectivization, promising them massive new harvests.

Lysenko trawled through past research to identify anyone who might challenge his ideas.

By 1932, Lysenko was effectively in charge of all Soviet agricultural science and research. He controlled the publishing of Soviet literature and journals, which he used to publicize his own work and suppress that of anyone who disagreed with him.

In 1935, Stalin gave Lysenko virtually unlimited power in the field of agricultural science when he was put in charge of the Academy of Agricultural Sciences of the Soviet Union. Hundreds of scientists found themselves dismissed from their posts or sent to the gulag labour camps. Lysenko trawled through past research to identify anyone who might challenge his ideas.

> *Hundreds of scientists found themselves dismissed from their posts.*

When Stalin died in 1953, Lysenko tried unsuccessfully to retain his influence under the new leader, Khrushchev. An official inquiry was convened and in 1965 it reported that Lysenko's work was false and fraudulent. He was dismissed from all his posts.

OTHER DECEPTIVE SCIENTISTS

Hwang Woo-suk (b.1953)
Dr Hwang was a leading biomedical research scientist until his work was discredited amid much scandal. Born into a Korean farming family, Hwang worked his way up to become one of his nation's top scientists. His work on human stem cells was highly regarded; two major breakthroughs in 2004 and 2005 made him an international hero. But in 2006, Seoul University announced that Hwang's work as published in the journal *Science* was fraudulent, and the results fabricated. He was fired from his professorship and charged with fraud.

Richard Owen (1804–1892)
One of the finest biologists and paleontologists of his day, Richard Owen is best known as the man who gave dinosaurs their name and for being a driving force in the creation of the British Natural History Museum. However, Owen was also disliked for his vindictive nature and dishonest work. He claimed the credit for discovering the dinosaur Iguanodon, suppressing the work of the actual finder, Gideon Mantell. He also feuded with Charles Darwin, and wrote anonymous articles pouring scorn on him and his evolutionary theories.

GROUNDBREAKING ASTRONOMER

"I do not know how I may appear to the world, but to myself I seem to have been only like a boy, playing on the sea-shore, and diverting myself, in now and then finding a smoother pebble or prettier shell than ordinary, whilst the great ocean of truth lay all undiscovered before me."

Humble words indeed from perhaps the greatest scientist who ever lived, and one with insights that profoundly changed the way we view the universe, and ideas that guided scientific thinking for three centuries.

A farmer's son from Lincolnshire, England, Newton's performance at school gave few clues to his future genius. Described as "sober" and "quiet", many of his teachers also thought him idle and inattentive. In 1661, he was packed off to Trinity College, Cambridge as a subsizar—a kind of 17th-century work-study scheme.

ISAAC NEWTON (1643–1727)

"If I have seen further it is by standing on the shoulders of giants." Isaac Newton

NEWTON & THE APPLE

The tale that Newton's law of gravity is inspired by a falling apple is one of the best known and apposite legends of all time. Ironically, the story's obvious symbolism has proved more durable than the theory it engendered as, evidently, has the tree itself. Today there are apple trees in both Cambridge and Lincolnshire revered as the descendants of Newton's "tree of knowledge".

In the intellectual crucible of Cambridge, Newton finally showed his true colours, and graduated with honours in 1665. The following year he went to his mother's home in Woolsthorpe, Lincolnshire to escape the Great Plague. It was to be a year of astonishing breakthroughs.

Newton used a prism to show how colours were simply components of sunlight. He made his own concave mirror to develop an improved astronomical telescope and he invented a whole new branch of mathematics for the computation of complex variables, which today

In the intellectual crucible of Cambrvidge, Newton finally showed his true colours.

we call calculus. These advances alone would have made 1666 a miraculous year. But the best was yet to come.

The concept of gravity was not new. Kepler, Hooke, and Halley had all wrestled with its understanding. But in that year Newton calculated that the force that held planets in orbit varied inversely with the square of their distance from the sun. It was an incredible piece of scientific deduction.

His law of universal gravitation provided the framework on which all cosmological models were based until the early 20th century. Then came his elucidation of the three laws of motion. Today, these laws seem as fundamental as gravity itself, and have become a fixture of every child's secondary science education.

> *Then came his elucidation of the three laws of motion.*

With his best work behind him, in his later years Newton intriguingly directed his energies towards the mysteries of alchemy and decoding hidden secrets from the scriptures. But when in 1699 he was appointed Master of the Mint, he had the opportunity to put his metallurgical knowledge to the more practical purposes of minting new coinage. Six years later he was knighted.

When Newton died in London on March 31, 1727, at the age of 85, he was given a funeral fit for a king and buried in Westminster Abbey.

Edmund Halley (1656–1742)

Halley was a gifted mathematician and astronomer who first won universal acclaim in 1676 for mapping 341 stars of the Southern Hemisphere. He also persuaded Newton to write his *Principia Mathematica*. But Halley is best remembered for realizing that the comets sighted in 1456, 1531, 1607, and 1682 were all one and the same, and for predicting that it would return again in 1758. When it did indeed return, it was named Halley's Comet.

Edwin Hubble (1889–1953)

While working at the Mount Wilson Observatory, Hubble made a discovery that changed our view of the universe. He found stars that lay way beyond our galaxy—in galaxies of their own. He also noted that the light from these galaxies was shifted to the red end of the spectrum. This meant they were moving away from each other, and suggested that the universe was expanding.

Karl Jansky (1905–1950)

In 1928, American physicist and one of the founding figures of radio astronomy, Karl Jansky joined the Bell Telephone Laboratories as a radio engineer. While exploring the sources of static that interfere with radio-telephone communication, he discovered a new kind of static emanating from the constellation Sagittarius, which lies at the centre of the Milky Way galaxy.

MEDICAL REFORMER

Florence Nightingale, the much loved "Lady of the Lamp", is one of the most revered and admired British women in history.

Born in Italy in 1820, and named after the city of her birth, Florence Nightingale was a bright child with a lively mind. At the age of 17, however, she experienced what she believed was a message from God telling her to do his work—but at that time she had no idea what this work was.

Her parents were appalled when she later announced her interest in becoming a nurse. Nursing was considered a lowly profession, pursued by women of dubious character. Initially forbidden to pursue her dream, Florence was encouraged to tour Europe with family friends. While in Germany, however, she visited the Kaiserswerth hospital, and the following year returned to train there. By 1853, she had become superintendent of a Harley Street clinic for gentlewomen.

> *She experienced what she believed was a message from God.*

FLORENCE NIGHTINGALE (1820–1910)

"It may seem a strange principle to enunciate as the very first requirement in a Hospital that it should do the sick no harm." Florence Nightingale

When the Crimean war broke out the following year, reports soon began appearing in *The Times* criticizing the care of wounded troops. The Secretary of War asked Nightingale to oversee the introduction of female nurses to the Turkish military hospital at Scutari. When Florence arrived with 38 companions in 1854, she received short shrift from the male doctors. But as casualties poured in from the Battle of Inkerman any objections were laid aside.

She rapidly won the hearts of the wounded and in less than two years, Florence Nightingale became the "Angel of Mercy". But despite her best efforts, the mortality of patients at the hospital actually went up during her stay, with ten times as many soldiers dying from illness as from their wounds. This was due almost entirely to her failure to appreciate

Perhaps her greatest achievement was helping to make the profession of nursing respected.

the health risks posed by the appalling sanitation at Scutari.

Treated like a saint on her return from the Crimea, Nightingale accepted her celebrity only in so far as she could use it to further her aims. At once she began the work for which she truly deserves to be remembered— tirelessly fighting to improve the health and conditions of British soldiers. She campaigned hard for higher standards of sanitation and cleanliness and in so doing significantly improved the health of the peacetime army.

But perhaps her greatest achievement was helping to make the nursing profession respected. In 1860, she opened the Nightingale Training School for nurses at St Thomas's Hospital, London. She was awarded the Royal Red Cross in 1883 and 24 years later, aged 87, became the first woman to receive the Order of Merit.

THE NUMERATE NURSE

One of Nightingale's lesser known skills was her mathematical prowess. She was a skilful statistician and one of the first to measure the incidence of illness and the success of treatment. In 1858, her contribution to Army health statistics and her work comparing hospital performace, led to her being the first women ever to be elected as a fellow of the Royal Statistical Society.

OTHER NOTABLE FEMALE MEDICAL FIGURES

Clara Barton (1821–1912)
In 1862, Clara Barton (above) organized supply lines for the Civil War soldiers on the front line. The following year she was granted a pass to travel with army ambulances to distribute "comforts for the sick and wounded". After the war, she went to Europe and became involved with the International Red Cross. Back in the USA she worked to establish the American Red Cross.

Margaret Sanger
(1879–1966)
Working as a nurse in New York's Lower East Side in 1912, Margaret Sanger (below) became acutely aware of how the burden of unwanted pregnancies could ruin the lives of women. Though she was initially met with fierce opposition, in 1916 she opened her first family planning clinic and subsequently founded the American Birth Control League.

Mary Seacole (1805–1881)
Pioneering nurse "Mother Seacole" (above) was born in Kingston, Jamaica and learned her nursing skills from her mother. She travelled to England where she requested transport to the Crimea to help support the nurses there. When she was refused, she funded her own passage. Rebuffed again on arrival she still managed to visit the battlefield to treat the wounded on both sides.

MODERN SCIENTIFIC VISIONARY

> **"The whole of my remaining realizable estate... shall constitute a fund, the interest on which shall be annually distributed in the form of prizes to those who, during the preceding year, shall have conferred the greatest benefit on mankind."**

So wrote Alfred Nobel in his last will and testament, forever linking his name with achievements in science, literature, and causes for peace. Yet when his will was first opened, this simple act of philanthropy caused such outrage and public opprobrium that even King Oscar of Sweden threw his crown into the ring and tried to have it amended.

Nobel made provision for five awards, in the fields of physics, chemistry, physiology or medicine, literature, and peace. The diversity of the prizes speaks eloquently of Nobel's own interests, and provides the perfect posthumous encapsulation of his life.

ALFRED NOBEL (1833–1896)

"I intend to leave after my death a large fund for the promotion of the peace idea, but I am sceptical as to its results." Alfred Nobel

NOBEL FACTS

Since the first Nobel prizes were presented in 1901 there have been nearly 800 winners. Up until 2008, however, only 34 of these have been women, with 23 of these being awarded prizes for Literature and Peace. Marie Curie, however, is one of only four people to win twice. In 1968, a sixth prize, "The Sveriges Riksbank Prize in Economic Sciences in Memory of Alfred Nobel" was added.

Born in Stockholm, Sweden on October 21, 1833, at the age of nine Nobel moved to Russia, where his father had built up a successful business as an engineer and inventor. There he received a first-class education from private tutors. By the age of 17 he was fluent in five languages and showed promise in both the arts and sciences. Keen to encourage the latter, Nobel's father sent him abroad to study chemical sciences.

In Paris, Nobel met Ascanio Sobrero, a young Italian chemist

Nobel branded his new invention "dynamite"—a name that would soon be known around the world.

who just three years earlier had invented nitro-glycerine. Although significantly more powerful than gunpowder, the new explosive was extremely unstable. Nobel was captivated by the challenge of taming this new compound.

From 1852 until 1863 he worked tirelessly with his father trying to create an explosive controllable enough to be useful to the construction industry. In 1864, a particularly bad explosion killed his brother Emil and several others. But Nobel's persistence finally paid off when he found that by adding a fine silicate called kieselguhr, the unpredictable liquid would become a more stable paste, one that could even be shaped into sticks. Nobel branded his new invention "dynamite"—a name that would soon be known around the world.

> Nobel's persistence finally paid off.

Before long, Nobel had more than 90 laboratories and factories in over 20 countries. As well as dynamite, he also invented synthetic rubber and artificial silk, and owned 355 patents.

When Nobel died of a heart attack on December 10, 1896, he left no wife or family. Perhaps conscious of his lack of heirs, he had decided that a series of awards would be a most appropriate use of his fortune. His will was contested by relatives, and it took five years of political and legal wrangling before the first Nobel Prizes were awarded in 1901.

Ernest Hemingway
(1899–1961)
Ernest Hemingway won the Nobel Prize for Literature in 1954—two years after writing *The Old Man and the Sea* and just seven years before his death. Universally recognized as one of the greatest American authors of the 20th century, much of his work, including the novels *A Farewell to Arms* and *For Whom the Bell Tolls,* has entered the American literary canon.

Robin Warren (b.1937) & Barry Marshall (b.1951)
In 2005, the Nobel Prize for Medicine went to two Australian scientists, Robin Warren and Barry Marshall, who proved that 90 per cent of duodenal ulcers and 80 per cent of stomach ulcers were caused by *Helicobacter pylori,* which meant they could be easily cured by antibiotics. Dr Marshall infected himself with the bacterium to prove their theory.

Richard Feynman (1918–1988)
In 1965, Richard Feynman won the Nobel Prize in Physics, with Sin Itiro Tomonaga and Julian Schwinger, for his work in the field of quantum electrodynamics. His "Feynman diagrams" depict the behaviour of subatomic particles, and help explain the motion of electrons—improving our understanding of atomic physics.

Muhammad Yunus (b.1940)
Banker and economist Muhammad Yunus was awarded the 2006 Nobel Peace Prize for utilizing the power of the free market to help alleviate poverty and inequality. As founder of the Grameen Bank in Bangladesh, he invented "microcredit" in which small unsecured loans are advanced to help people start businesses and so escape the poverty trap.

DANGEROUS INVENTOR

At 7.15am on November 1, 1952, the countdown reached "T-zero", and a small Pacific atoll was illuminated with a light of blinding brightness.

As the fireball grew like a huge rising sun, a plume of dirty smoke soared more than 25 miles (40 km) into the sky, before billowing out into an eight-mile (12-km) wide mushroom-shaped cloud. It was an iconic image that would fill TV screens for months to come, and haunt the world for longer.

Five hundred times more powerful than the weapon dropped on Nagasaki, "Ivy Mike" was a hydrogen bomb—the brainchild of physicist Edward Teller. With this successful test, Teller had seriously upped the ante in the arms race and, he believed, brought the world a step closer to a Cold War peace based on the principle of mutually assured destruction.

> *Teller had seriously upped the ante in the arms race.*

Throughout his long and distinguished professional career, Edward Teller was as controversial as the bombs he helped invent, drawing both devotion and disdain. Andrei Sakharov, Teller's Soviet opposite number, offered a clue to understanding the disparate opinions, when he said, "In Dr Teller I see a man who has always acted, his whole life, in accordance with his convictions."

EDWARD TELLER (1908–2003)

"We had a wonderful record on the hydrogen bomb. We tested it, perfected it, and never used it— and that served to win the Cold War." Edward Teller

And there were few things Teller was more convinced about than his belief in the value of nuclear weapons and nuclear power.

Born in Budapest, Hungary, in 1908, Teller went to Germany to study. Quantum mechanics held a particular fascination for him, and while at Leipzig University his enthusiasm was stoked by the acclaimed physicist Werner Heisenberg. But with the rise of the Nazis, Teller chose to head west, to the George Washington University in the USA.

When Otto Hahn and Fritz

Edward Teller was as controversial as the bombs he helped invent, drawing both devotion and disdain.

Strassmann split the atom in Berlin in 1938, Teller feared that the Nazis might soon develop atomic weapons. He thus eagerly joined President Roosevelt's Manhattan Project, set up expressly to develop the first nuclear bomb. But even before the first viable fission bomb had been developed Teller had set his sights on the next horizon: the fusion bomb.

After the appalling devastation of Hiroshima and Nagasaki, the role of scientists in creating weapons of mass destruction had become a matter of public debate. Teller's insistent advocacy of the hydrogen bomb therefore made him increasingly out of step with public mores. When Russia tested its atom bomb in 1949, however, Teller got his way, and by 1952 all his theorizing came to an explosively successful conclusion with the detonation of Ivy Mike.

Always the bête noir of the liberal left, in 2003 Teller nonetheless received his adoptive country's highest award: the Presidential Medal of Freedom, in recognition of his contribution to science and national security.

BOMBS A TO H

Under the Manhattan Project, in July 16, 1941, the first atomic weapon was successfully detonated in New Mexico. These bombs, often referred to as A-bombs, or atom bombs, exploited the power of nuclear fission—the breaking up of the nuclei of uranium or plutonium. H-bombs, however, have the potential to be thousands of times more powerful. Also referred to as "thermo-nuclear" devices, they employ a small atomic explosion to create enough heat to cause the nuclear fusion of hydrogen into helium.

OTHER FAMOUS BOMB-MAKERS

Wernher von Braun (1912–1977)

Von Braun (above) was one of the greatest rocket scientists of the twentieth century, for the Germans and the Americans. Working for the German army, he helped develop the V-2 rocket bombs used to attack London. After the war he and some of his team worked at Fort Bliss in Texas developing ballistic missiles for the US Army.

Samuel T Cohen (b.1921)

Cohen was one of the Manhattan Project's physicists who witnessed the power of atomic fission in the Nevada desert. His role was to calculate how the neutrons behaved. Cohen's so-called neutron bomb involved a much smaller explosion than that of an A- or H-bomb, but it released deadly high-energy neutrons. Cohen argued that while such a bomb would be lethal to enemy troops, it would leave the hard landscape of buildings, roads, and vehicles virtually untouched. Despite successful testing of the neutron bomb between 1958 and 1961, there was no political appetite for the weapon. The Pope did, however, award Cohen a peace medal in 1979.

Barnes Wallis (1887–1979)

British aviation engineer Wallis (below) was made famous by the "Bouncing Bomb" used in the Dambusters Raid to breach the Mohne and Eder dams. In 1943, he developed the idea of attacking German dams in an attempt to disrupt the industrial output of the Ruhr. His bomb was drum-shaped and to make it bounce he designed it to rotate.

COMPUTING INNOVATOR

With more than 18 million users, and a rapidly growing presence in the world of entertainment media and mobile phones, the computer operating system Linux has become a major player in computer technology.

All the more remarkable then that it was created by a 22-year-old Finnish computer science student, who then gave it away for free. Linus Torvalds was a student at Helsinki University when he wrote the core code —the so-called kernel—of what would become Linux.

His goal at the time was simply to empower his home PC with some of the features of the university's UNIX machines. He already had a teaching program called MINIX, but he was frustrated by its limitations. So he began by trying to improve on it.

> *His goal at the time was simply to empower his home PC with some of the features of the university's UNIX machines.*

LINUS TORVALDS (b.1969)

"Really, I'm not out to destroy Microsoft. That will just be a completely unintentional side effect." Linus Torvalds

Today Torvalds is often portrayed as a freedom-fighting hacker challenging the evil axes of copyright and capitalism, a Finnish David, fearlessly flinging code at corporate Goliaths. But while Linux and the huge Open Source movement it has helped spawn have become the adopted tools of those opposed to proprietary software, Torvalds remains an "accidental revolutionary", as his biography describes him.

When on September 17, 1991, he gave the world Linux, he gave permission for anyone to improve on it—but, importantly, he requested that any changes be shared with everyone. Initially he also prohibited anyone from making money out of Linux. But Torvalds freely admits that he wasn't being altruistic. "My reasons for putting Linux out there were pretty selfish... I wanted help." And help he got.

With each improvement of his embryonic operating system,

With each improvement of his embryonic operating system, more users picked up on it.

more users picked up on it. And with more users Torvalds received more improvements, bug fixes, and suggestions. As the popularity of Linux grew, Torvalds' reputation as a revolutionary grew with it. His lack of financial reward was widely contrasted with the fortunes of Microsoft founder Bill Gates.

Quite simply, Linux is a computer operating system just like Microsoft's Windows Vista and Apple's Mac OS X, but one of the first requests Torvalds received—and one of its great strengths—is that it can run on almost any hardware, however decrepit. There are even versions so compact that they can be run from a USB memory stick.

The feature that perhaps most obviously distinguishes Linux from its rivals, however, is that it is free. Linux may also be the largest collaborative project ever organized in the history of the world, both in terms of the number of people involved and the hours contributed to it.

PENGUIN POWER

Five years after the birth of Linux, its supporters decided it should have a logo. Torvalds happened to mention his liking of penguins, and in an email in 1996, he outlined how it might look: "think cuddly... cute... contented... stuffed on herring..." Larry Ewing's painting of Tux failed to win any of the contests held, but Torvalds thinks it epitomizes Linux: "It's supposed to be kind of goofy and fun. Linux is... the best operating system out there, but it's goofy and fun at the same time!"

Charles Babbage (1791–1871)

Babbage was one of the true pioneers of computing. Having graduated in mathematics at Cambridge during the 1820s, he began work on what he called the "Difference Engine". This was a mechanical device that could perform mathematical calculations. Although Babbage died before its completion, his work laid the foundations for the development of the modern computer.

Alan Turing (1912–1954)

Alan Turing was a brilliant mathematician and original thinker. After graduating from Cambridge in 1934, he wrote his famous paper in which he postulated the so-called "Turing machine", which was effectively the blueprint for the modern computer. During World War II, Turing applied his talents to cryptanalysis, developing a machine to break the German Enigma code—an achievement that saved countless lives.

Bill Gates (b.1955)

At the age of 13 Bill Gates began programming computers, and while at Harvard University developed a version of the programming language BASIC for the first microcomputer. In 1975, he and Paul Allen set up Microsoft, which has effectively cornered the personal computer software market. When Gates retired in 2008, he was believed to be the third-richest man in the world.

Douglas Engelbart (b.1925)

Along with Bill English, Douglas Engelbart is most famous for inventing the computer mouse. The first prototype comprised a hand-carved wooden shell with two wheels and one button. It was initially called the X-Y Position Indicator, but was soon nicknamed "the mouse" because its wire resembled a tail. Although Engelbart was granted a patent in 1970, by the time the personal computer market took off, the patent had expired. In 1997, however, he was awarded the Lemelson-MIT prize for his inventions.

MODERN MEDICAL MASTERMINDS

In a Cambridge lab in 1953 two young scientists effectively cracked the code of life. It was one of the most significant scientific breakthroughs of the twentieth century.

On February 28, 1953, as James Watson later recalled, Francis Crick burst into the Eagle pub in Cambridge and announced that they had "found the secret of life". For they had finally worked out that the structure of the DNA molecule—the molecule that contains the genetic code of all living things—was a double helix.

Watson and Crick made an interesting team. Watson had completed a degree in zoology at the University of Chicago by the time he was 19; then switched focus to do a PhD in genetics.

Watson and Crick made an interesting team.

WATSON (b.1928) & CRICK (1916–2004)

"In the game of science—or life—the highest goal isn't simply to win, it's to win at something really difficult." James Watson

Crick was a physics graduate who had worked for the Admiralty during World War II. After the war he turned to biology. Working at the Cavendish Laboratory in Cambridge, he found himself in a highly competitive environment as the director, Sir Lawrence Bragg, was eager to beat both the distinguished American chemist Linus Pauling, and a team at Kings College, London, and be first to unlock the mystery of DNA.

When Watson and Crick met for the first time in Cambridge in 1952, they both shared the suspicion that DNA could contain genetic information, and that understanding its structure would be a major breakthrough.

Meanwhile, in London, Maurice Wilkins and Rosalind Franklin were hard at work trying to unravel the mystery of DNA using X-ray crystallography. After attending a seminar given by Franklin in 1951, Watson and Crick began building a model of the DNA molecule. But they had misinterpreted Franklin's data, and their model was way off base; Watson and Crick were told

to return to their official research. So they passed on all their ideas to the Kings' pair. Then, in January 1952, Dr Pauling announced he had cracked the code. But his structure had three chains and was proved incorrect. Seizing the opportunity, Watson persuaded Dr Bragg to let them resume research and Bragg agreed.

Wilkins then fell out with Franklin, and showed her latest X-ray image to Crick and Watson. Crick deduced from the images that DNA must comprise two

Watson then famously made cardboard cut-outs of the four DNA bases.

spiral chains with chemical bases running up the centre like a ladder. Watson then famously made cardboard cut-outs of the four DNA bases: adenine (A), thymine (T), guanine (G), and cytosine (C), and noticed that an A-T pair was identical in shape to a G-C pair. He saw how the chains paired up and how, when separated, each could be the basis for a new molecule.

It was a rare discovery, and it won Watson, Crick, and Wilkins the 1962 Nobel Prize for Physiology.

CHERCHEZ LA FEMME

Rosalind Franklin was a gifted biophysicist and crystallographer whose brilliant X-ray diffraction images helped Watson and Crick unravel the mystery of DNA. So why is her name virtually unknown? Franklin undoubtedly suffered from the sexism prevalent in the scientific community at that time and was often described as prickly. Her preference for working alone also meant that she wasn't always aware of the progress her colleagues were making.

OTHER LEADING GENETICISTS

Gregor Mendel (1822–1884)

It is difficult to overemphasize the contribution of Mendel to the science of genetics. Born in Austria, Mendel was an Augustinian monk before training in mathematics and biology. Between 1856 and 1863, he cultivated and tested at least 28,000 pea plants. This led to him becoming the first person to trace inherited characteristics in successive generations. He also noted that certain characteristics appeared in mathematical ratios that could only be explained by the concept of dominant and recessive "hereditary units", later discovered to be genes.

Professor Ian Wilmut (b.1944)
& Professor Keith Campbell (b.1954)

In 1996, at the Roslin Institute, Edinburgh, Wilmut and Campbell created the sheep Dolly—the first mammal ever to be cloned from an adult cell. A huge scientific breakthrough, it proved that a whole organism can be recreated from virtually any cell in the body. In this historic case, the team began with cells taken from an adult sheep's mammary glands. Dolly was born 148 days later. DNA testing confirmed that she was a true clone—her genes coming from the tissue culture and not from the ewe that gave birth to her.

Sir Alec Jeffreys (b.1950)

During the 1970s, British geneticist Professor Alec Jeffreys (below) and his team at Leicester University were searching for DNA variability between individuals, in the hope of identifying genes for inherited diseases. Then on September 10, 1984, Jeffreys found something special. X-ray films of a myoglobin gene showed large areas of variation in DNA between individuals. By the afternoon they had named their process "DNA fingerprinting"—and a whole new science had been invented.

The Arts

"I think most of the people involved in any art always
secretly wonder whether they are really there because
they're good or there because they're lucky."

Katharine Hepburn

ACCLAIMED OPERA SINGER

The opera singer Maria Callas dominated the world of opera in the mid-20th century with her stunning acting ability and highly versatile voice.

To the general public she was rather more widely known for her temperamental behaviour, professional feuds, and her love life. She was a true celebrity, as well as a highly talented singer.

Born in the USA to Greek parents, Callas moved to Greece with her mother in 1937 when her parents split up. During the war the family fell on hard times and Callas was forced to go out and sing to raise money.

Her musical education proceeded as much as the war allowed. In February 1942, she took a small role in a professional opera. Later that year, she starred as Tosca, gaining rave reviews.

After the war, Callas went to the USA to make contact with her father and try to break into the American opera circuit. In 1946, she was hired to play

MARIA CALLAS (1923–1977)

"Don't talk to me about rules, dear. Wherever I stay I make the goddam rules." Maria Callas

THE CALLAS VOICE

The singing voice of Maria Callas was controversial. It lacked classical purity and elegance but it had an astonishing range of timbre and weight. At the height of her career it was claimed by one critic that she could sing anything written for a female voice. However, she remained primarily a soprano, often singing coloratura roles, as well as dramatic roles, and occasionally mezzo roles.

Turandot in *Chicago*. The show didn't make it to the stage, but she was spotted by Giovanni Zenatello who hired her for his next showing in Verona, Italy. It was in Verona that she made her name and entered into the most productive part of her career. In 1949, she also met and

married the wealthy industrialist Giovanni Battista Meneghini.

In Venice, in 1949, she took on the role of Elvira in *I Puritani*, moving her career into the bel canto repertoire, as well as dramatic soprano. By the mid-1950s she was at the top of her profession, appearing in prestigious

In Verona she made her name and entered into the most productive part of her career.

opera houses worldwide. In 1950, she decided to lose weight, and promptly shed almost six stone. This dramatic change sparked the first of various controversies. It was suggested that she had swallowed tapeworms to achieve the weight loss. At the same time, rumours began to circulate of a feud between Callas and the Italian soprano Renata Tebaldi. The newspapers delighted in printing their snipes at each other.

The scandals continued to envelop Callas. In 1957, she refused to extend a series of performances at the Edinburgh Festival due to fatigue, but rumours abounded of temper tantrums. She was sacked by The Metropolitan Opera in New York in 1958 amid gossip about artistic differences. Nevertheless, Callas performed into the late 1960s.

Meanwhile, her love life had also been making the headlines. Her marriage broke up in 1959, by which time Callas was having an affair with the Greek shipping magnate Aristotle Onassis. She died of a heart attack alone in her Paris apartment aged 53.

OTHER MEMORABLE OPERATIC DIVAS

Conchita Supervía (1895–1936)

Conchita Supervía (above) made her stage debut at the age of 15 in Argentina. In 1912, she returned to her birthplace, Barcelona, to sing *Carmen*; it was this performance that really established her as an opera diva. Her voice was instantly recognizable as it was capable of perfect enunciation.

Anna Renzi (c.1620–c.1670)

One of the greatest opera singers of her era, Anna Renzi's acting ability did much to revive the concept of musical drama. She sang the role of Ottavia in the premiere of Monteverdi's *L'incoronazione di Poppea* in Venice, but also appeared frequently in Rome. In 1644, she was the subject of what was probably the first celebrity fan book when the volume *Le glorie della signora Anna Renzi* (The glories of the lady Anna Renzi) was published by Giulio Strozzi. She was a member of the Accademia degli Incogniti, a group of musicians who met to discuss philosophy and other subjects. Her fate after she retired from the stage still remains a mystery to this day.

Cecilia Bartoli (b.1966)

Cecilia Bartoli (below) is best known for her work in Baroque music, especially Mozart and Rossini. Her lively stage persona has done much to assure her popularity with the public. She has also become a major recording artist. In 2007, her CD *Maria* went to the top of the Classical Charts in the USA.

SILENT MOVIE STAR

Charles Chaplin was the greatest comic of the silent era. His films were enormously successful during his lifetime and are still shown around the world today.

Born in London to a musical family, Chaplin first sang on stage at the age of five. He moved into comedy as a teenager and in 1910 began an extended tour of the USA with a comedy troupe led by Fred Karno. In 1914, film producer Mack Sennett saw the act and hired Chaplin to appear in a series of short comedy films. In one of his first films, *Kid Auto Races at Venice*, Chaplin was cast as a tramp. He dressed in what was to become his trademark outfit of baggy trousers, tight jacket, big shoes, walking cane, and too-small Derby hat.

> *Film producer Mack Sennett saw the act and hired Chaplin.*

As *The Tramp*, Chaplin began to inject more subtle characterization and sympathetic storylines than was usual in film comedy. In 1916, he moved to the Mutual Film Company, which gave him greater artistic freedom. His first film for Mutual, *Easy Street*, remains a classic to this day. It was here that he put together the acting team that would remain with him for years: love interest Edna Purviance, villain Eric Campbell, and support actors Henry Bergman and Albert Austin.

CHARLIE CHAPLIN (1889–1977)

"At first I had no idea of the character. But the moment I was dressed, the clothes and the make-up made me feel the person he was… by the time I walked on stage, he was fully born."
Charlie Chaplin, talking about his Tramp character.

In 1919, Chaplin co-founded United Artists with Mary Pickford and Douglas Fairbanks. The company was a distribution network that gave independent directors and producers the chance to make films outside of the studio system. Chaplin set up his own studios and, after a few moderately successful films, made *The Kid* (above) in 1921. The dramatic storyline, combined with superb comedy acting was a major breakthrough in the

The uncompromising political message of the movie was considered unwise in Hollywood.

cinematic arts; it was a huge box office success.

When sound movies arrived, Chaplin at first produced essentially silent movies with music and sound effects. He finally entered the talkies with *The Great Dictator* in 1940. The film had its comic moments, but was essentially a hard-hitting satire on Adolf Hitler and the fascist regimes then dominating Europe. The USA was at peace at the time, so the uncompromising political message of the movie was considered unwise in Hollywood. But the public loved the movie, Chaplin's most profitable ever.

In 1952, Chaplin went to Britain, but permission to return to the USA was refused. Although he had been largely resident in the USA for 40 years, he had retained his British nationality. His outspoken left-wing views had angered many in the US government. Chaplin returned to the USA only once, in 1972, to receive an honourary Oscar, his third. He chose not to return permanently and lived in Switzerland until his death.

CHAPLIN'S ETHNICITY

Chaplin was baptized into the Protestant Church of England. Despite this, there have been recurring rumours that he was born of a Jewish background. Certainly, he was never a church goer and some details of his ancestry are obscure. Some elements of his work do seem to draw on Jewish traditions. He may, however, have picked these up during his childhood years in London.

Buster Keaton (1895–1966)
A leading comic of the silent cinema, Buster Keaton (right) is widely considered to be one of the most innovative screen comedians of all time. His successful career as a stage comedian was cut short when he met Roscoe "Fatty" Arbuckle in 1917 and moved into films. In 1920, he left Arbuckle to make his own shorts and in 1923 began making feature-length comedies, such as *The General* of 1927.

Douglas Fairbanks Snr (1883–1939)
Douglas Fairbanks Snr (left) was the greatest swashbuckling action hero of the silent film era. Always an astute businessman, in 1919 he joined with Chaplin, Pickford, and DW Griffiths to start United Artists. In 1920, he made *The Mark of Zorro*, beginning his definitive list of roles in costume adventure epics.

Mary Pickford (1892–1979)
A Canadian actress who moved to Hollywood, Pickford (right) became one of the industry's biggest stars. Born Gladys Smith, Pickford adopted her stage name when she appeared on Broadway in 1907. There she was spotted by director DW Griffiths. She got her first lead role in 1914 and subsequently starred in 52 movies, becoming the first actress to earn $1 million in a year.

PROLIFIC MOVIE DIRECTOR

For nearly half a century, US film director Cecil B DeMille shone as brightly as the stars that he helped place in the Hollywood firmament.

A quintessential showman, his mastery of special effects and management of spectacular crowd scenes enabled DeMille to create celluloid epics the like of which will never be seen again.

His attention to detail is visible in every frame of his films. One of the first directors to use artificial lighting, DeMille's innovative use of art directors and costume designers also broke new ground—helping him to produce films so vibrant that they influenced fashion both on and off the silver screen.

DeMille had always wanted to be a performer. He attended the American Academy of Dramatic Arts, making his stage debut in 1900 playing a small role in *Hearts Are Trumps*. At this time his mother was managing the DeMille Play Company. Her young son would often help with direction and stage management.

His attention to detail is visible in every frame of his films.

It wasn't until DeMille was in his early thirties that he first began exploring the exciting new medium of movies. Together with producer Jesse Lasky and his brother-in-law Samuel Goldfish (later Goldwyn), DeMille formed

CECIL B DEMILLE (1881–1959)

"God means us to be free. With divine daring, He gave us the power of choice." Cecil B DeMille

a company to turn popular plays into films. In 1914, their impressive first effort, *The Squaw Man*, was well received, and the following year DeMille produced *Carmen* to even greater acclaim. It would, however, be another eight years before he would achieve a similar success. But for many it was worth the wait. DeMille's 1923 *The Ten Commandments* is regarded as one of the most successful films of the silent era. Unfortunately, it also went spectacularly over budget, and when his contract expired DeMille found himself looking for a job.

For its authentic grandeur and gravitas The Ten Commandments *is a film with few equals.*

With the Great Depression looming, hard times lay ahead for the film industry. But in 1932, DeMille returned to Paramount and made The Sign of the Cross.

Although he became known for holding strong views against "leftist" union practices, he redeemed himself in the eyes of many when he hired formerly blacklisted actors and technicians for the 1954 remake of The Ten Commandments. This biblical epic, which starred Charlton Heston and Yul Brynner, was filmed on one of the largest film sets ever constructed. For its authentic grandeur and gravitas it is a film with few equals, and one with which DeMille will always be closely associated.

By the time DeMille died in 1959, he had not only proved to be one of the few successful film-makers to survive the transition from silent movies to sound, he had also effectively redefined the role of director.

CELLULOID PROPHET

With his remake of *The Ten Commandments*, DeMille was extending his religious canon of *The King of Kings*, *The Sign of the Cross*, and *Samson and Delilah*. The son of a lay Episcopal minister, DeMille was always pleased to hear that his films had a positive effect on his audience's feeling towards religion, and evangelist Billy Graham even referred to DeMille as "a prophet in celluloid".

"Creativity is a drug I cannot live without." Cecil B DeMille

OTHER GREAT FILM-MAKERS

Howard Hawks
(1896–1977)
Both for the quality and realism of his films' dialogue and for some inspirational casting, Howard Hawks is highly regarded. His pairing of Humphrey Bogart and Lauren Bacall in To Have and Have Not and The Big Sleep created an on-screen chemistry never equalled.

Stephen Spielberg
(b.1946)
Frequently described as a latter-day Cecil B DeMille, Spielberg has enjoyed a huge run of box office successes, including ET, Jaws, Jurassic Park, and Indiana Jones. An enthusiast, Spielberg once said: "I always like to think of the audience while I'm directing, because I am the audience."

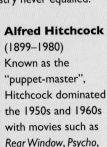

Alfred Hitchcock
(1899–1980)
Known as the "puppet-master", Hitchcock dominated the 1950s and 1960s with movies such as Rear Window, Psycho, and The Birds. A master of suspense, his popular, cleverly manipulative movies frequently wrong-footed and shocked their audiences.

Francis Ford Coppola (b.1939)
Coppola is a five-time Academy Award-winning film director, producer, and screenwriter. His first film was Dementia 13, in 1963. Nine years later, he directed the film that made him a household name, and became one of the highest-grossing movies of all time: The Godfather.

NOTABLE HOLLYWOOD BAD BOY

Dashing and handsome, Errol Flynn played a succession of wild characters in flamboyant period dramas in which he fought and romanced his way around the world. His real life was no less colourful and dramatic.

Flynn was born in Australia to a respectable lawyer and was sent to the prestigious Shore School in Sydney. He was expelled for fighting and for having seduced the school's laundress. He moved to New Guinea where he worked in copper mining and coffee and tobacco growing.

In 1933, Flynn moved to England and worked in provincial theatre for a year. He was then spotted in a minor British film by a Warner Brothers talent scout and shipped to Hollywood as a contract actor.

Flynn was an immediate success in his first movie, *Captain Blood*, in which he played a 17th-century English buccaneer. He went on to play a series of

ERROL FLYNN (1909–1959)

"The only thing that you could rely on Errol to be was unreliable."
David Niven

FLYNN'S WAR RECORD

Despite his image as a fighting hero, Flynn did not serve in the armed forces of either Australia or the USA during World War II. This later led to rumours and allegations that he had been a fascist sympathizer, though these are generally thought to be groundless. In fact, Flynn volunteered for both the army and the navy in 1941, but was turned down on medical grounds.

swashbuckling heroes in hugely successful historic adventure films, of which some of the best were *The Charge of the Light Brigade* (1936), *The Dawn Patrol* (1938), *The Adventures of Robin Hood* (1938), *Dodge City* (1939), and *Adventures of Don Juan* (1948).

Despite his good looks and magnificent physique, Flynn did not enjoy good health. He suffered recurring attacks of malaria; his heart was weak, and he had a bad back. In part, the ill health may have been responsible for his heavy drinking and increasing

Despite his good looks and magnificent physique, Flynn did not enjoy good health.

use of drugs such as cocaine and opium, but his own devil-may-care attitude was also to blame.

Flynn was famous for his heavy drinking, propensity to turn violent when drunk, and inability to see a pretty woman without making a pass at her. Scandal ensued in 1942, when two teenagers, Betty Hansen and Peggy Satterlee, alleged they had been seduced by Flynn. Since they were both underage, the allegations led to criminal charges. The case came to court in February 1943, and Flynn was found not guilty. Many believed that Flynn had been lucky to get away with the case.

> *His own devil-may-care attitude was also to blame.*

Despite his constant womanizing, Flynn was married three times. His first marriage to actress Lili Damita took place in 1935 but ended in divorce in 1942. His second marriage to Nora Eddington in 1943 lasted only five years. Finally, in 1950, he married actress Patrice Wymore. Despite still being with her, in 1958, Flynn fell for 17-year-old Beverly Aadland who had a role in his final film *Cuban Rebel Girls*.

By this time, Flynn was seriously ill. He was grossly overweight and a heavy drug user. His acting abilities were, however, undimmed and he was still working when, during a trip to Vancouver, he suffered a massive heart attack and died during a wild party. Many people felt it an apt end.

David Niven (1910–1983)

The British film star David Niven resigned his army commission in 1934 to go to Hollywood. He had no acting experience but impressed producer Samuel Goldwyn with his impeccable English accent, military bearing, and perfect manners. Goldwyn cast him in a series of starring roles as English gentlemen. Niven was a notorious drinking partner of Errol Flynn—even sharing a home with him for a while—and a well-known womanizer. When World War II began he returned to the British army and saw much active service, ending the war as a Lt Colonel. The early death of his wife never saw him return to his wild pre-war days.

Heidi Fleiss (b.1965)

Fleiss was arrested in June of 1993 on charges of running a high-class call girl service to the rich and famous of Los Angeles. The press dubbed her "The Hollywood Madam" and speculated about which actors, directors, and other movie industry figures would be named and shamed in the course of her trial. In the event, charges involving prostitution were dropped and Fleiss was convicted of tax evasion instead.

William Desmond Taylor (1872–1922)

The murder of William Desmond Taylor revealed a sordid side to the booming Hollywood film industry. An Irish émigré, Taylor became a successful silent-movie director. In January 1922, he made a series of odd, enigmatic statements to friends, then, on February 2, he was found shot dead. Suspects included his bisexual negro valet, a homosexual former servant, actresses, and his rumoured lovers Mabel Normand and Mabel Minter. The sex, scandal, and rumour that followed did much to discredit Hollywood.

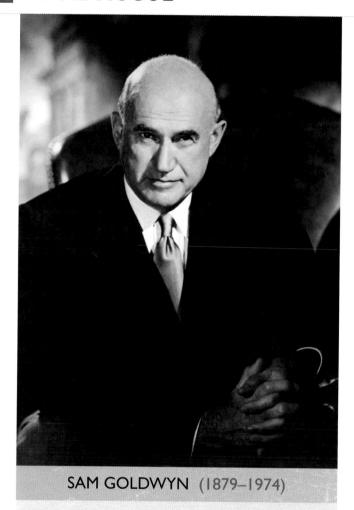

SAM GOLDWYN (1879–1974)

"I think luck is the sense to recognize an opportunity and the ability to take advantage of it…The man who can smile at his breaks and grab his chances gets on."
Samuel Goldwyn

Perhaps the archetypal movie mogul of Hollywood's golden era, Samuel Goldwyn was born into an impoverished Jewish family in Warsaw, Poland in 1879.

Schmuel Gelbfisz left Poland as a teenager to live with relatives in England, where he anglicized his name to Samuel Goldfish. In 1898, he moved to Canada, then to New York where he became a glove salesman—something that

his innate marketing skills made him hugely successful at.

He invested his savings in founding a movie production company with comedy stage star Jesse L. Lasky, theatre owner Adolph Zukor, and playwright Cecil B DeMille. The company would later become Paramount Pictures, but Goldwyn did not stay to enjoy the success. He fell out with Zukor and in 1917 sold his share in the business to found Goldwyn Pictures. The name Goldwyn, which he subsequently adopted, came from merging his own name with that of his partner Archibald Selwyn. That company later became part of Metro-Goldwyn-Mayer (MGM), and Goldwyn moved on again.

> *He invested his savings in founding a movie production company.*

He then founded Samuel Goldwyn Inc, and set about the making of high-quality films. Those films were released through United Artists, and Goldwyn's quality productions were largely responsible for that company's success for many years.

Known for his ruthless business manner and explosive temper, Goldwyn was both loved and hated by the stars and directors that he catapulted to fame. Among the stars that he discovered were actor Gary Cooper, director William Wyler, and writers Ben Hecht, Sidney Howard, and Lillian Hellman. In the 1930s, he turned

Among the stars that he discovered were actor Gary Cooper and director William Wyler.

to making musicals with stars such as Danny Kaye and Frank Sinatra.

He was one of Hollywood's most prominent producers for more than 30 years. After World War II, he received an honorary Oscar while his films garnered numerous nominations. Goldwyn retired in 1959.

GOLDWYNISMS

Goldwyn's limited grasp of the English language and his excitable temperament led him to utter a huge number of "Goldwynisms". Among those that have entered film legend have been:

"In two words: im-possible."

"Gentlemen, include me out."

"They stayed away in droves."

"Give me a couple of years, and I'll make that actress an overnight success."

"I'm willing to admit that I may not always be right, but I am never wrong."

"Our comedies are not to be laughed at."

"A bachelor's life is no life for a single man."

"What we need now are some new, fresh clichés."

"Never make forecasts, especially about the future."

"A wide screen just makes a bad film twice as bad."

"Give me a smart idiot over a stupid genius any day."

"A verbal contract isn't worth the paper it's written on."

"Never let that SOB in here again unless we need him."

"Color television! Bah, I won't believe it until I see it in black and white."

"Let's bring it up to date with some snappy nineteenth century dialogue."

Louis B Mayer (1882–1957)

Russian-born film producer Louis B Mayer (right) was most famous for co-founding and leading the film studio Metro-Goldwyn-Mayer. Mayer acquired a reputation for ruthless business behaviour but went on to make it the most successful studio in Hollywood. He had under contract many of the outstanding screen stars of the day, including Greta Garbo, Judy Garland, and Clark Gable.

Mack Sennett (1880–1960)

In 1912, Mack Sennett set up Keystone Studios in California to produce slapstick comedy movies. He was the first director of comedies to develop a distinctive style; the films became famous for a group of bumbling policemen—the Keystone Cops. He sold Keystone and set up Mack Sennett Comedies, continuing his madcap short comedies.

David O Selznick (1902–1965)

David O Selznick (left) is best remembered for the epic *Gone with the Wind*, which he produced after leaving RKO in 1936 to found his own studio. But his body of work was vast and of unvaryingly high quality. As head of production at RKO, he was responsible for the first *King Kong* movie in 1939.

Darryl F Zanuck (1902–1979)

Unlike other movie moguls, Zanuck (right), the co-founder of 20th Century Fox, was neither a self-publicist nor a source of anecdotes. He was more noted for his ability to produce a string of movies popular with both critics and audiences, including one of the greatest ever musicals, *The Sound of Music*.

LEGENDARY ROCK GUITARIST

JIMI HENDRIX (1942–1970)

"The time I burned my guitar it was like a sacrifice. You sacrifice the things you love. I love my guitar." Jimi Hendrix

Jimi Hendrix burst onto the music scene in 1967. In four years he expanded the vocabulary of the electric guitar more than anyone before or since.

On thunderous walls of distortion Hendrix would spray his sonic graffiti, before laying soft melodies above the musical mayhem. From "All Along the Watchtower" to "Little Wing", Hendrix created the most original music ever to issue from an amplifier.

To many of the fans who saw Hendrix that year, he appeared to have stepped right out of another dimension. Tall, black and playing a right-handed Stratocaster upside down, Hendrix was a strange mix indeed. And that was before he had even played a note. But he had paid his dues—for four years, he had toured the clubs and bars of America's "chitlin' circuit", and played sessions for the likes of the Isley Brothers and Little Richard.

It was in a New York club that Animals' bassist Chas Chandler spotted Hendrix and persuaded him to come to England. Backed by Noel Redding on bass and Mitch Mitchell on drums, the Jimi Hendrix Experience was born. It was an inspired combination, and their every release became a classic. "Hey Joe", "The Wind Cried Mary", and "Purple Haze" all made the Top Ten, and their first album, *Are You Experienced*, went double platinum.

> It was an inspired combination.

In 1967, Hendrix returned home to play the huge Monterey International Pop Festival, climaxing his set with an incredible version of the Troggs' "Wild Thing". Hendrix pulled out every trick he knew. As a finale he set his guitar alight, to painful howls of feedback before smashing it against the stacks. The audience was shocked and awed.

Like his guitar, however, Hendrix would burn brightly for but a brief while. In the next year he would release two more albums: *Axis: Bold as Love* and the double LP *Electric Ladyland*. With *Ladyland*,

As a finale, Hendrix set his guitar alight, to painful howls of feedback.

Hendrix not only pushed the limits of the electric guitar, he also began using the studio as a tool, with which he could construct even stranger worlds of sound.

Now internationally famous, Hendrix began to suffer the pressure of stardom. He became entangled in legal wrangles over old contracts, band members came and went, but most serious of all, he appeared to lose his way musically. Much of his inner chaos was exemplified by his performance at Woodstock in 1969, where the most poignant part of his act was his rendition of the "Star Spangled Banner", played to a departing crowd.

Then on September 18, 1970, Hendrix's genius was snuffed out forever. Amid speculation that he had committed suicide, the coroner reported death due to an inhalation of vomit following barbiturate intoxication.

OTHER ROCK STARS WHO DIED YOUNG

Sandy Denny (1947–1978)
Regarded as one of Britain's finest singer-songwriters, Denny fronted Fairport Convention and Fotheringay before establishing herself as a solo performer. In 1971 and 1972, *Melody Maker* voted her Britain's best female singer for songs such as "Who Knows Where the Time Goes". She died, aged 31, of a brain haemorrhage.

Janis Joplin (1943–1970)
Rated one of the greatest rock 'n' roll singers of all time, Joplin's gravely, gutsy voice has few equals. Fronting Big Brother and the Holding Company at the Monterey festival in 1967, her performance of "Ball and Chain" marked her out as one of the finest white blues singers ever. An accidental overdose tragically ended her career.

Jim Morrison (1943–1971)
Best known as the charismatic, leather-trousered front-man of The Doors, Morrison was renowned for his unpredictability on stage. But with sales of more than 70 million albums and classic songs such as "Light My Fire", his work remains an important contribution to rock music history. At 27, Morrison was found dead in the bath of his Paris apartment.

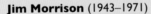

OSCAR-WINNING ACTRESS

KATHARINE HEPBURN (1907–2003)

"I think most of the people involved in any art always secretly wonder whether they are really there because they're good or there because they're lucky." Katharine Hepburn

On Katharine Hepburn's mantelpiece stand four golden Oscars, an achievement unmatched in Hollywood history. But even more inspiring is the fact that her achievements span her entire career.

Hepburn made up her mind that she would act while at Bryn Mawr College, Pennsylvania studying History and Philosophy. After graduating in 1928 she soon managed to pick up a few parts both on and off Broadway. But it was when she landed the starring role in *A Warrior's Husband* that Hollywood began calling.

A few screen tests later and Hepburn was playing opposite John Barrymore in the 1932 *A Bill of Divorcement*. Impressed with their new starlet, RKO offered her a five-film contract. By the third of these, *Morning Glory*, she repaid their confidence with an Academy Award-winning performance.

But there were rumours that "The Great Kate" could be a touch difficult at times. And what really disappointed her fans was her unwillingness to play the star. As far as Hepburn was concerned, once the director had said "Cut!" her job was over. She wouldn't pose for photos, she wouldn't give interviews, and she wouldn't even try to look like a star—she seldom wore make-up and almost always wore trousers.

> *Once the director had said "Cut!" her job was over.*

But the public would have their revenge. Her Broadway outing of 1934 *The Lake* was abandoned by the audience. When her films failed, too, she even became known as "box office poison". Undaunted, Hepburn went back to Broadway in 1938 and had a smash with *The Philadelphia Story*. Cannily buying the film rights, she then repeated her triumph in Hollywood, playing opposite heartthrob Cary Grant.

Her next film, *Woman of the Year*, would rescript her personal life, too. Paired with Spencer

In The African Queen she delivered an amazing performance opposite Humphrey Bogart.

Tracy the two quickly formed a bond both on and off screen that would last until Tracy died.

As Hepburn moved into a new decade, she began taking the kind of gritty spinster roles she is perhaps best remembered for. In the 1951 *The African Queen* she delivered an amazing performance opposite a perfectly cast Humphrey Bogart. But with Tracy ailing, she cut back on her workload until in 1967 they made their last movie together,

Look Who's Coming to Dinner.

By now the times had changed, and Hepburn's less glamorous, sometimes hard-nosed manner was respected, and she became widely regarded as a feminist icon. It was alongside another screen legend that Hepburn would make her last movie. As the wife of Henry Fonda in *On Golden Pond,* Hepburn's touchingly beautiful and believable performance provided the perfect swan song for a truly remarkable actress.

HEPBURN'S MOST FAMOUS MALE LEADS

Cary Grant (1904–1986)
Debonair and sophisticated, Cary Grant's almost deadpan style served him well in both straight and comedic roles. In the highly acclaimed 1940 romantic comedy, *The Philadelphia Story,* Grant (below) played Hepburn's playboy ex-husband. But he is perhaps best known for his Hitchcock blockbusters *Notorious* and *North By Northwest.*

Humphrey Bogart (1899–1957)
Voted by the American Film Institute in 1999 as the Greatest Male Star of All Time, Bogart (below) is mostly identified with tough yet good-hearted roles. His on-screen chemistry with Ingrid Bergman in *Casablanca* was matched only by his sizzling performances opposite his fourth wife, Lauren Bacall.

Henry Fonda (1905–1982)
A Hollywood legend, Henry Fonda's career spanned 50 years and included numerous outstanding performances, from Abraham Lincoln in the 1939 *The Young Mr Lincoln* to Tom Joad in *The Grapes of Wrath* the following year. But it was for his performance of Norman Thayer in the 1981 *On Golden Pond* that he won an Oscar as Best Actor.

CONTROVERSIAL ARTIST

In 2007, *For the Love of God*—a diamond-encrusted human skull created by the British artist Damien Hirst—sold for £50 million ($100 million), a record price paid to a living artist for a single piece of work.

Hirst grew up in Leeds. As a teenager he excelled in art, though otherwise did not do well at school, managing to enter the Leeds College of Art and Design only at his second attempt. He later moved to Goldsmiths at the University of London in 1986, where he worked part-time at a funeral directors to fund himself. While at university, Hirst helped organize an independent show called "Freeze" in a disused warehouse. The show attracted several wealthy art benefactors, including Charles Saatchi.

After graduating, Hirst continued with "warehouse shows" in a variety of disused industrial buildings. In 1990, he had his first real success when Saatchi bought his work *A Thousand Years*, a glass case containing a rotting cow's head covered in maggots.

DAMIEN HIRST (b.1965)

"Painting is so poetic, while sculpture is more logical and scientific and makes you worry about gravity." Damien Hirst

> *The show attracted several wealthy art benefactors.*

Hirst was later to claim that his concentration on works about death and decay derived from his time working at a funeral parlour. The following year Hirst met the art dealer Jay Jopling who took on the young artist and promoted his works assiduously.

Meanwhile, Saatchi funded a show which took place in 1992 under the title Young British Artists—soon to be referred to as YBA and used as a term to refer to works by Hirst and a group of fellow conceptual artists. Hirst's contribution to the exhibition was a shark preserved in formaldehyde that sold for £50,000 ($100,000).

In 1993, Hirst went to Venice to show *Mother and Child Divided*, a cow and a calf cut into sections, preserved in formaldehyde, and displayed in a number of glass

In 1993, Hirst went to Venice to show Mother and Child Divided, *a cow and a calf cut into sections.*

tanks. In 1994, this was followed by a sheep in formaldehyde entitled *Away from the Flock*.

By this time, the press were noticing Hirst's work, more often to criticize its "good taste" or in order to ridicule contemporary art than to praise its merits. When Hirst won the Turner Prize in 1995, his fame was assured. He has subsequently produced a range of controversial and highly publicized works in various mediums.

By 2007, Hirst had to some extent given up actually doing the art works himself, in favour of hiring assistants to put his concepts into reality. Two of these assistants are thought to have produced around 300 of Hirst's famous "spot" paintings. Asked why he hired others to do them, Hirst explained that the real creative thrust came from the original conception of the work, not the execution of it.

CATERING TO ART

Hirst has been linked to a number of restaurants. He part-owned and flamboyantly opened a restaurant called Pharmacy in London's fashionable Notting Hill area. When the restaurant closed in 2003, he removed all of his artworks with which it had been decorated and has subsequently sold them for £11 million. He has since opened a seafood restaurant in Ilfracombe, Devon.

OTHER CONTENTIOUS ARTISTS

Tracey Emin (b.1963)
Tracey Emin is a British sculptor belonging to the YBA (Young British Artists) movement who in 2007 received the ultimate in establishment respectability when she was invited to join the Royal Academy of Arts. She entered art college in 1980 and achieved instant fame in 1999 when her work *My Bed* (above) was shortlisted for the Turner Prize. The piece was an unmade bed festooned with condoms and soiled underwear. Emin has since focused more on painting.

William Etty (1787–1849)
Etty (below) caused a sensation in his day with his highly skilled, sensual paintings of nudes. After training to be a printer in the north of England, Etty moved to London to study art. At first, Etty painted scenes that were ostensibly Baiblical or based on Classical Greek myths, but he later began painting naked women in contemporary settings and so sparked great controversy.

Riefenstahl (left) filming in Nuremberg at the 1934 Nazi Party Congress.

Leni Riefenstahl (1902–2003)
Riefenstahl was a German film-maker of great talent whose career was forever blighted by her association with the Nazi regime of Adolf Hitler, of whom she became a devoted follower. She made a series of propaganda documentaries for the Nazi Party that were made all the more powerful by the innovative techniques she employed. Her masterpiece is generally thought to be *Triumph of the Will* (1934).

LE CORBUSIER (1897–1965)

"Space and light and order. Those are the things that men need just as much as they need bread or a place to sleep."
Le Corbusier

Le Corbusier dreamed of cities where vertiginous towers pierced the sky, and broad thoroughfares arched through the air above wide green open spaces. His was a vision of a "Radiant City".

Le Corbusier believed that his new century deserved a new kind of architecture. "Modern life demands, and is waiting for, a new kind of plan, both for the house and the city," he once declared.

Charles-Édouard Jeanneret (as he was then called) was born in La Chaux-de-Fonds, Switzerland. He started as a watch-case engraver before exploring architecture. Before long he began to develop a utopian vision of planned development, with the home as a "machine for living" at its centre.

In 1920, he took Le Corbusier as a pseudonym, a modified version of his grandfather's name. To complete his reinvention, he took to wearing bow ties and starched collars which, together with his dark horn-rimmed glasses, soon made Le Corbusier as recognizable as his buildings.

> *To complete his reinvention, he took to wearing bow ties and starched collars.*

Inspired by the creative possibilities of concrete, he soon demonstrated his talent. The Notre Dame du Haut chapel at Ronchamp in France is a Le Corbusier masterpiece. With its thick, curved walls and huge shell-like roof, the chapel has a sculptural form that is both naturalistic and modern.

Le Corbusier's effect on the cityscape, however, was more controversial. A utopian at heart, he was eager to imprint his urban vision on the post-war world. His buildings were typically built on stilts, had walls independent of the structure, open floorplans, and were lit by regimented rows of windows. A garden or swimming pool would be on the flat roof.

Despite some success applying these principals to his up-market

Le Corbusier's effect on the cityscape, however, was more controversial.

development in Marseilles, Le Corbusier's urban vision proved flawed. The scale and geometric regularity of his architecture made it impersonal and disorientating. Beneath the damp skies of northern Europe, his beloved concrete became water-stained and dreary; his planned separation of work, home, and amenities into discrete areas simply created sterile ghettoes of uniformity.

Today, while some of Le Corbusier's work, such as the Geisel Library at the University of California, is still admired, much of the urban regeneration he inspired is being bulldozed in favour of developments that are being built a little closer to the ground and also on more neighbourly terms with the past.

BRUTALISM

Le Corbusier is considered the father of the architectural style known as Brutalism, popular in the 1960s and 1970s. The name derives from the French for raw concrete (*bréton brut*), Le Corbusier's material of choice. Architects Alison and Peter Smithson (above) coined the term and were involved in the regeneration of many of the post-war British communities in the Brutalist style.

Frank Lloyd Wright (1867–1959)
Hugely prolific, American architect Lloyd Wright is best remembered as a proponent of organic architecture. This philosophy is the antithesis of Brutalism, as it seeks to establish harmony between human constructions and the natural world, so that the resulting building becomes one with its surroundings. Lloyd Wright carried this concept further, to a point where every part of a building is organically connected—from the windows to the doors—including the contents.

Antonio Gaudí (1852–1926)
Born in Reus, Spain, Gaudí abandoned his family's metalworking tradition for architecture. Initially associated with the Catalan Modernismo movement and Art Nouveau, Gaudí developed an architectural style that was both unique and controversial. The finest examples of his organic creations are in Barcelona, and include the Park Güell, Casa Batillo (left), and Sagrada Familia, the church that he worked on for 43 years, and yet never saw completed.

Jørn Utzon (b.1918)
Danish architect Utzon is best known for designing the Sydney Opera House in Australia. Although many see the building as an evocation of the spinnaker sails that ply Sydney Harbour, Utzon says that the dramatic roof structure was inspired by the segments of an  orange. Budget overruns and political intrigue led to Utzon's withdrawal from the project, and to his not being invited to the opening ceremony. In 2003, his design won him the Pritzker Prize.

TRAGIC STARLET

A Molotov cocktail of curves, innocence, and allure, Marilyn Monroe's incendiary Hollywood career made her a legend.

Voted the sexiest woman of the 20th century, four decades after her death she remains the most famous woman in the world.

Monroe possessed an appeal that went way beyond her obvious sexuality. She exuded a vulnerability that not only affected the people she met, but which somehow she communicated through the camera to the millions who adored her.

Marilyn Monroe was born Norma Jeane Mortenson to a single mother fighting a battle with mental illness. Norma Jeane's childhood was characterized by insecurity, poverty, and abuse.

While working at a local munitions factory, she was photographed by David Conover for a feature on women and the war effort. From the first click of the shutter it was obvious to all that the camera loved her.

MARILYN MONROE (1926–1962)

"I don't mind living in a man's world as long as I can be a woman in it." Marilyn Monroe

CONSPIRACY THEORIES

Not long after Marilyn's death a number of conspiracy theories emerged. The one accorded most credence linked her death with Robert Kennedy. In 1993, Peter Brown and Patte Barham published their book, *Marilyn: The Last Take*. In it they proposed two conspiracies, one involving 20th Century Fox and the other implicating John and Robert Kennedy with a cover-up by the CIA.

Conover began putting work her way, and within two years she had a successful modelling career.

She enrolled in acting classes and by 1946, the now blonde Norma Jeane was starting to become known. Twentieth Century Fox put a contract pen in her hand first; casting director Ben Lyon suggested the name Marilyn, she appended her grandmother's surname, and the transformation was complete.

For seven long years Monroe played more than 20 inconsequential roles in as many forgettable films. Then, in 1953, she scored two box-office

From the first click of the shutter it was obvious to all that the camera loved her.

Marilyn at a rehearsal for a benefit performance at Madison Square Gardens, New York, in 1955.

smashes with the comedies *Gentlemen Prefer Blondes* and *How to Marry a Millionaire*.

Desperate to ditch her reputation as a dizzy blonde and sharpen her acting skills, in 1956 Monroe moved to New York to train with coach Lee Strasberg. When *Bus Stop* was released to critical acclaim it appeared that her efforts had paid off. And with a Golden Globe award for *Some Like it Hot* in 1959 Monroe was apparently on top of the world.

Behind the scenes, however, her personal life wasn't so "hot". In 1956, she had married playwright and intellectual, Arthur Miller. Four years and two miscarriages later, their marriage was in ruins. Monroe was beginning to unravel.

Two months after being fired from her last film, *Something's Got to Give*, Marilyn Monroe was found dead in bed by her housekeeper, with a bottle of sleeping pills beside her.

OTHER MOVIE STARS WHO DIED YOUNG

Jayne Mansfield (1933–1967)
One of the leading sex symbols of the 1950s, Mansfield's breakthrough came in 1956 when she starred in *The Girl Can't Help It*. With more talent than she was often given credit for, she aspired to more serious acting roles. But Mansfield would forever be typecast as the archetypal "dumb blonde". She died in a car accident aged 34.

River Phoenix (1970–1993)
River Phoenix was acting on TV by the age of ten but it was his performances in the 1986 box-office hits *Stand By Me* and *Mosquito Coast* that really got him noticed. Three years later he was nominated for an Academy Award, but a drugs overdose on Halloween in 1993 ended his life midway through the filming of *Dark Blood*.

Bruce Lee (1940–1973)
A superb athlete of enormous talent, American-born Lee's 1970s movies transformed a niche Asian film genre into international box office gold. After a spell back in Hong Kong, he returned to Hollywood to film the seminal 1973 *Enter the Dragon*. That same year, however, he died of a brain haemorrhage.

James Dean (1931–1955)
James Dean had one of the most spectacularly ephemeral careers of any Hollywood star. Epitomizing the credo, "live fast die young", in one short year he made three films before crashing to his death in his Porsche Spyder. Of all his roles it was the tense, brooding Jim Stark of *Rebel Without A Cause* with which he is most closely identified.

MACABRE WRITER

American poet, critic, and author of such macabre masterpieces as *The Fall of the House of Usher*, Edgar Allan Poe is regarded by many as one of the high-priests of gothic fiction.

Poe's passport to travel through the dark lands of despair was stamped early on with the death of his mother and later with the loss of his brother to alcohol, and his wife to tuberculosis. But while Poe clearly wasn't short of inspiration for his dark themes, he was less the madman driven by inner devils and more the astute journalist, attempting to satisfy public demand for Gothic horror.

Born in Boston, Massachusetts, Poe lost both parents by the time he was three years old and was raised by Frances and John Allan in Richmond, Virginia. After a brief spell with the army in 1831, Poe decided to focus on a career as a self-supporting writer.

In 1835 he secured a job with the *Southern Literary Messenger* as a contributing critic and essayist. In his spare time he continued to write—poetry mostly—pausing only briefly to controversially marry his 13-year-old niece.

In 1838 *The Narrative of Arthur Gordon Pym* was published, Poe's only complete novel. Although essentially an adventure story, within it ran the darker themes of murder and cannibalism. The following year Poe took a job as assistant editor of *Burton's Gentleman's Magazine*, one of a

EDGAR ALLAN POE (1809–1849)

"Deep into that darkness peering, long I stood there, wondering, fearing, doubting, dreaming dreams no mortal ever dared to dream before."
From *The Raven*, 1845, by Edgar Allan Poe.

number of literary periodicals for which he would work. He soon established his reputation as a lively and sometimes harsh critic.

One night in 1842, however, while singing at the piano, Poe's young wife Virginia began coughing up blood—she had tuberculosis. Poe took comfort in his two most loyal friends, alcohol

and poetry, and managed to produce his most successful work to date, *The Raven*. But although the poem helped to make Poe a household name, he only received $9 for its publication.

During his last years, Poe allegedly became increasingly dependent on alcohol, and late on Sunday, October 7, 1849, he

In 1849, Poe was found dying in the street, inexplicably dressed in someone else's clothes.

was found dying in the street, inexplicably dressed in someone else's clothes. The newspapers reported the cause of death as a "congestion of the brain"—but accounts of the author's last days are so rare that the truth may never be known.

> Poe took comfort in his two most loyal friends, alcohol and poetry.

The day after Poe's burial, a long, vituperative obituary appeared in the *New York Tribune*. Its author was one Rufus Wilmot Griswold, an anthologist who had held a grudge against Poe since 1842. In Griswold's subsequent *Memoir of the Author* appended to a collection of Poe's work, he described Poe as: "a depraved, drunk, drug-addled madman". A mixture of fiction and forgery, some of the mud stuck— partly because no authorized biography contradicted it, but also because a section of Poe's public were secretly thrilled at the idea of reading the dark works of a depraved author.

THE FIRST DETECTIVE

When Poe wrote *The Murders in the Rue Morgue* in 1841, he inadvertently created the very DNA of detective fiction. From the creation of locked-room and cipher-based mysteries, to their subsequent deduction, Poe blueprinted the modern whodunit. And, through the character of Auguste Dupin, Poe established a lineage that lead to the birth of Sherlock Holmes and Hercule Poirot.

Bram Stoker (1847–1912)

Abraham "Bram" Stoker was born in Ireland. In 1890, he began researching European folklore and vampire legends for a book to be called *The Un-Dead*, chronicling the blood-sucking exploits of "Count Vampyre". Only at the eleventh hour was the title of the sharp-toothed Count changed to give us the eponymous chiller we know today as *Dracula*.

Mary Shelley (1797–1851)

In 1816, Mary Shelley spent a summer sojourn at the Geneva home of poet Lord Byron. The party spent much time reading ghost stories and discussing the work of Erasmus Darwin and galvanism—the concept of using electricity to revive the dead. It was here that Shelley gave birth to her tragic masterpiece: *Frankenstein*.

H P Lovecraft (1890–1937)

American writer Howard Phillips Lovecraft wrote mostly at night, creating stories that were mysterious and macabre, mostly for the pulp magazines of his day. Following his death, many of his weird and wonderful tales, including *The Color Out of Space*, were rescued from obscurity.

Algernon Blackwood (1869–1951)

By turns a journalist, British secret agent, and psychic researcher, Blackwood is today remembered as one of the greatest ghost-story writers of the early 20th century. Informed by his interest in spiritualism, Blackwood's stories had a vibrant realism about them that sought less to frighten the readers than to make them marvel at the mysteries of the supernatural.

CONTROVERSIAL POET

THE ARTS

If there is one thing that can be said with certainty about American poet Ezra Pound it is that he was never shy about controversy and often seemed to revel in it as he promoted the modernist art movement.

Pound was born in Idaho, but grew up in Philadelphia where he had a conventional middle-class upbringing and education. He went to the University of Pennsylvania, where he gained a Master of Arts degree in Romance Philology in 1906. While at university, Pound fell in love with Hilda Doolittle and was devastated when she left him for a relationship with a woman named Frances Gregg. Soon afterwards, he resigned from his teaching job in Indiana in somewhat murky circumstances and moved to London.

Until his arrival in London, Pound's poetry had been workmanlike but conventional. Once in England, he met William Butler Yeats, whose work he soon declared to be the greatest poetry in the world. Working with Yeats, he promoted what he termed "imagism" in poetry, and enthusiastically supported the work of writers such as James Joyce, Jacob Epstein, and Rebecca West. He edited TS Eliot's *The Waste Land*, which achieved enormous critical acclaim. In 1914, Pound married Dorothy Shakespear, the daughter of Yeats's

EZRA POUND (1885–1972)

"America is a lunatic asylum."
Ezra Pound on his release from hospital in 1959.

lover, with whom he would have a close but uneasy relationship for the rest of his life.

World War I proved to be a defining experience for Pound. He lost all faith in modern technology and civilization, left London, and moved to Paris. In France, he met and mixed with artists

who were striving to change the world through the movements of Dadaism and Surrealism. He began work on what would prove to be his defining work, *The Cantos*, and started composing. He also took a lover in the shape of musician Olga Rudge. In 1924, he abruptly left Paris and moved to Italy.

When the USA joined the war against Italy, Pound was indicted for treason.

There he came to admire the exciting new fascist regime of Benito Mussolini. At this time, the more unpleasant sides of the fascist regime had not yet become obvious and Pound chose to ignore the lack of democracy in favour of the rapidly improving Italian economy.

> He came to admire the exciting new fascist regime of Benito Mussolini.

When Italy declared war on Britain and France, he decided to support the German-Italian cause. He gave radio talks and published articles alleging that multinational banking and commercial interests were the driving force behind the Allied cause. When the USA joined the war against Italy, Pound was indicted for treason.

In 1945, he surrendered to the American troops. Pound was declared insane and committed to St Elizabeth's Hospital where he spent 12 years. After his release, he lived in Italy until his death.

INSANE TREATMENT

Pound's stay at St Elizabeth's Hospital is controversial. For somebody supposedly suffering a severe mental illness, his treatment was odd. He was given a private room where he was allowed to receive visitors and write books. It has been alleged that his insanity plea was accepted by the authorities to avoid the embarrassment of putting a major artistic talent on trial for treason.

Amiri Baraka (b.1934)
American poet Amiri Baraka was born Everett LeRoi Jones, but in 1967 adopted the more African name that he now uses. His poetry and other writings have been highly acclaimed and he became a professor of literature. However, his links to Black nationalism and Marxism have always been controversial while his writings have used violent imagery directed against whites, women, gays, and Jews.

Philip Larkin (1922–1985)
Widely recognized as the most important English poet of the later 20th century, Larkin's poems, especially *Whitsun Weddings*, remain hugely popular. However, he courted controversy that often harmed his career. He was apparently obsessed with pornography, expressed racist views on several occasions, and could be outrageously rude to those he did not like.

Walt Whitman (1819–1892)
The works of American poet Walt Whitman continue to be highly influential, but his writings were hugely controversial at the time for their often highly charged sexual content. It was the publication of his collection of poems *Leaves of Grass* in 1855 that began the controversy. The poems were immediately hailed by critics, until they realized the underlying homosexual theme, which was unaccepable at the time.

THE KING OF ROCK 'N' ROLL

Elvis Presley was a musical phenomenon. Fusing country and blues first into rockabilly and then rock 'n' roll, he provided the soundtrack for a generation.

His high-energy, sexually charged performances tapped into a new teenage zeitgeist and sent his audiences wild. As John Lennon succinctly said, "Before Elvis there was nothing". Today, his achievements remain awesome. With record sales of more than a billion, Presley has had more gold, platinum, and multi-platinum disks than any artist in history.

Born in Tupelo, Mississippi during the Great Depression, Presley grew up poor. Having moved to Memphis when he was 13, he graduated from the local high school in 1953. He then had a series of low-paid jobs before ending up as a truck driver.

> *Born in Tupelo, Mississippi during the Great Depression, Presley grew up poor.*

That same year, Presley went to the Memphis Recording Service, where you could make a record for $4. In January 1954, he went back for a second attempt and this time bumped into owner Sam Phillips, who ran the business as a sideline to Sun Records. Phillips had been looking for a white artist with a black sound who could take rhythm and blues to a white audience. And as he

ELVIS PRESLEY (1935–1977)

"Some people tap their feet, some people snap their fingers, and some people sway back and forth. I just sorta do 'em all together, I guess." Elvis Presley

watched Presley belting out Arthur Crudup's "That's All Right Mama", Phillips could hear the ker-ching of the cash registers.

The song became the first of five singles Presley would record for Sun. It was arguably his finest work and it wasn't long before

bigger fish took an interest. In 1955, Sam Phillips sold Presley's contract to RCA for $35,000, and Colonel Tom Parker became Presley's manager.

At first it was business as usual. Presley's next few records for RCA—"Heartbreak Hotel",

Love Me Tender was the first of 33 movies Presley would make, each one a box office smash.

"Hound Dog", "Jailhouse Rock", and "All Shook Up"—all had much of the same energy as his earlier recordings. But Parker had bigger plans for his protégé.

In 1956, he encouraged Presley to move into films and later that year *Love Me Tender* was released. It was the first of 33 movies Presley would make, each one a box office smash. But by the late 1960s, fame was beginning to take its toll on the King. Suffering from insecurity and depression, he had become inward and reclusive and would rent out whole movie theatres and amusement parks so that he could visit them alone.

After a period in the 1970s that saw Presley try to revive his career performing in Las Vegas, his lifeless body was found at Graceland on August 16, 1977. Cause of death was first given as heart failure. Later investigation suggested that drugs also played a part.

OTHER ROCK 'N' ROLL "KINGS"

Chuck Berry
(b.1926)
One of the greatest influences on the genre, Chuck Berry's blues-country records of the 1950s fused teenage-friendly lyrics with an infectious rocking rhythm. With his flamboyant stage act, featuring his trademark "duckwalk" and his string of hits, for many Berry is Mr Rock 'n' Roll.

Gene Vincent
(1935–1971)
A frenzied stage act matched by the hit "Be Bop A Lula" made Gene Vincent a teenage idol. Credited with helping define the rockabilly sound, he was also one of the first musicians to star in a film—with Jayne Mansfield in the 1956 *The Girl Can't Help It.*

Little Richard
(b.1932)
With his falsetto voice, made up face and effeminate hair style, Little Richard added rebellious sexual confusion to his take on high-energy piano-pounding rock 'n' roll. Never shy about proclaiming himself the "king of rock 'n' roll", with hits including "Tutti Frutti", "Long Tall Sally", and "Good Golly Miss Molly", few would argue his pedigree.

Jerry Lee Lewis
(b.1935)
In the early days of rock 'n' roll, Elvis was not without competition. The piano-slammin' Lewis, was easily Presley's match for enthusiasm and energy. Selling over six million copies of "Whole Lotta Shakin' Going On", Lewis even followed Presley into movies with *High School Confidential.*

WILLIAM SHAKESPEARE (1564–1616)

"All the world's a stage, and all the men and women merely players: they have their exits and their entrances; and one man in his time plays many parts, his acts being seven ages."
From *As You Like It* by William Shakespeare.

William Shakespeare is widely regarded as the greatest poet and playwright the world has ever known, and his impact on the English language is beyond comparison.

In over 150 sonnets and 37 plays he created a body of work that remains popular with theatre audiences, and critics, nearly four centuries after his death.

Today, Shakespeare's plays are often thought highbrow, but back in the Bard's day plays were very much popular entertainment. And for every speech of nodding erudition he penned, there would be another equally eloquent belch just to make everyone laugh. For the young playwright to fill his purse, he first had to fill the theatres.

Shakespeare's success grew from his ability to create wonderfully believable characters. He placed these characters in situations that best explored the human condition. From love and marriage to greed and avarice, his plays wrestled with issues that his audience could relate to.

> *He placed these characters in situations that best explored the human condition.*

Thanks to his popularity, we know more about Shakespeare than any other playwright of the period. As the son of a successful glovemaker and wool importer, he almost certainly attended school until he was about 14. At school he would undoubtedly have learned Latin, and studied the classics, from which he would later draw great inspiration.

His early life is only documented by his marriage to Ann Hathaway, and the birth of his children. But by 1592, we know his reputation was established in London, as a rival dramatist referred to him as an "upstart crow". During this period, Shakespeare wrote *Henry VI*, *Two Gentlemen of Verona* and *Titus Andronicus*, and

Building on his success, in 1599 his company built the Globe Theatre on the south bank of the Thames.

in 1594 helped form The Lord Chamberlain's Men players with Richard Burbage as its lead actor.

For the next 20 years Shakespeare wrote almost two plays a year, providing such classic roles for Burbage as Richard III, Hamlet, and King Lear. Building on his success, in 1599 his company built the Globe Theatre on the south bank of the Thames.

Shakespeare wrote his plays on sheets of folded paper, and few were printed. But seven years after his death, in 1623, the *First Folio* was published, a collected edition of 36 plays assembled from the Bard's original quarto scripts, playbooks, transcriptions, and the memories of actors.

However, his influence on the language he so cleverly used goes far beyond his plays. Possessed of a vocabulary of in excess of 21,000 words, Shakespeare is credited with inventing or, at the very least, popularizing, some 1,700 new words, ranging from accessible to zany by way of bedazzle, courtship, fashionable, homely, majestic, and puke.

TRULY THE AUTHOR?

Many have questioned the authorship of Shakespeare's plays, suggesting he lacked the education to write so eruditely. Sir Francis Bacon, Christopher Marlowe, and Edward de Vere have all been put forward as contenders, but none stands serious scrutiny. Many of his contemporaries frequently praised and criticized his plays, and Ben Jonson even contributed to the *First Folio*.

Arthur Miller (1915–2005)
Pulitzer Prize winner, Arthur Miller was one of the greatest post-war American playwrights. His 1949 play *Death of a Salesman* remains one of the classics of the modern theatre. Miller further established his ability with *The Crucible*, first performed in 1953. In 1956, Miller married Marilyn Monroe for whom he wrote the film comedy, *The Misfits*.

Anton Chekhov (1860–1904)
Chekhov initially set out to become a doctor, only writing short stories in rooms to support himself and his family. Gifted with a deep sense of the ridiculous, he found he could make his audiences laugh. His acclaim as a writer steadily grew with such masterpieces as *Uncle Vanya*, *The Three Sisters*, and *The Cherry Orchard*.

Tom Stoppard (b.1937)
British playwright and screenwriter Tom Stoppard was a freelance drama critic who then began to write plays for radio and TV. His first major success came with *Rosencrantz and Guildenstern Are Dead*. Opening in London in 1967, it made Stoppard an almost overnight sensation. During the next decade he had further successes with *Jumpers* and *Travesties*.

Tennessee Williams (1911–1983)
Tennessee Williams (right) drew heavily on the inspiration of his turbulent family life to become one of America's greatest and best-loved playwrights. With some 30 plays to his credit, many of them have been made into equally successful films.

MISUNDERSTOOD ARTIST

If ever an artist could claim to be misunderstood, it is Vincent van Gogh. Today, his works sell for millions, but in his lifetime, van Gogh was derided as being without talent, lived in poverty, and endured the horrors of depression.

He was born near the village of Breda in the Netherlands as the eldest of three brothers and three sisters. He did well in art classes at school and, at the age of 15, went to work at an art dealers in The Hague. He later moved on to work at the company's London office, where he earned steady promotion through hard work and talent.

In 1875, Vincent moved to Paris but he became increasingly frustrated that his employers concentrated more on the commercial value of the art they handled than on its artistic merit.

> *He did well in art classes at school.*

In 1876, he resigned and drifted through a number of jobs before, in 1879, becoming a preacher at a Protestant church ministering to the very poorest industrial workers in Belgium. He was dismissed after arguing with his superiors, moved home, and fell out with his parents.

Finally, in 1880, van Gogh decided to become an artist, apparently at the suggestion of his brother Theo. He threw himself into his art and even proposed marriage to his widowed cousin Kee Vos-Stricker, who refused him. He then went to stay with a relative, the painter Anton Mauve, but soon fell out with him and moved in with a prostitute named Clasina Maria Hoornik. Within 18 months he was back with his parents due to a lack of money.

As an artist, van Gogh was largely self-taught, which allowed him to experiment with colour and unusual ways of applying paint without the constraints that training might have brought to his style. He drew much inspiration from the Impressionists without

VINCENT VAN GOGH (1853–1890)

"For my part I know nothing with any certainty, but the sight of the stars makes me dream." Vincent van Gogh

He drew much inspiration from the Impressionists without being subservient to them.

being subservient to them and delighted in experimenting with the effects of light and colour.

By 1885, Theo van Gogh was an art dealer in Paris and agreed to try to sell some of Vincent's paintings. There was not much interest, but enough money came in to allow Vincent to pay rent, buy food, and paint. Vincent lived with Theo for a while, then moved on to Asnières and met Paul Gauguin, who later stayed with van Gogh in his house in Arles. It was after a quarrel with Gaugin that van Gogh famously grabbed a razor and sliced off his own earlobe. Gauguin left.

In May 1889, van Gogh commited himself to a mental hospital in Saint Rémy de Provence. There he continued to paint, drawing admiration from Toulouse-Lautrec and Monet. He left there after a year and moved to Auvers-sur-Oise under the care of a private doctor. On July 27, 1890, however, he shot himself in the chest, then retired to his hotel where he died two days later.

VAN GOGH'S MADNESS

That van Gogh was mentally disturbed throughout much of his adult life is widely acknowledged. His family did all they could to cover up his behaviour, so details of symptoms have not survived. Recent diagnoses suggest that he may have suffered from schizophrenia, bipolar disorder, syphilis, or even lead poisoning caused by licking his paintbrushes. On one fact most people are agreed—his heavy drinking did not help, nor did the fact that his drink of choice was absinthe.

OTHER TROUBLED ARTISTS

Paul Gauguin (1848–1903)

The French post-Impressionist Paul Gauguin (right) had a life best described as troubled. He was born in Paris but grew up in his mother's native Peru after his father died. He returned to Paris as a teenager, became a stockbroker, married, and seemed set for a conventional life. But in 1885, he abandoned his family to take up his hobby of painting full time. None of his work sold well and by 1891 he was bankrupt. Gauguin then moved to Tahiti to escape his debtors and it was there that he produced his finest work.

James Thurber (1894–1961)

American humourist James Thurber (left) is often portrayed as a misogynist, or at least as a man deeply suspicious of women. It was in New York in 1930 that he began his artistic career when some of his cartoons were published by *The New Yorker* magazine. His artworks were simple but surrealistic and often centred on small, inoffensive men being bullied or intimidated by larger women. The character Walter Mitty was probably his best-known and best-loved creation. In fact, he had several rewarding friendships with women and was twice married.

CONTROVERSIAL WRITER

Oscar Wilde was a poet and dramatist gifted with formidable wit and artistry. In six brief years of incandescent creativity he wrote a collection of stories and plays that brought him worldwide critical acclaim.

Oscar Wilde was born in Dublin to unconventional and gifted parents. His mother was a poet, journalist, and translator; his father, a specialist in eye and ear diseases, an antiquarian, and author.

After excelling in classics at Trinity College in Dublin, Wilde won a scholarship to Magdalen College, Oxford where he received a First Class degree. After graduating, he moved to London where he proceeded to sharpen his wit among the gay young blades of the city.

By 1881, the foppishly eccentric Wilde had become a spokesman for Aestheticism, which advocated "art for art's sake". And that year he embarked on a tour of the USA, giving 140 lectures in 260 days. While there, he met several of his heroes including Henry Longfellow and Walt Whitman.

In 1884, to the surprise of some of his friends, Wilde married Constance Lloyd and the couple had two sons. To support his young family, Wilde settled down and began a two-year stint at *Woman's World* magazine.

Over the next six years Wilde's creative flame burnt at its brightest. In 1888, he

OSCAR WILDE (1854–1900)

"It is only an auctioneer who can equally and impartially admire all schools of art." Oscar Wilde in *The Critic as Artist*.

published *The Happy Prince and Other Tales,* followed by *A House of Pomegranates* in 1892—two collections of children's stories that he wrote for his sons.

In 1890, he completed his first and only novel, *The Picture of Dorian Gray.* But it was in his plays that Wilde gave full rein

to his crackling wit and acerbic observations on Victorian life and manners. His first, *Lady Windermere's Fan,* opened in 1892 to critical and financial success; in 1885 *An Ideal Husband* opened. His last mainstream production came later the same year: *The Importance of Being Earnest.*

It was in his plays that Wilde gave full rein to his crackling wit and acerbic observations.

But while many marvelled at Wilde's rapier wit, others recoiled from his feminine foppishness. And with homosexuality illegal at that time in Britain, it wasn't long before a war of words became a battle of beliefs. In the trials that followed it wasn't just Wilde in the dock, but the very Victorian values he had so often pilloried.

> *It wasn't long before a war of words became a battle of beliefs.*

Despite support from many of his contemporaries, Wilde was ultimately sacrificed. As his wife Constance fled to Switzerland, a defiant Wilde was led away to Wandsworth prison. From there, he was transferred to Reading, and on his release two years later he wrote *Ballad of Reading Gaol*. But his creative fires were never rekindled, and his once adoring audiences abandoned him. For the last three years of his life, Wilde wandered Europe, where he contracted meningitis, and the world lost one of its sharpest wits.

WILDE ON TRIAL

It was his relationship with **Lord Alfred "Bosie" Douglas** that proved to be Wilde's downfall. Douglas's father detested Wilde. But when he publically called Wilde a sodomite, Wilde sued him for libel. At the trial, Wilde's wit initially delighted the court, but after personal letters had been read and a string of young boys had taken the stand, not only was the Marquess exonerated, but Wilde had effectively been convicted.

Dylan Thomas (1914–1953)

One of the best-known and perhaps greatest poets of the 20th century, Swansea-born Thomas infused most of his work, including his sublime *Fern Hill*, with his deep love for the Welsh countryside. Known to be a perfectionist, he would sometimes labour for several days on a single line. A number of his richly-accented readings were recorded, including his renowned radio play, *Under Milkwood*.

Percy Bysshe Shelley (1792–1822)

A contemporary of Keats and Byron, Shelley is remembered as one of the most passionate of the English Romantic poets. His best-loved works include *Ozymandias* and *Ode to the West Wind*. Throughout his life, however, Shelley was a controversial character, with outspoken views on religion and politics. He died by drowning, after his yacht sank at Spezia in Italy.

James Joyce (1882–1941)

Dublin-born James Joyce is remembered for his experimental use of language in his seminal works, *Ulysses* and *Finnegans Wake*. The result is a unique blend of invention and classic symbolism woven around internal monologues and streams of consciousness. But while Joyce's writing has always impressed the critics, his public often proved to be more resistant to his genius.

RENOWNED STAGE ACTOR

DONALD WOLFIT (1902–1968)

"Dying is easy—it is comedy that is hard."
Sir Donald Wolfit on his deathbed.

Known as "the last of the great actor-managers", Donald Wolfit was a dominating character in British theatre during the mid-20th century. He had a profound influence on many of those who worked with him.

Wolfit was born in Newark, Nottinghamshire, and had a major success on London's West End stage aged only 22 when he played in the drama *The Wandering Jew*. After this meteoric rise, he failed to make much impression for the following few years. This did nothing to dent

Wolfit's confidence in either his abilities or his eventual success. In 1930, he attracted a good deal of positive critical acclaim when he played Claudius in the Old Vic Theatre's production of *Hamlet*. Wolfit was annoyed that his performance was eclipsed by the younger actor playing Hamlet, John Gielgud. The ill feeling this caused led to a life-long rivalry between the two men.

Wolfit's breakthrough came when he himself played Hamlet at the Shakespeare Memorial Theatre in 1936. Critical acclaim was unbounded and the audiences flocked to the show. Wolfit drew up plans to take the production on a tour of provincial theatres. However, the producers were unimpressed and turned down the idea.

> *Wolfit drew up plans to take the production on a tour of provincial theatres.*

Wolfit then drew out all his savings and founded his own touring company. He never looked back. As he took his company around the country, Wolfit specialized in the classics by Shakespeare—in particular *King Lear* and *Richard III*—Ben Jonson, and Christopher Marlowe. His dramatic style was hugely popular with British audiences.

Anecdotes about Wolfit were widespread; in fact, he often encouraged them himself to publicize his shows. One has it that at the close of one

Anecdotes about Wolfit were widespread; in fact, he often encouraged them himself to publicize his shows.

play, Wolfit announced to the audience, "Next week my company will be performing the wonderful Shakespearean tragedy of *Othello*. I shall be playing the role of the moor Othello and my wife will be playing the role of Othello's beautiful wife, the fair Desdemona."

"But your wife is an ugly old rat bag," someone shouted back. Wolfit smiled and replied: "Nevertheless, as I said, she will be playing the fair Desdemona".

In 1940, as World War II raged, Wolfit further endeared himself to British audiences by returning to London to put on his shows as bombs fell. He even put on Shakespeare plays abridged to 45 minutes so that workers could see them in their lunch breaks.

After the war he appeared at the prestigious Royal Shakespeare Company as King Lear, but he was never quite as popular with critics and the arts establishment as he was with the provincial audiences. Although he is best known for his stage work, Wolfit also appeared in several films.

THE DRESSER

After Wolfit died, his dresser, Ronald Harwood, wrote a play called *The Dresser*, which was closely based on their working relationship. The play was filmed in 1983. Although the great but declining actor who is the focus of the story is never named, nobody was in any doubt that he was based on Sir Donald Wolfit. The film was nominated for five Oscars but failed to win any.

Sir Alan Bates (1934–2003)

Sir Alan Bates became a star with his first role on the West End stage in 1956 when he starred in the controversial play *Look Back in Anger*. He subsequently became the darling of the British stage, and was particularly successful when appearing in plays by Simon Gray—including *Otherwise Engaged*, *Stage Struck*, and *Simply Disconnected*. Bates was knighted and made an Associate Member of the Royal Academy of the Dramatic Arts (RADA). He also appeared in numerous films, most memorably *Whistle Down the Wind* and *Far From the Madding Crowd*.

David Garrick (1717–1779)

David Garrick dominated the British stage in a way that few actors have done before or since. Although a wine merchant by trade, Garrick took up a professional career as actor and playwright. In 1747, he took over management of the Theatre Royal, Drury Lane, which he ran until his death. Garrick's acting style was to avoid flamboyant, dramatic gestures and act quite naturally, as if he really were experiencing the emotions he portrayed. The style caught on and within a decade all actors were following his lead.

Julie Harris (b.1925)

One of the true greats of the American Theatre, Julie Harris has also had a respectable film career. She won a Tony Award for Best Actress in 1952 for the role of Sally Bowles in the stage play *I am a Camera*, which was later turned into a musical and filmed as *Cabaret*. More than 20 years later, she won a second Tony for her role as Mary Lincoln in *The Last of Mrs Lincoln*. In all, she has won five Tony Awards, more than any other performer.

SHAMELESS LIBERTINE

The English nobleman John Wilmot, 2nd Earl of Rochester, had a difficult early life but he was determined to make up for it in grand fashion after his luck changed.

Wilmot's subsequent dedication to pleasure and vice became the talk of London, and gossip about him spread across Europe.

He was born in Oxfordshire during the English Civil War. The fact that his father had fled abroad to serve the exiled King Charles II meant that the family in England were under suspicion of the republican government.

After the death of Oliver Cromwell, conditions eased and Wilmot was able to go to Oxford, where he developed talents for poetry, learning, and heavy drinking. He managed to gain a degree as Master of Arts and set off on a tour around Europe to further his education—and to get into a number of scrapes and scandals involving women.

The return of King Charles II to rule Britain allowed Wilmot to regain his family estates and he returned to London to take up a position at court. Unfortunately for Wilmot, he did not have the money to live in the style he favoured. His eye then fell on the rich, intelligent heiress, Elizabeth Malet. King Charles himself arranged a formal introduction. The girl returned his affections but her family disapproved so the young couple decided to elope.

JOHN WILMOT (1647–1680)

"God bless our good and gracious king, Whose promise none relies on; Who never said a foolish thing, Nor ever did a wise one."
Wilmot writing about King Charles II in his satire of 1674.

Rochester arranged for a coach with two women servants to be waiting at Charing Cross on the night of May 28, 1665, when he knew that Elizabeth and her father would be driving past. Rochester pounced on the coach with a gang of supposed footpads and abducted Miss Malet. But Mr Malet had, meanwhile, recognized Wilmot and raised the forces of law and order. When he was dragged in front of Charles, the King was furious and

Unfortunately for Wilmot, he did not have the money to live in the style he favoured.

threw Wilmot into the Tower of London until such time as Miss Malet returned to her family.

Despite this escapade, he eventually won over the Malet family and married his love. The new Duchess of Rochester took up residence on the family estates, where Wilmot proved to be a perfect husband. During his visits to London, however, he continued to indulge in womanizing and scandalous behaviour. He joined an informal group of rakes known as the Merry Gang, notorious for its sexual adventures.

> *During his visits to London, however, he continued to indulge in womanizing.*

In 1674, Wilmot angered the king by writing a satirical poem and was forced to withdraw from court. Wilmot returned to London society in the disguise of a "Doctor Bendo", who promised to be able to cure infertility. When his final sickness struck, Wilmot renounced his lifelong atheism and converted to Christianity.

SODOM

Wilmot was a noted poet and playwright during his lifetime. His most famous work was the play *Sodom*. The work was not only deeply pornographic, but also contained much satire about contemporary noblemen, ladies, and even the King himself. It was written in 1672, but performed only privately for a few friends, and did not appear in print until after Wilmot's death.

Giuseppe Balsamo (1743–1795)

Alessandro, Count of Cagliostro, was the false name adopted by Giuseppe Balsamo, a Sicilian bookseller, when he embarked on his life as an adventurer. Cagliostro left home in 1764 after defrauding a wealthy local merchant. An adept forger, he spent the next 30 years travelling around Europe claiming to be an Italian nobleman, alchemist, and a magician who had fought against the Moslem Turks.

Francis Dashwood (1708–1781)

The English rake and debauchee Francis Dashwood inherited a fortune when he became the 15th Baron le Despencer. Despite being a talented politician, he led a scandalous private life. At his family seat he built a mock-medieval chapel and chambers at which he hosted parties that featured vast quantities of drink, prostitutes, and quasi-sacrilegious ceremonies.

Antoine Gombaud (1607–1684)

Antoine Gombaud, Chevalier de Méré, was a notable French 17th-century gambler. He gained great fame when Blaise Pascal used de Méré's favourite bet as the basis for the new mathematical discipline of probability. Pascal eventually proved that de Méré had a 51.77 per cent chance of winning.

Francis Charteris (1672–1732)

The Scotsman Francis Charteris became widely known as "The Rape-Master General" due to his sordid private life. Charteris made a fortune gambling. He also acquired a reputation as a serial seducer of young women and in 1730 was convicted for the rape of a servant. He was pardoned but then contracted a fever and died.

Index

Credits

The Automobile Association would like to thank the following photographers, companies and picture libraries for their assistance in the preparation of this book.

Abbreviations for the picture credits are as follows: (t) top; (b) bottom; (c) centre; (l) left; (r) right; (AA) AA World Travel Library; (BAL) The Bridgeman Art Library; (B/C) Bettmann/Corbis; (C) Corbis; (CS) Corbis Sygma; (GI) Getty Images; (HA) Hulton Archive; (HDC) Hulton-Deutsch Collection; (JSC) John Springer Collection; (KC) The Kobal Collection; (MEPL) Mary Evans Picture Library; (Pf) Popperfoto; (RF) Rex Features; (SC) The Stapleton Collection (SPL) Science Photo Library; (TAA) The Art Archive; (TF) TopFoto; (TLP) Time Life Pictures; (TP) Topham Picturepoint.

6(i) © Illustrated London News Ltd/MEPL; 6(ii) ©2005 Roger-Viollet/TF; 6(iii) Imagno/Austrian Archives; 6(iv) © B/C; 6(v) © The Gallery Collection/C; 7(i) © Interfoto Pressebildagentur/ Alamy; 7(ii) © MEPL 2008; 7(iii) © 2004 Stock Montage/C; 7(iv) © B/C; 7(v) © B/C; 12 Dreamworks/ KC/Cooper, Andrew; 13t 'Soapy' Smith's Saloon Bar at Skagway, Alaska, 1898 (b/w photo) by American Photographer, (19th century), Library of Congress, Washington D.C., USA/BAL; 13b ©PA Photos/TF; 14 ©TF; 15t Imperial War Museum; 15b © B/C; 16 Blackbeard the pirate (coloured engraving) by English School, (19th century), Private Collection/Peter Newark Historical Pictures/BAL; 17t| Blackbeard the pirate killed in combat 1718 (coloured engraving) by American School, (19th century), Private Collection/ Peter Newark Historical Pictures/BAL; 17tr Blackbeard the pirate killed in combat 1718 (coloured engraving) by American School, (19th century), Private Collection/Peter Newark Historical Pictures/ BAL; 17cl Captain Kidd Hanging in Chains, from 'The Pirates Own Book', pub. by the Marine Research Society, 1924 (engraving) (b/w photo) by American School, (20th century), Library of Congress, Washington D.C., USA/BAL; 17br © The British Library/HIP; 18 © HDC/C; 19tr © Photodisc/Alamy; 19cr © B/C; 19bl Jimin Lai/AFP/GI; 20 © 2005 Roger-Viollet/TF; 21t © B/C; 21b Pf/GI; 22t RF; 22b Mirrorpix; 23tr HA/GI; 23cl Hans Neleman/GI; 23bc HA/GI; 24 © B/C; 25t © The British Library/HIP; 25c © 2003 TP; 25b © TF; 26 MEPL; 27 © MEPL 2008; 27 Tomas Hudcovic - isifa/GI; 28 Keystone/GI; 29tr Sipa Press/RF; 29cl © MEPL/Alamy; 29br © Koren Ziv/CS; 30 © B/C; 31t © 2003 TP; 31c © Austrian Archives/C; 31b Joaquin Murieta (1829-53) (litho) by American School, (19th century), Private Collection/ Peter Newark American Pictures/BAL; 32 © The Print Collector/Alamy; 33t © MEPL 2008; 33b © MEPL 2008; 38 © Classic Image/Alamy; 39tcr Photo Researchers/SPL; 39bcr Library of Congress/SPL; 39cl © MEPL 2008; 39c © 2000 TP; 40 © B/C; 41t © MEPL 2008; 41c NASA / SPL; 41b Ria Novosti/SPL; 42 © C; 43t © PA Photos/TF; 43b Pf/GI; 44 Everett Collection/RF; 45cl Jan Sonnenmair/Aurora/GI; 45cr AFP/AFP/GI; 45b © B/C; 46 © The Gallery Collection/C; 47cl Library of Congress/SPL; 47br © MEPL 2008; 48 © B/C; 49t NASA/SPL; 49bl © C; 49br © C; 50 Peter Dench; 51t Roger-Viollet/RF; 51c © Illustrated London News Ltd/MEPL; 51b Keystone/GI; 52 © B/C; 53tl © B/C; 53cr © Jerry Cooke/C; 53bl © Franck Seguin/ TempSport/C; 54 © MEPL 2008; 55tl © North Wind Picture Archives/Alamy; 55cl © North Wind Picture Archives/Alamy; 55cr HA/GI; 55bl © mediacolor's/ Alamy; 56 ©ullsteinbild/TF; 57 © Royal Geographical Society/Alamy; 58 © Pictorial Press Ltd/Alamy; 59t Sipa Press/RF; 59c Allsport UK/Allsport; 59b Pf/GI;

60 © B/C; 61cl © B/C; 61cr © B/C; 61bl Alfred Eisenstadt/TLP/GI; 61br © B/C; 62 © B/C; 63t SNAP/RF; 63c © MEPL 2008; 63b © CS; 68 © Fine Art Photographic Library/C; 69t © MEPL 2008; 69c © MEPL 2008; 69b B/C; 70 © HDC/C; 71cl © World History Archive/Alamy; 71cr © MEPL 2008; 71bl © The Gallery Collection/C; 72 © The Gallery Collection/ C; 72t © MEPL 2008; 73bl © DLILLC/C; 73br © MEPL 2008; 74t © SC/C; 74b © MEPL/ Alamy; 75t © MEPL; 75b © Photodisc/Alamy; 76 © The Print Collector/Alamy; 77t © HDC/C; 77bl © Illustrated London News Ltd/MEPL; 77br © B/C; 78 © TAA/C; 79cl © MEPL 2008; 79cr © MEPL 2008; 79b © MEPL 2008; 80 HA/GI; 81tc TLP/Mansell/ TLP/GI; 81cl © C; 81br HA/GI; 82 ©2004 TP; 83tr Leonard McCombe/Picture Post/GI; 83cr © ullsteinbild/TF; 83bl © C; 84 © ullsteinbild/TF; 85t © 2000 TP; 85c; 85b Public Record Office/HIP; 86 © MEPL 2008; 87tl © MEPL 2008; 87tr © B/C; 87b Imagno/GI; 88 © B/C; 89c TLP/Mansell/TLP/GI; 89bl © MEPL 2008; 89br © MEPL 2008; 90 Terry Fincher/ Express/GI; 91t © MEPL; 91b © MEPL 2008; 92 © B/C; 93t © Illustrated London News Ltd/MEPL; 93b © C; 94t © TF; 94b An Accident Aboard the 'Victoria', the Death of Admiral Tyron and 359 Officers and English Sailors, illustration from 'Le Petit Journal', 8th July 1893 (coloured engraving) by Meyer, Henri (1844-99), Private Collection/Giraudon/BAL; 95l © Ria Novosti/TF; 95r © MEPL; 100 © MEPL 2008; 101cl © Nikolai Ignatiev/Alamy; 101cr Keystone/GI; 101b © Terry Fincher.Photo Int/Alamy; 102 © Ivy Close Images/Alamy; 103c HA/GI; 103bl © B/C; 103br © MEPL 2008; 104 © B/C; 105t Evening Standard/GI; 105c © B/C; 105b © 2002 TP; 106 © MEPL 2008; 107t TP,TopFoto.co.uk; 107c © C; 107b © B/C; 108 © Hans Gedda/CS; 109c © B/C; 109c Mark Peters/GI; 109b David Hume Kennerly/GI; 110 © MEPL 2008; 111tc © MEPL 2008; 111tr © HDC/C; 111b RIA Novosti/TF; 112 TLP/Mansell/TLP/GI; 113tl Clifford Collection/ Canterbury Museum; 113tr © C; 113b Pf/GI; 114t © HDC/C; 114b Topham/PA TopFoto.co.uk; 115t Sipa Press/RF; 115c © MEPL 2008; 115b Sipa Press/ RF; 116 HA/GI; 117c © B/C; 117bl © HDC/C; 117br © C; 122 © B/C; 123t Keystone/HA/GI; 123c © Universal/TempSport/C; 123b Keystone/GI; 124 © B/C; 125c Sam Bass (1851-78) (b/w photo) by American Photographer, (19th century), Private Collection/Peter Newark American Pictures/BAL; 125bl © 2002 TP; 125br Henry Plummer (1837-64) (b/w photo) by American Photographer, (19th century), Private Collection/ Peter Newark American Pictures/BAL; 126 © Print Collector/HIP /TF; 127t © B/C; 127c © C; 127b © B/C; 128 © Leonard de Selva/C; 129t © Interfoto Pressebildagentur/Alamy; 129bl © Visual Arts Library (London)/Alamy; 129br Beamish Collection; 130 Pf/GI; 131t © MEPL; 131b © 2005 Fotomas/TF; 132 © B/C; 133c © MEPL; 133bl TAA/Private Collection MD; 133br ©TF; 134 TAA/Musée Fabre Montpellier/Dagli Orti; 135l TAA/ Harper Collins Publishers; 135r © MEPL 2008; 136 Caligula Caesar (12-41 AD), 1596 (engraving) by Italian School, (16th century), Private Collection/SC/ BAL; 137t © MEPL 2008; 137c © MEPL 2008; 137b © MEPL 2008; 138 © B/C; 139l © The National Trust Photolibrary/Alamy; 139r © Lynn Goldsmith/C; 140 Imagno/Austrian Archives; 141t Image by © SC/C; 141b © 2003 TP; 142 Filmstudio, S.A./Antonio Isasi; 143t © 2004 The Image Works/TF; 143bl Topical Press Agency/GI; 143br TLP/Mansell/TLP/GI; 144 © SC/C; 145t National Redding Museum; 145b © HDC/C; 146 © MEPL; 147t Rodrigo de Vivar, 'El Cid' (c.1043-99) and his father, Don Diego, c.1827 (oil on canvas) by Fragonard, Alexandre Evariste (1780-1850), Private Collection/Stair Sainty Matthiesen Gallery, New York, USA/BAL; 147b TAA/Haghia Sophia Istanbul/Dagli Orti (A); 148 © B/C; 149cl © B/C; 149cr © B/C; 149br American Stock/GI; 150 © MEPL; 151t ©World History Archive/TF; 151cr © HDC/C; 151bl HA/GI; 152 © B/C; 153t © Elisabeth Baranyai/CS; 153c © Epix/CS; 153b © Brooks Kraft/ CS; 154 ©ullsteinbild/TF; 155t © 2002 TP; 155c © 2000 UPP/Topham; 155b © Joi; 156 © Christie's

Images/C; 157t © B/C; 157c © C 157b Kean Collection/GI; 158 TAA/Windsor Castle; 159t © MEPL; 159c © MEPL/Alamy; 159b © MEPL/MARY EVANS ILN PICTURES; 160 © John Van Hasselt/CS; 161c © B/C; 161bl 20th Century Fox/KC; 161br Jon Brenneis//TLP/GI; 162 © MEPL/Alamy; 163t © Ian Patrick/Alamy; 163b © David White/Alamy ; 163b Everett Collection/RF; 164t TAA; 164b © C; 165t Media H/O, © Newspix/News Ltd; 165c © MEPL; 165b © Newspix/News Ltd; 166 Douglas Miller/ Keystone/GI; 167t -/AFP/GI; 167b KC/Costa, Tony; 168 © 2004 TP; 169t © MEPL; 169c © MEPL 2008; 169b © The British Library/HIP; 170t TAA/Musée du Château de Versailles/Dagli Orti; 170b TAA/Private Collection/Marc Charmet; 171l © 2003 TP; 171r © B/C; 172 © 2006 TF/Fortean; 173t © B/C; 173cl akg-images; 173br The Fall of Simon Magus, from 'La Chronique de Nuremberg' by Hartmann Schedel, Nurnberg, 1492 (colour woodcut) by German School, (15th century), Bibliotheque Mazarine, Paris, France/ Archives Charmet/BAL; 174 © The Gallery Collection/C; 175l Fox Photos/GI; 175r TLP/ Mansell/TLP/GI; 176 STR/AFP/GI; 177c © HDC/C; 177bl © Underwood & Underwood/C; 177br © HDC/C; 182 © B/C; 183t © B/C; 183c © B/C; 183b © Stefano Bianchetti/C; 184 TAA/Culver Pictures; 185t © B/C; 185c © C; 185b © B/C; 186 © MEPL 2008; 187t © Michael Nicholson/C; 187c © B/C; 187b © HDC/C; 188 © MEPL 2008; 189l © MEPL; 189r © MEPL 2008; 190 Arthur Schatz/US Library of Congress/ SPL; 191t © B/C; 191c STR/AFP/GI; 191b © Colin McPherson; 192 © MEPL 2008; 193t © MEPL 2008; 193c SPL; 193b © MEPL 2008; 194 Sheila Terry/SPL; 195cl ©World History Archive/TF; 195cr © B/C; 195b © B/C; 196 © MEPL 2008; 197t © B/C; 197b © B/C; 198 © B/C; 199tr © HDC/C; 199cr © You Sung-Ho/Reuters/C; 199bl © MEPL; 200 HA/GI; 201t SPL; 201 © 202 © Illustrated London News Ltd/MEPL; 203cr © 2005 Fotomas/TF; 203b © B/C; 204 © 2004 Stock Montage; 205t © HDC/C; 205c Cern/SPL; 205b Sipa Press/RF; 206 © C; 207l © B/C; 207r Chris Ware/Keystone Features/ GI; 208 © Jim Sugar/C; 209t © HDC/C; 209b Jeff Chistensen; 210 A. Barrington Brown/SPL; 211tr Science Source/SPL; 211cl James King-Holmes/SPL; 211br ©PA Photos/TF; 216 © MEPL 2008; 217tr © MEPL 2008; 217cl © HDC/C; 217br Geoff Wilkinson/RF; 218 © JSC/C; 219t KC/Metro-Goldwyn; 219c KC; 219b © HDC/ C; 220 Ralph Crane/TLP/GI; 221cl © JSC/C; 221cr © Marcel Hartmann/CS; 221bl © CinemaPhoto/C; 221br © Stefani Kong Uhler/CS; 222 KC; 223c © JSC/C; 223b © B/C; 224 GI; 225t © JSC/C; 225c From the Jewish Chronicle Archive/HIP/TF; 225b © B/C; 226 Ray Stevenson/RF; 227cr © The Image Works/TF; 227bl Ray Stevenson/RF; 227br Michael Ochs Archives/GI; 228 © TF; 229c © JSC/C; 229bl KC; 229br © MEPL 2008; 230 © Andrew Winning/ Reuters/C; 231cl © Elder Neville/CS; 231cr © C; 231b © MEPL; 232 Nina Leen/TLP/GI; 233tr TAA/ Culver Pictures; 233c © Bass/Evening Standard/GI; 233c © eye35.com/Alamy; 233br Keystone/GI; 234 KC/20th Century Fox/Reisfeld, Bert; 235tr © B/C; 235bl Ronald Grant Archive; 235br KPA/HIP/TF; 236 © B/C; 237t ©2006 TF/Fortean; 237c © B/C; 237b © HDC/C; 238 © MEPL 2008; 239c © Christopher Felver/C; 239c © 2006 John Hedgecoe/ TF; 239b ©2005 Roger-Viollet/TF; 240 KC ; 241cl © MEPL 2008; 241cr © HDC/C; 241bl © B/C; 241br © Neal Preston/C; 242 Stock Montage/GI; 243t © B/C; 243c © B/C; 243b Alfred Eisenstaedt//TLP/GI; 244 Francis G. Mayer/C; 245l © B/C; 245r HA/GI; 246 © B/C; 247t © MEPL 2008; 247c © MEPL 2008; 247b © HDC/C; 248 © SC/C; 249t © JSC/C; 249c Roger Viollet Collection/C; 249b © JSC/C; 250 HA/ GI; 251t ©2003 Charles Walker/TF; 251c © MEPL 2008; 251b © MEPL;

Every effort has been made to trace the copyright holders, and we apologise in advance for any accidental errors. We would be happy to apply the corrections in the following edition of this publication.